The Natural Laws
of Good Luck

The
Natural Laws *of*
Good Luck

A Memoir of an
Unlikely Marriage

Ellen Graf

TRUMPETER
Boston & London · 2009

Trumpeter Books
An imprint of Shambhala Publications, Inc.
Horticultural Hall
300 Massachusetts Avenue
Boston, Massachusetts 02115
www.shambhala.com

9 8 7 6 5 4 3 2 1

First Edition
Printed in the United States of America

Distributed in the United States by Random House, Inc., and in Canada by
Random House of Canada Ltd

⊗This edition is printed on acid-free paper that meets the American National
Standards Institute z39.48 Standard.
♻This book was printed on 30% postconsumer recycled paper. For more
information, please visit www.shambhala.com.

Designed by Daniel Urban-Brown

Library of Congress Cataloging-in-Publication Data
Graf, Ellen.
The natural laws of good luck: a memoir of an unlikely marriage/Ellen
Graf.—1st ed.
p. cm.
ISBN 978-1-59030-691-8 (hardcover: alk. paper)
1. Graf, Ellen—Marriage. 2. Intercountry marriage—United States—Case
studies. 3. Intercountry marriage—China—Case studies. 4. Women—United
States—Biography. 5. Divorced women—United States—Biography.
6. Married people—United States—Biography. 7. Troy Region (N.Y.)—
Biography. 8. China—Biography. 9. Chronically ill—Case studies. I. Title.
HQ1032.G73   2009
306.84'5092—dc22   [B]2009004257

For my husband

Wanting

IT'S EASIER to say where you are than what or who you are. I
am on an old farm in upstate New York where lichen-covered
stone walls hug the hummocks of a forest floor that once was
treeless pasture. Seventeen generations of sheep farmers tended
these walls to separate into four-acre parcels what was not in essence different—grass and sheep from grass and sheep. These art-
ful divisions remain today, separating trees from trees.

Leaves ruffle the sound waves in the half mile to the highway,
where the trucks rumble past a barn someone once leaned a ladder
on to paint ragged and red: "No Zoning!" Box springs and old cars
with no wheels are allowed in front yards. Junk is not a category.
Horses, goats, llamas, and Highland cattle all qualify as livestock—
also allowed. This is a hinterland of survivors. Bald eagles nest here
above secret waterfalls where teenagers leap off cliffs into deep pools.
There are deer, mink, bear, lynx, and packs of coyotes.

What I am is an artist who cannot follow instructions. One customer commissioned a sculpture of two lovers joined at one root,
twisting from the earth and parting at the sky end, all arms extended in praise. I confused this request and made the lovers' feet
large, each pair planted in a firm, wide stance on its own ground.
Their arms embraced only each other, tight enough to hurt. The
customer pointed out crossly that the end result was "the opposite

of what we talked about." And so I have needed to scour the landscape for work to supplement my art.

Who we are, it seems to me, is in relation to others. I am a mother. Five children finished growing up in this old yellow farmhouse. The first four witnessed my slow progress toward solvency after an early divorce. They jostled under the low ceilings until the space was too small for them and their heads threatened to poke right up through the roof. Three showed their readiness to go by sparking stones with the lawn mower and chopping potatoes in half with the spade instead of carefully lifting them from the dirt. The fourth found the potatoes with her hands, sorted them by size, and left home more reluctantly. (The walls had barely stopped trembling when my fifth child arrived, tall and quiet, not exactly a baby and not exactly mine. I will tell it.)

These rustling leaves and bare bones of where, what, and who describe my situation as well as I understood it myself when I answered the personal ad in the *Want Ad Digest* placed by the "real good looking workaholic handyman looking for SBF or SWF."

I wasn't thinking only about how this unknown person could make my life easier by knowing how to fix things that I didn't. I was thinking what a joy it would be to see the circling of a red-tailed hawk and call out "Look!" or just point, saying nothing. What a joy to be with someone when the late sun turned red in the pignut branches or when other astonishing things happened. Educated by now in the trickeries of my heart, I knew I would not thrive alone, even though I am a solitary person who likes empty surroundings and complete quiet. My energy would spin around and around inside crying "Look!" and I might become crazy. I hankered after an imaginary companion to whom I could say "Good morning" or "Excuse me" as we pushed past each other in the bathroom. I thought this daily brushing against flesh and blood might keep me in the middle space where life is lived.

I wrote long letters to my handyman, telling him about wilderness trips with my untalkative father, and the world above the tree line, where nothing with fur and four legs could thrive and miniature alpine flowers trembled in the crevices of rocks. I told him about the time when I got lost for fifteen hours. Just as the forest rangers were calling for a helicopter, I appeared from a tunnel in the night woods, blood dribbling out of my nose. My father said simply, "Hi, kiddo." But why would a stranger want to know all that? Why would anyone?

When he replied to my letter, the handyman was very formal and respectful. He made no comment on the nose story or other personal revelations. He said things like: "I work in construction. I like dancing, parties, am a great social drinker. Sometimes enjoy quiet times." I didn't drink and disliked socializing. But no matter—I had an old house that needed a lot of help. In my fantasy, he had a sweet and burly personality, and he came over after work in his tight, dirty blue jeans. He was wily and strong and always smiling. He would swing me up over his head, I would bubble with laughter, and then we would fix stuff.

In the next letter, the handyman informed me that his old girlfriend had unexpectedly come back to town. He was very sorry, he had no idea this would happen, but there she was and what could he do? He said he had a buddy who sold used cars, was a real nice guy, and would like to be my pen pal. He enclosed the address. But I didn't want the used-car buddy; I wanted the handyman of my dreams. I had a good cry in the barn about someone I didn't know and had never even had coffee with while my two dogs looked on, the old wolf-crossed Socrates, who liked to lie on my feet disdaining to be touched, and his constant companion Loki, an oddball spaniel with curly hair, a stocky build, and a gaze of impatient optimism. As darkness fell, disdain and anticipation snored, and infinity advised. I picked the straw out of my hair. I threw the *Want Ad Digest* away for good.

That spring the peepers were so loud outside the window that my teenage daughter Paroda, the only one still at home, couldn't fall asleep. She lay there thinking of ways we could improve our standard of living, and in her mind, this should be accomplished by acquiring more things. The want ads resurrected, we found a television, a sewing machine, and a free trampoline that was two hours away. The black rubber top draped over the roof of the car, concealing the upper half of all the windows. As we crept home with pipes looming up between the passenger's seat and the driver's seat and out the back windows, the muffler scraped swollen bumps of asphalt, and by the time we drove up our own road, the tailpipe was dragging in the dirt.

Bouncing up into blue sky and flapping our arms was ecstatic fun at first. The dogs sat below, spotting us with the rising and falling of their noses. It hadn't occurred to Paroda or to me that it was too late for the trampoline or that the empty sky could not fulfill our longings. We tried alternate jumping, my weight propelling her upward and vice versa, but she said I had no rhythm, and each impact caused me to pee my pants on ascension. At fifteen, she was more interested in boys than backward flips and decided to use the trampoline to lie on her back in a two-piece bathing suit.

In redoubled efforts to make my own sovereign sense of life, I employed my hands more than my head, because knowing how to do things seemed vitally important to a feeling of belonging to the world. I started with the old doorknobs, which were forever coming off in our hands. It had taken some years of tightening and re-tightening the screws to no avail before I realized that the threads were stripped. Even that simple thing had presented a mystery. I pulled porcupine quills out of my dog's gums with pliers and cleaned his fight wounds with Betadine. I sliced the throats of my chickens, tied their legs, and hung them upside down, their little assholes curiously identical to my own.

Every time I stepped out the back door, several toads blinked their gold-rimmed eyes in the porch light. I felt this amphibious wealth as an omen; I could smell a fragrant storm on the horizon. Outside my house was a small pond, surrounded by cattails and birch trees and rapidly filling in with mud and islands of grass. The nostrils of box turtles, bullfrogs, and blacksnakes appeared and disappeared at the amber surface. The great blue heron reigned supreme. Never caught arriving, he was just suddenly and completely there, as if the sky had opened and closed behind him. Leaving, he would step once and rise into air thickened by his own wings. If there were someone somewhere in the world available to share all this with me, then I guessed that person would have to appear like the heron, out of a tear in the sky.

From the dew of toad-attended nights came an unexpected spring. My friend invited herself over for "talking together." I had known her for nine years, since the day after she arrived from China—about three years after her husband, Zhang Bei-hu, my Tai Chi teacher. Before my teacher brought her to class, he described his wife as not pretty, only "so-so" by Chinese standards. He repeated this three times so slowly and pointedly that it seemed an incantation to repel potential admirers. I thought she was the most beautiful person I had ever seen, especially her curly lips with their never-ending vocabulary of pouts, presses, hesitant poses, and different-shaped portals for her high-pitched, musical laughter. She had a full, round face with dimples and a smooth, honey-colored expanse of forehead. I felt her bewilderment with her husband's new American personality and his impatience with her need for him to slow down to help her adjust. I identified with her saddened but hopeful spirit, fighting off bitterness while holding out for a taste of sweetness.

Now, years later, my friend still found the English language an excruciatingly clumsy vehicle of expression, so her announcing that she wanted to have a talk with me aroused suspicion. Usually we just ate lunch, laughing when food fell from my chopsticks or her napkin disappeared under the table. She winced when I tried to pronounce her name, Yiliang, while she did quite well enunciating mine: "Eh-lin-ah." She imparted sisterly wisdom to me, such as, "Before twenty year old, daughter no good, don't listen mother. After twenty, daughter not too bad. I think all daughter same way. You don't worry." On husbands she said, "Men all same way too.

5

Doesn't matter Chinese, not Chinese. Men not understand what the lady need. This traditional Chinese saying." She dubbed any aphorism she deemed worthy a "traditional Chinese saying."

The afternoon she came over, she summoned all her powers to make the few words she knew convey a startlingly clear message. We sat facing each other, she on my grandmother's rocker and I at her feet on a low footstool. She said that she had noticed I was lonely—no good. Loneliness was a demon that could detach you from the world. Having two old people together is better than one old person all alone. These two can take care of each other and try to understand each other. Understanding required many years; therefore, the two must help each other live a long, long life. Her brother in China was lonely too. Maybe we would like each other. She would send me to China to find out.

That was her speech, and she had exhausted her vocabulary. She grasped the arms of the chair and stood up. I, too, stood up. She drew a huge breath and said, "OK, all done." She had caught me off guard with this strange idea, unnerved the atmosphere and lowered the barometric pressure in the low-ceilinged room. We walked arm in arm toward the door, and I said I wasn't so sure. "You think about," she said.

Thinking back a few months, I realized that Yiliang had been cooking this idea of hers ever since February. I had been sitting next to her in the high school auditorium in the midst of the four-hour-long Chinese New Year's talent show. Besides the natural songbirds and weapon-flashing acrobats, there were nose singers, forgetful dancers, and bad joke tellers, but all held their heads high, supported by the precept that anything worth doing is worth doing badly. I agreed with this, for almost two hours.

A young man in a suit and tie wielded a yo-yo with solemn finesse, but Yiliang wasn't watching. She was pressing her nose with her forefinger, squishing it down to meet her curly upper lip. "Maybe," she murmured, tapping the finger, then turning to address my lap, "maybe could work."

I didn't ask her what could work. Answering questions only stranded her in the mire of the English language. Instead, I shared with her that I had gotten a speeding ticket on the way over, on a dark, doglegged back road, for going forty-two in a thirty-five-mile-an-hour zone. "Police catch you now is good thing," she said. No stranger to upside-down logic, I accepted her statement. On the way home, even though I took a different route, I was pulled over again.

Later, anticipating my blind date in China, I looked up the Chinese zodiac, which is based on the twelve-year orbit of Jupiter, the planet of luck. Each year has its own animal whose traits are reflected in the people born under that sign. I found that her brother was a dog person, and I was a snake. The astrologer's commentary, informed by centuries of folk wisdom, was simply "This could work."

When Yiliang first proposed that I meet her brother, it seemed an odd and disturbing idea, since I knew nothing about him and had never considered going to China. Still, I thought that not choosing for myself might possibly work better for me. Allowing my own attractions to steer my life had only battered my heart.

Yiliang's husband, Zhang, was leading a small tour group to China, and I could come along. I asked Yiliang, "What's your brother like?"

"He is very kind, very weak."

"He's very weak? Oh dear."

"Oh dear? I think you don't need 'oh dear.' What does *weak* mean in English?"

"*Weak* means 'not very strong.'"

"No, no. He is not this word, because he is very strong. I cannot translate. He is not exactly weak, maybe just some way weak, sometime weak, but not exactly weak. You know, my brother doesn't like fighting, arguing something. My brother is very peaceful, quiet, very nice. He very love painting something, but he painting all no good. *Weak* is wrong word, but my English no good. So sorry, cannot find right word for brother."

7

Yiliang's husband's sister, having met the man in question at family gatherings back in China, volunteered that he had a face that was *bu cuo*. The literal translation of *bu cuo* is "not bad," but the actual meaning is "really cute." She elaborated that he looked better than his sister because his upper lip did not pout over his lower lip—not pretty, by her standards. No one on her side of the family had the undesirable lip configuration.

"My side all not too ugly—don't you agree?"

I nodded awkwardly, still unaware at that point in time that "not too ugly" meant "pretty cute."

With only one wrong word and several bland words, including the two blandest of all—*nice* and *cute*—I discarded them all and asked no more questions. My mind remained empty of ideas, except one: her brother's name was Zhong-hua. I learned that *zhong* means "middle" and *hua* "flower," "bloom," or "flowering." Therefore, *Zhong-hua* translates as "Middle-Flowering," referring to Middle Kingdom, the ancient name for China. Other than flowers, maybe fields of poppies, no images enticed.

We never spoke on the phone or exchanged letters because neither of us knew enough of the other's words. He would have been capable of saying an economical "I am Lu Zhong-hua," and I just *"Ni shenti hao bu hao"* (How's your physical health?). We both knew our limitations and chose the silent way. I tried to imagine all the water, stars, sand dunes, storms, and trembling leaves between this man and me.

I am an anxious person and not eager to trust. How can I explain that when I thought of this man I had agreed to meet, I felt immense calm? I had never felt calm before and wondered if *calm* and *weak* meant the same thing in Chinese. In the months before I traveled to China, we had a fervid courtship, impossible as it may seem. I felt as if he were speaking right into my soul: "Don't worry. You can relax."

People reacted differently to my decision to go to China to meet a man. Paroda, a great romantic, was excited and pleased. My older

three children reserved both judgment and enthusiasm and said later that, having but one mother, they had no alternate standard for what a mother should be or do. Two wise old friends said, "Yes, of course, this is your destiny." The common wisdom is that people, by seeking love, risk losing themselves. I did not fear this loss. The very essence of me was in that unfinished part ever tipping toward the unknown or somersaulting, completely without grace, except in its willingness to be changed.

I got off the plane in Beijing to a surge of Chinese people politely pushing, shuffling, and nudging past one another. This was not the politeness of words but the politeness of no words and no eye contact. Jowl to jowl and hip to hip, they managed not to invade one another's capsules. Everywhere I turned, there were people pressed so closely that any one of them could stand on one leg and lean without falling down. They averted their eyes and baby-stepped purposefully, all without offending other people by noticing them. In China's public places, you can still feel a private space despite being hotly pressed from all sides. This was unlike the experience of American crowds, where you end up feeling harried, invaded, and even accosted. Rocked in the personal houseboat of my own body, I sailed comfortably, for the first time in my life, into a sea of introverts.

A voice said, "There he is—that one, you see, with the flowers." I saw one solid figure standing absolutely still. A multitude swayed around him. I had never seen a photograph of him, yet recognized this density, this shape—its decisive statement, "I am here." Condensed and contained, he appeared at the same time to have been waiting there for a thousand years and to have just parachuted down through a hole in the world above this one. He was rooted like a tree to the center of the earth, and he had roses. Other people pushed and bumped him as if he were invisible to them. His eyes remained fixed on nothing.

The temperature was ninety-nine degrees Fahrenheit. Beads of moisture clung to his firmly closed jaw and to the unfurled petals.

He had a strong-boned face, ruddy skin, and an ultra-flat-topped crew cut. Large wire-rimmed glasses seemed about to slide off the low bridge of his nose. A green plaid short-sleeved shirt and loose-fitting pants, belted high, clothed a short, stout, no-frills package.

His eyes met mine, and with a quick bow of the head, he looked down, smiling inwardly. I smiled this way, too. It was the most no-nonsense, needing-no-further-elaboration, sincerely silent communication I would ever receive from another human being. I should have remembered its completeness in times to come better than I did.

The Middle Flowering

THE ROSES HAD BEEN HIS SISTER'S IDEA. "American women like," she had instructed. Zhong-hua would never again resort to this kind of romantic gesture. With him I was to learn a strange and separate language of love.

Our first meal together was shared with a group at a large, round table. The entrées were placed on a revolving Chinese-style lazy Susan, a tiny plate and teacup placed before each guest. I reached for a dish in the center, but before my hand closed around a serving spoon, someone had spun the circle and the desired food revolved to the other side of the world. Whisking food away from other people by spinning the lazy Susan was evidently not considered rude, but other things were. Zhong-hua never took the last few morsels of a savory dish, for example, and he carefully picked from the sides of a shared dish with his chopsticks rather than mining the center.

Zhong-hua sat at my right and leaned toward me, attending to me as if I were a baby bird. He fed me by placing each delicacy on my plate and watching without ever making eye contact or smiling. Of the locusts and sea slugs, he gave me just a little and nodded once encouragingly to say, "Try." He saw I loved shrimp and piled more on the plate. If I could not eat something for its strangeness, he would eat it himself off the plate. Out of necessity, the first new phrase I learned in China was *chi bao le*, "I am full."

During our first evening together, we used a big red English-Chinese/Chinese-English dictionary to talk. While we sat across from each other, I on the hotel bed and he on a chair, our heads bent together over the fat book, I told him I was *yi shu jia* (an artist). He told me in English that his daughter was in middle school. He announced this carefully rehearsed phrase a dozen times, from which I inferred that, should I wish it, they would both become part of my life.

He said he liked to draw flowers, or rather, he drew a flower and said, "I love." I said I would grow some for him. He said, "Thank you very much." I said, "You are welcome." Later I figured out that he always said "Thank you very much" when he had no idea what had been said. That evening the surplus of feeling spilled out as laughter over the edges of our small words. He forced out the English words with too much vigor of breath, and I deprived my Chinese words of oxygen and punch. It was fun for a while, until my body wanted to cave in under the strain of earnestness.

Little could jump from the fat book complete. We were both communicating mainly the sincerity of our effort. Suddenly, I felt an iron grip on my knee. I turned my face, but he was looking straight down at the open dictionary. I knew all his strength and ardor at that moment. Zhong-hua closed the fat dictator and set it on the floor.

After spending a few weeks together in China, we decided to get married. It could work, we knew it, and if we did not have official papers, Zhong-hua would not be able to come to America. Even this way, we would have to wait many months.

Zhong-hua called his sister's husband *Da Ge* (big brother). His sister, who had stayed home, he called *Da Jie* (big sister). Da Ge took us to the hospital for physicals and then to stark government offices to apply for marriage documents. The officials smiled big; they made long speeches assuring us that the Chinese government would not stand in the way of two people in love. They smugly wished us long life, as if to say, "Look, if things go wrong, it's not our fault!" Da Ge talked to them and handed them an envelope of money, although we had already paid the fee. I looked at Zhong-hua, and he said, "Must be." For a thousand years, bribery has been the grease of commerce and social interaction in China. Recent laws have made bribery grounds for imprisonment, but a person might invite equally serious disasters by not taking out this insurance.

There were other rituals over the next few days, following the ritual first feeding of the baby-bird bride. There was the ritual of washing each other. This spouse washing was done with great care and thoroughness in the shower. It was not an occasion for lusty overtures. Perhaps by middle age, experience had sobered us to the potentially harmful outcome of loving another. We didn't want to hurt each other. I was tentative and shy. I had been naked before, but this was the first time I actually felt naked.

There was no hiding from this man. Zhong-hua had flabby breasts and a hanging belly, which he guided my hand to scrub. Under the soft outer layers, I could feel the hardness of his body. His thighs were massive swells of muscle. All of this was rather surprising because the roomy business clothes and little black shoes he always wore disguised his powerful physique. Zhong-hua was rigorous and solemn scrubbing me. I had always been horribly self-conscious about my flat chest. I hated to disappoint him, but he didn't seem disappointed. He was meticulous and unsentimentally gentle. He said, "Yeah" and "Turn." His sonorous voice was balm to my nerves. I turned and turned, breathing deeply. He dried my hair and passed the towel to me. He bent his head.

Before I went to China, I had banished expectations and moved beyond the amusement of imagining what my perfect person should be like. Expectations I didn't know I had would rear up much later, but in China I had none and so was allowed to see, feel, and appreciate with the extrasensory powers granted anyone whose critical mind is in suspension. I knew something about

Zhong-hua, not because of what his sister had told me but because he had been willing to open his heart to possibility. How awful it could be to reach halfway across the world to someone with whom you could find no rapport. That he also risked this disappointment assured me he intended to try his best and let me love him, sight unseen. We shared the implicit trust of mountain climbers, based solely on the certainty that the other will not purposely let you fall.

I am a mountain climber's daughter. My father's people came from Switzerland, so his mountains had craggy profiles, caped with fields of snow and skirted with slopes of scree. They required a strategy to reach the summit, and he knew how to make an inch on a map into many difficult steps by reverse magic. I learned that the mountain's head makes its own thoughtstorm, and wind and hail blow fiercest at the pass. I learned several unkosher methods of starting fire in the rain, but I never learned to plan my footsteps ahead of time or to employ a strategy. I had no strategy in China and yet, without ever knowing, had been prepared.

From my father, I had learned of the silences of men, silences whose sparse emissions of words burst like seminal flowers high in the air. Camping in a pup tent with him, to whom I did not complain when groundwater soaked the bottom of my sleeping bag, I sometimes felt lonely, but there was a lot of space in the silence, space that had its own slow-motion speech, its own eons of time. I was in my world, he was in his longer, dryer one, but we were together at the feet of great mountains.

In our hotel room, Zhong-hua ordered our few belongings. How quickly that random room became our world. We unpacked and hung up clothes, sat on the floor and stretched our backs, sat on the toilet or sat on the bed with our notebooks and pens. We ate snacks and brushed our teeth. In this wordless matrix, the objects around us shone with new importance and a kind of radiant energy. From every thing in the room two different names slipped off, and they carried on in an unlabeled democracy reflected in the big wall mirror. Stomach rumbles and farts made perfectly articulated statements. The absence of words let things be themselves. I felt the air warm and tingling with companionship sheltered from discourse. I looked often at Zhong-hua's resolute profile but did not need to look.

Zhong-hua stood at the foot of the bed where I was reading. *"Anmo,"* he said, which meant "massage." He gestured for me to roll over. I did. His hands were astonishingly warm and powerful. He massaged not the muscle but whatever was underneath and inside. He pressed intensely on certain points, such as the sole of my foot. A warm, liquid feeling spread from my stomach to my limbs. He pressed my knee, and my head cleared. He slapped and chopped and rolled as if preparing flour and water for dumpling dough. I was grunting "Ouch, ouch, uh, ugh, hey!" This was not exactly what the word *massage* referred to, but then again, maybe *anmo* did not exactly mean "massage." When it was over, I staggered to my feet and said, "Holy crap." Zhong-hua smiled, satisfied that he had revealed to me another hidden dimension of himself.

Over the next few days, Da Ge took his small group to visit some tourist sites. Zhong-hua and I went along, lagging behind the others. In the daylight, Zhong-hua seemed invisible. Others hardly noticed him. He did not project outward at all. On the bus, he sat immovable, usually with his eyes closed. He seemed to ignore everything around him unless directly spoken to. Then he politely nodded or laughed. That's all. If I sighed or yawned, he pressed my head into his lap. The lap was heavenly.

We visited the Forbidden City, the Great Wall, and other grand remnants of power. Zhong-hua's face remained expressionless. Sometimes I asked him *"Ni xiang shenme?"* (What are you thinking?). He said, *"Bu xiang"* (Not thinking).

At night in the room, he held me. His heavy body felt luminous and lithe; it was a fluid body that emanated energy from every part. I felt bathed in affection and treasured beyond measure, but could not breathe very well. I had to punch out an airhole in the covers and lunge for it.

Da Ge was ten years older than Zhong-hua, and both had been sent away during the Cultural Revolution (1966 — 1976) to teach school and labor in the fields of small farm villages. Mao's Cultural Revolution attacked the four "old elements" of Chinese society: old customs, old habits, old culture, and old thinking. Schools were closed and students banded into Red Guard squads appointed to implement the attack. The repressed rage of powerlessness was unleashed into unspeakable acts of sadism. Thousands of intellectuals—including writers, artists, musicians, and teachers—were beaten to death. Countless others committed suicide or spent years in prison.

Da Ge had spent six years as a teacher in a one-room school. With no fuel through the long winter, he had warmed up the children with jumping jacks and Qigong exercises until their fingers and toes thawed and they could concentrate. Nobody had winter clothes, gloves, or warm shoes. There was almost nothing to eat.

Now, thirty years later, we walked the hardened dirt between the village huts. One of his former students lived in the old schoolhouse with his aged mother. The mother seemed made of dry sticks dressed in rags and was barefoot, grinning a toothless welcome. Her son was also barefoot, dressed in rags, and grinning, but his belly was round. The rural people now had food, if little else. In a shed there was a motorized press for extracting oil from soybeans, a process that Da Ge remembered being carried out by human donkeys leaning their bodies against a pole that turned the gears.

The former schoolhouse was a small brick square with no windows, a dirt floor, and a thatch roof. A sleeping platform with a straw mat occupied most of the space, and a low stove made of sheet metal held the corner. There was dry grass heaped on the floor for making fire. That was all. In front a few chickens pecked listlessly behind a fence made of short branches stuck in the ground to form a semicircle against the house. All the villagers lived in similar barren simplicity, except for the director, whose house was larger and had a poured concrete floor, a furnished tearoom, a food-storage room with tall baskets and urns, a walled courtyard, and a fat pig.

We continued by train to Da Ge's hometown, Qufu, birthplace of Confucius. Not far away was Yi Mountain, one of many Taoist mountains riddled with caves. Temples remained on such mountains, but they were ghost temples. Legends of both shamanism and early Taoism speak of sages and mystics, often called "immortals," who lived in harmony with nature, eating herbs and alchemical elixirs, until they were four hundred or even eight hundred years old, when they just disappeared into the landscape. Da Ge said one Taoist monk meditated for forty years in front of a rock, keeping warm with Qigong practice. When he died, his shadow image was imprinted on the rock.

During the Cultural Revolution, spiritual practices were banned, spiritual leaders imprisoned or killed, and devotees ordered to marry and return to secular life as farm or factory laborers. Perhaps some fled to their sacred mountains. This particular mountain was made of many huge egg-shaped boulders. The trees were lush and hung with mist. I recognized many of my familiars from home: pine and oak, maple and birch. Even the flowers hugging the ground resembled their blue and yellow relatives in upstate New York. Sometimes Zhong-hua nudged me and pointed. His nudges were heavier than would be acceptable in American culture, but I was beginning to appreciate that these were conjugal nudges. "Umm," I said.

Sometimes I tapped his knee and pointed. His eyes found the spot of sunlight that had rolled under a rock or the tree making its way up the mountain like a bent old man. He nodded with a barely audible grunt. A grunt is a sound in Chinese that can mean "oh," "yeah," "so what?" "OK," "thanks," "very, very good," "oh, really?" "I'll be there," "I'll think about it," "good-bye, then," or "I'm disgusted." In this case, though, it meant "perfect."

Halfway up the mountain, a path dipped under the boughs of long-needled pine and into a cave. A tiny old woman guarded the entrance. She ushered us inside to the dark circle of water brimming at the mouth of the spring. She handed Zhong-hua a wooden ladle and bade him drink. He drank greedily and passed the ladle to me. Pure water in China is precious. Candles burned on a small altar, and there were unlit sticks of incense in a bowl. Zhong-hua knelt before the altar and lowered his head to the soil. He lit incense and stuck it into the dirt. I knelt and lowered my head, paying my respects to the spirits of this place, whoever they were, and to the god of my husband. Using the Chinese Fo (Buddha), I asked if he followed Buddha. He said no, because when he grew up under the rule of Chairman Mao, people could not believe. I asked if we had just prayed to Buddha. He nodded. Just to make sure, I asked again. He shook his head rapidly, "No, no, no."

We left and joined the main path climbing upward. Small boys from the village at the bottom of the mountain bounded behind us, laughing and shouting. Their eyes sparkled with glee. They warned us in Chinese, "You cannot get to the top unless you are willing to crawl on your belly!"

"Like a dog!"

"Yes, yes, like a dog!" They laughed uproariously. I had no problem crawling on my belly but had to leave Zhong-hua behind where the tunnel became narrower than his. He and two portly ladies on the tour named Alice and Myrtle turned back on two legs to wait for us. The small boys, Da Ge, and I continued. The top was a smooth stone forehead sticking up into the swirling mist. This mountain where legendary Taoist monks had lived clandestine lives protected by the mountain spirits was the one place in China where I felt at home. On top, taking gulps of wind for nourishment, I felt elated. I sat in a crease of the bald head so as not to be swept off the mountain into oblivion. After a while I missed the dirt below. When we came back through the tunnel, Zhong-hua was waiting.

Waiting is a Chinese art. Just waiting in a fold of time. Travelers often find themselves waiting: waiting for a train or a bus, waiting for breakfast or lunch to be served, or waiting on a bench, as Zhong-hua was, between the footsore Alice and Myrtle. There is no dishonor in this kind of waiting. No need to try to make something happen or fill up the emptiness. When Zhong-hua waited on a stone bench, he became stone. When he leaned his body against a tree, he became wood. Whenever possible, he combined waiting with sleeping. I learned from him how to conserve energy this way. He seemed to think that talking just to talk wasted energy. It was better to keep it inside and make no extra effort until conversation rode out clomp-clomp on the horses of intent. If the horses were relaxing, then what need for words? Perhaps it was possible to listen to another's thoughts as horses listen to one another chewing grass.

Zhong-hua excelled in the art of being simultaneously absent and present. He wore no expression on his face. Walking, he stared ahead and never walked farther than necessary. When a bench presented itself, he sat down. If the group lingered, he soon dozed.

During our travels, Da Ge sometimes grunted something in his ear. Zhong-hua nodded and disappeared into the crowd, reappearing later with a cryptic message for Da Ge. They exchanged sharp, explosive words and never smiled. When he returned with packages, Da Ge tucked them in his bag, and Zhong-hua resumed gliding stoutly along with no agenda of his own while concealing an exquisite readiness for action. If Alice tripped, he righted her before anyone else knew she was falling. If Myrtle dropped her purse, he caught it before it hit the ground.

Word quickly spread in Da Ge's native Qufu that he had returned for a visit with American friends. A young university woman, Kong Hui, appeared at our lunch table, hoping to practice some English. Kong Hui followed me around for several days. I had only a small paper book of poetry with me, translations of Antonio Machado by Robert Bly. I read these poems to Kong Hui, and we decided to translate one of them into Chinese. Of course, it had already made one crossing from Spanish to English.

I have never wanted fame
Nor wanted to leave my poems
Behind in the memory of men
I love the subtle worlds,
Delicate, almost without weight,
Like soap bubbles.
I enjoy seeing them take the color
Of sunlight and scarlet, float
In the blue sky, then
Suddenly quiver and break.

Kong Hui was uncommonly sincere and honest. When she re-appeared the next day after examining the poem, her smooth oval face was troubled, her straight eyebrows furrowed.

"Ellen, I do not understand this poet. I believe he must be confused. I feel very sorry; you share with me, and I don't want to hurt you."

"Go ahead, Kong Hui, tell me what you think."

"He says he would like to see beautiful things break and die."

"Kong Hui, perhaps he means that a person can appreciate beauty but need not grab it. He is accepting that all things pass away and are lost."

"This is a very sad thing."

"He very much loves the beauty of the world."

"He very much enjoys watching this beauty break."

"Well, he notices that the best things cannot be fully known; they float by, and you can't tell if they are real or reflections of something, maybe of your own eye."

"No, I still don't understand him. Why does it make this poet so happy to see things break and die?"

"Hmm. Yeah. Is that strange to you?"

"Very strange. I believe this man has a terrible heart."

Kong Hui helped me find the red shoes to wear with the red dress for the fake wedding. Zhong-hua and I were already married in a government office by virtue of official signing of papers. But Da Ge had invited many old friends to come to a wedding "show" that included martial arts stunts and a wedding orchestra. We were supposed to appear onstage and dance a wedding dance. This exhibitionist idea was repugnant to Zhong-hua, but he could not say no to an older brother-in-law.

Da Ge and Zhong-hua were opposite personalities. Da Ge relished the limelight. He loved to show off his skill with sword or staff and leap high in the air in his pink silk pantaloons. Wherever we went, he demonstrated to people he had just met how he could make qi energy by concentration. He captured their attention and then made them feel the heat collected in his palms. He said he could blow off the end of a Coke bottle with this heat, but it would make a mess. I asked Da Ge if Kong Hui and I could share our poem translation at the show, since his brother was also going to perform with his yo-yo in what seemed to be shaping up as a hodgepodge talent show. He said, "OK, OK, if there is time." I didn't yet know enough to realize that this meant "No way."

The night of the show we were supposed to meet everybody to catch the bus that would take us to dinner. We hurried down the main street lined with vendors selling from small tables or makeshift platforms made of crates. They sold bunches of greens, eggs and watermelons, jade bracelets, and small statues of Confucius. Zhong-hua shouldered me onto a side street and up an alleyway strewn with cardboard and vegetable refuse. Stucco walls smelled of urine, and flies feasted on melon rinds. We made a few more turns into the labyrinth and ducked into a restaurant.

The restaurant was the living room of an old man and his wife who were on the couch watching TV. Two bottles of wine stood at attention on top of the TV, and one small table occupied the middle of the room. The man motioned for us to sit, and Zhong-hua pointed to the wine atop the TV. Soon we were served a gigantic dish of dumplings with another huge bowl of chopped cucumbers on the side. Zhong-hua linked his arm through mine and downed the wine while I downed mine. We smirked like two outlaws stealing time. It took only an ounce of Chinese wine to paralyze my lips and set my head on fire. I vaguely remembered that we were supposed to be going somewhere, but where?

I thought of the two small china vessels on my mother's shelf, a portly middle-aged man with a knapsack and cane and his pleasingly plump wife in her bonnet and long-aproned skirt with a basket on her arm. The inscription on the base under the man's feet said, "I am going on a journey." The inscription beneath the woman read, "And I am going with him." I would follow Zhong-hua anywhere. Zhong-hua's face was beet red, but I trusted him no less. I asked, "*Women yin'gai qu nar?*" (We should go where?)

"*Bu yao.*" (No need.) He filled my glass again. We finished our meal and careened back into the alley. Zhong-hua bought a watermelon from a farmer, who slashed it open with one stroke of his big knife. We sat on the dusty curb and ate it, slurping and spitting seeds. One landed on my shoe. I realized Zhong-hua did not care about red shoes or about my appearing in them to please his brother-in-law. Ordinarily, I could not detect any trace of negative attitude in this man, but he had drunk the tall bottle of wine from the top of the TV, and I could plainly see that he disdained to go among the people Da Ge had summoned.

"Da Ge is waiting for us."

Zhong-hua waved his hand in dismissal. As the younger relative, he must always defer to his elder. Da Ge used him as a shopping cart, a hat rack, a bellboy, and a secretary, according to the order of the Confucian universe. Zhong-hua sauntered down the alley with deliberate slowness, his arm draped heavily over my shoulder. He began to sing a melody. The notes of his magnificent voice floated over the dirty puddles like wind-borne blossoms. No, he surely did not want to appear in a spectacle or to be anywhere but here. I thought of Da Ge, generous and voyeuristic, presenting his friends with sword dancing, wedding music, and us—the bride and groom puppets.

When we arrived at the school where the stage had been set, Da Ge met us frantically at the door and said we must run because the music was already playing. We ran up on the stage. By magic, Da Ge was already there before us, gesticulating to make us walk faster. We were both drunk and full of dumplings. Da Ge directed everything with the mastery of a circus trainer. He stepped around us and between us, pushing here, pulling there, brushing our ears with garlic-breathy orders. I vaguely recall eating from opposite sides of an apple that Da Ge dangled between us. I do remember at the end of the routine Zhong-hua lifted me over a wooden bench and carried me off the stage while Da Ge's friends clapped and laughed. Then Da Ge thrust bowls of candy into our arms and told us to distribute it to these guests whom we did not know. Next came Tai Chi Sword, Wushu Tiger, Monkey, and Snake demonstrations. These are dancelike fighting forms based on diligent observation of animals in motion. Da Ge was in his glory.

I saw Kong Hui with the poem in her hand. She saw my face fall in realization that we hadn't gotten to read our poetry after dinner as we planned because I had been drunk in the alley with my new husband, and because Da Ge had never intended to allow a poem to infiltrate his show. I had let her down. She read my heart and rushed to me. "Ellen, don't worry about this small thing. We can read this terrible poem next time. I know when you return, we will translate many things. You will return home to China and live here forever. Forever. I am sure of this." In what time or manner return or forever might manifest, I could not imagine. I folded her curious words away.

I tried to hug my husband good-bye in the hotel room. He moved back and said, "Airport."

"OK." That seemed frugal to me. Couldn't we hug twice? Maybe the last hug would be a big bear hug. I would have to wait and see.

At the airport we waited in line. Da Ge chattered to anyone

who would listen. Zhong-hua stood stiffly with his lips pressed together. I took my cue from him and stood straight and motionless. As it turned out, this was a quite tolerable way to deal with the situation; it contained the swells of emotion and conserved energy. A few tears rolled down my face, but I didn't wipe them or move.

At the last minute, Da Ge turned to Zhong-hua and ordered, "*Yongbao*, American-style." Zhong-hua looked shocked, as if pinned to the wall by a dart. "*Kuai yidiar, yongbao! Meiguoren xihuan zuo zheyang*" (Quickly hug! Americans like doing things this way). I don't remember feeling this public hug, only that it was a swift, uninvested motion. Other Chinese people were standing in line watching us; I sensed Zhong-hua did not wish to entertain them. Zhong-hua turned to Da Ge and said, "*Ta dei geiwo xie henduo xin*" (She must write me many letters), then hurried away without saying good-bye.

A Sovereign Sense

I RETURNED HOME TO AMERICA and waited a year and a half for Zhong-hua to be granted a visa. We communicated over the phone in Chinese bookended with English for hello and good-bye; in letters we both wrote Chinese characters and English words, one underneath the other. Translating with a dictionary, I sometimes wrote down characters that had been out of popular use in China for centuries. When I asked after his father, it probably sounded something like "I prithee, how fareth thy honorable ancestor?" Zhong-hua wrote things like "I am writing you together with my miss and wishes from the brootom of my heart." So I was surprised to receive a perfect love poem in English:

Love doesn't ask why
It speaks from the heart
and never explains
Don't you know that love doesn't have to think twice
It can come all at once,
or whispers from a distance
Don't ask me if this
feeling's right or wrong
It doesn't have to make much sense

It just has to be this strong
cause when you're in my arms I understand
we don't have to have a voice
when our hearts make the choices
there's no plan
it's in our hands.

Impressive! I thought he had labored over this poem for me and didn't discover until five years later that it was a Céline Dion song his English teacher had handed out in class.* At Christmas the kids grew some fondness for Zhong-hua based on the messages he left on the phone asking after their welfare: "This is Lu. Uh. Merry Crimma! How are your cho-co-lates?"

After one failed attempt and two long train rides from Linyi to Guangzhou, Zhong-hua was finally granted a visa. He would be coming soon, he said, after he sat by the bed of his dying uncle and journeyed to his mother's grave with delicious food and paper money.

I wanted to have everything neat and tidy when my husband came—no junk, no broken, useless things. Paroda helped me clean the cobwebs and wood ash from the corners of the house and rearrange our possessions. She made a list of yet more products needed for decent living, adding up to thousands of dollars, including things like a color-matched bath mat and toilet seat cover, but in the end we just painted the walls the color of Granny Smith apples.

On the way home from the airport, according to our notions of American hospitality, Paroda and I kept the banter going, and my husband kept saying "Oh!" and "Yes!" even though he could not yet understand or speak English.

It was winter. As soon as we entered the house, Zhong-hua made

*Written by Cynthia Weil, Barry Mann, and Phil Galdston.

himself deftly at home. First he stood before the woodstove and removed the business pants he had traveled from China in. There he stood in his baggy quilted long underwear. "Very comfortable," he said. This phrase, along with "not comfortable," "yes," "no," and "hello," completed his vocabulary.

It must have been the moment when the pants came off that Paroda and I simultaneously adopted our policy of no judgment. It was clear that Zhong-hua was living by a different set of rules. We didn't know those rules—we only knew we adored him. Supper that night was a piece of salmon. Zhong-hua nudged me aside and, with experienced hands, sliced garlic and scallions. He pulverized a big handful of peppercorns under a stone pestle and dumped the pile into sizzling oil. I began sneezing uncontrollably and had to run outside. Paroda ran upstairs.

While we recovered from the meal, Zhong-hua rummaged around in the bathroom until he found the mop, bucket, and Murphy Oil Soap. He then proceeded to methodically scrub all the floors, upstairs and down. Afterward he went outside and stood on the snowy porch in the shiny business shoes and baggy long johns. He looked up at the starry sky and had a smoke.

I wasn't yet used to the poker face that I had become comfortable with in China as the normal and correct facial expression. There were no random smiles, no effort at small talk, no hand squeezing or patting on the shoulder. My husband would no sooner pat my hand or kiss my cheek than pat his own hand or kiss his own image in the mirror. I had to feel the airwaves to know whether everything was OK or not OK. I decided it was OK and went to bed, leaving my husband out in the snow. When he came to bed, he held me as if I were something long lost and precious that might not live until morning. Words became necessary: "*Wo bu neng huxi!*" (I can't breathe!)

After the first night of floor mopping had come the much more rigorous second night of filling in holes between the foundation stones with mortar. The crawl space of our cellar slanted upward to the far end under the kitchen; we had to hunker down more and more and then waddle on our haunches to complete inspection with the flashlight. Cobwebs clung to our faces, and a chill rose like well water from the clammy bedrock up our pant legs. Zhong-hua mixed small batches of mason's mortar in a dishpan and troweled it into the crevices. It was very dark, so first he held his wrist close to the wall to feel the stream of cold air, then aimed the laden trowel. This subterraneous boundary set apart a ten- by twenty-foot space in the middle of a windy pasture where successive hearty souls had improvised lives. Zhong-hua remained silent and focused throughout the somber ritual, communicating with a turn of the shoulder or by holding the trowel out to his side without looking. I kept the trowel full of mortar and held the flashlight. By dawn the two bags of mortar were empty shreds of brown paper. Cold had turned my fingertips white. Cement dust had turned his eyes red. He said, "*Wanle,*" meaning "finished," and we went to sleep.

This was just the first of many "concrete solutions" to daily problems. My husband put great store in concrete, a material that, though at first solid and unyielding, could be flowed around, over, and under; quaked from below; smashed from above; and exploded in slow motion by delicate crystals of frost, proving the fundamental Tai Chi principle that soft overcomes hard by turning, retreating, infiltrating, waiting, and shape-shifting.

Shortly after arriving, Zhong-hua suggested we sell the refrigerator. "Just three people—no need." In China many people do not own a refrigerator. They shop daily for fresh meat and vegetables and after a meal leave leftover food uncovered on the table until it is consumed. The first time Zhong-hua and Paroda went shopping together, she reported, laughing, that instead of getting a cart, Zhong-hua had just transferred each item to her arms until piled-up stuff hid her face. After more trips and more looking around, my husband noticed that other men were not loading their merchandise onto their female companions and switched to using the cart.

I found four dozen eggs in the cupboard, and Zhong-hua said that was "no problem" because in China eggs are kept unrefrigerated for up to two months. I said the eggs were different here and convinced him to wait on selling the refrigerator. It soon became a hazard. His sister, whom we both now called *Da Jie*, "Big Sister," showed up once a month with poppy-colored plastic bags from the Chinese grocery bursting with Chinese cabbage, bok choy, spinach, and daikon resembling short, pale baseball bats. She brought cases of mangoes and stacks of eggs six dozen high. Every time the refrigerator door was opened, a Chinese cabbage or two tumbled to the floor and sharp-clawed chicken feet startled me from under bunches of cilantro and watercress. Bags of frozen cuttlefish stacked in the freezer had a way of sliding out like bobsleds and hitting me in the chest.

I had never eaten giant sea slugs or sheep's stomach. I tried them, once. He had never eaten cheese or mashed potatoes. He tried them, once. He tasted small, tentative half spoonfuls of ice cream. He stirred it vigorously to warm it up and, when that didn't work, poured hot tea over it. We both went hungry or suffered indigestion when the other made supper. We endured this food trauma for six months. He lost fifteen pounds. I lost ten. After that, he still would not touch cheese or homemade chicken potpie but could devour an entire half gallon of chocolate ice cream in one sitting and eat the entire crust off the top of a cherry pie. He seemed surprised at my indignance. "You make this crust is very good. I like!"

He said if food could not be eaten until it was all gone, then it was no good. "One time, eat all gone" was the rule. He was also fond of repeating his father's maxim that a craving is your body telling you what it needs to be healthy. I still hated slugs but became accustomed to my lips burning while eating his hot Shandong Province cuisine. I enjoyed wood ears, a kind of fungus that feeds on dead branches. Dried wood ears soaked in water were slippery and crunchy and not exactly tasty, but not bad either. I also came to relish squid and what I called "smelly fish." This salted fish, when deep-fried, "smells very bad but tastes very good," just as Zhong-hua said. Its smell filled the house with an odor like that of a men's wrestling team locker room. In early spring, Zhong-hua purchased a large package of tripe but was disgusted by how dirty it was, unlike the clean tripe he could buy in China. Scrubbing the gritty sheets of intestines under running water took more than an hour. While the huge open pot bubbled on the stove, Zhong-hua again reassured me, "Smells very bad but tastes very good."

Later the same day I was outside hanging laundry when I heard my daughter screech, "MOM, MOM, the house is on fire!" I ran up from the garden. Green, foul-smelling smoke poured out of the windows. The electric burner glowed fiery red, and the water had boiled from the pot, leaving smoking cinders of pig's bowels. The house was not on fire, just the tripe. We threw open all the doors and windows. This only chilled the hideous smell without decreasing it.

When Zhong-hua reappeared, he broke his rule of "never say sorry to your wife." "Sorry! Sorry!" he said, grinning, though technically the apology was directed at my daughter. This ban on "sorry" is part of a cultural model that considers it not only unnecessary but also inappropriate and offensive to extend certain polite or conciliatory gestures to one's spouse. It is as if doing so would identify him or her as "other." Additional forbiddances include "thank you," "hello," "good-bye," "excuse me," and "please." Whenever he used one of these phrases, he said it as if on stage, with great gusto and enunciation. It struck him as so funny that he burst into uncharacteristic laughter, especially with "excuse me."

He routinely bumped into me in a deliberate manner if I was in his path. The collisions usually happened in the kitchen while we both prepared food. He pushed me along, using his ample stomach as a snowplow, until he had enough counter space. I didn't realize that bodily rudeness was a privilege of intimacy, and I made a point of being offended. When I tried to explain the concept of "excuse me," my husband looked at me with impatient disbelief. He said, "This kind of thing in our home no need, because this is *family*.

Family no need these kind of words." Understanding that he was operating out of a belief system and not out of rudeness, I tried his way. Pushing him out of the way with a forceful thrust of the hip was fun, though he was very solid and removing him to another location took several tries.

As the weather warmed, Zhong-hua loved to sit on a purple plastic milk crate at the edge of the pond smoking and studying the food chain. Within the pond were grassy islands where painted turtles sunned themselves and deeper parts where blacksnakes preyed. Birds also loved this food bowl, full of bugs and catfish. The great blue herons ruled over kingfishers, orioles, woodpeckers, swallows, finches, jays, and hummingbirds.

A dove flew over our heads. "This is a very good bird."

"Yes, their call is lovely. We call this a mourning dove. To mourn is to be sad about someone, and this bird sounds sad."

He seemed not to be listening to me. "This bird is very, very good! In China people love to eat this one."

"Really?"

"Yes. Very delicious! Gooder than chicken. Also free." When he purchased a cheap air gun at the Elks' tool sale, I didn't make the connection. I suppose I thought he was going to shoot at outdated cans of beans, as my son Athan had done with high school friends. He shot dead one bird, a downy woodpecker. I panicked. "Zhong-hua, our neighbor Flippy fills five feeders every day for those birds. You can't shoot them. You just can't!"

Zhong-hua had a way of not reacting to shrill utterances, as if they were outside his auditory frequency range. This made me all the more strident, "No, Zhong-hua, I mean it. You just can't!"

Still gazing up at the sky, he nodded. "OK, OK. You right. Make neighbor happy is right way." He didn't shoot any more birds at home, but every time we went to Troy, he eyed the plump pigeons waddling up and down on the sidewalks and asked if it was OK to shoot those birds. I said that would be a bad idea. He said there were a lot and nobody else was eating them.

Food gave us trouble, but words gave us more. Food presented itself to our bodies in unfamiliar packages that eventually broke down into universal molecules. Words presented themselves as the world and, undigested, made the world strange.

I had striven hard during our separation to master a conversational level of Chinese and assumed he had been in China wrestling with English. To my dismay, I learned that his English class had come after luncheons with company clients, during which he was obliged to drink competitive rounds until negotiations became optimal. He managed to find his way to English class, then promptly fell asleep. Dinner meetings followed, with more drinks to be downed and deals to be sealed. Finding his way home on his motorbike was not straightforward. He sometimes rode in wobbly circles until the policeman, a pal he had gone to high school with, pointed him home. Before he left, he gave the bike to his best friend. In America he almost never drank, deciding that one major vice—smoking—was enough, and citing the case of Deng Xiaoping, who smoked three packs a day and lived ninety-three years.

One of his English assignments dealt with daily schedules. He had sent me his: "Get up at four thirty, go to meet Tai Chi teacher in the park, eat something, go to work, after work go to English class, then go back to work until ten thirty." He concluded with, "I'm tired, wanna sleep." His English teacher, from the Philippines, was teaching them "American English" from a book called *Speak English As You Wish*. After he arrived, I looked over his class book. There were several pages of sentences that began "I wanna . . ." Another book called *A Trip to the United States* included a conversation between two erudite young men:

"I thought Jack went for the busty, well-padded types. What happened to his little broad?"

"What's he doing casting eyes at my girl?"

"Maybe he likes the way she swings—most of us do. . . ."

"It's not her fault she's stacked."

His second month here, we enrolled Zhong-hua in the free

English classes in Troy, which included students from many parts of the world. One day Zhong-hua jumped into the car after class and said, "*Fuckyou*. What do you mean, *fuckyou*?" It turned out that rather than teach something useful, the teacher had spent the day teaching them expressions that he then told them never, ever to use. Between this teacher and the Filipino teacher, Zhong-hua had a very small vocabulary of appropriate things to say.

My husband had two degrees, one in Chinese cultural studies that he had paid for by working in a candy factory shortly after Mao's death, and one from a technical institute he attended while employed at a machine parts factory. At the factory, he wore protective clothing to tend a giant furnace. Hot metal tempered in a chemical solution hissed toxic fumes that affected the workers' lungs and sinuses. After thirteen years, the prolonged exposure to intense heat caused Zhong-hua's heart to beat irregularly. A friend helped him get reassigned to a management job at a steel building materials company, where he became chief manager of negotiations. Arriving in America, he said, "Now I need start from zero." (*Xianzai wo dei cong ling kaishi.*) In Chinese, the verb phrase was inverted to "from nothing start," which was locomotively more logical.

Early on, a friend's husband with kind intentions hired my husband to help him with a house painting job. I thought that would be a great job for him. I didn't know that in China houses are not painted. Walls are usually stone block, cement, or plastered wood. The two returned after dark, the rumble of the truck engine drowned out by the oldies station blasting "Wooly Bully," by Sam the Sham and the Pharaohs. Zhong-hua had white paint all over his hair. He looked wildly wretched. The friend's husband comported himself with shell-shocked dignity, managing a tight, haggard smile. They had gone into a convenience store for lunch, where Zhong-hua did not recognize anything as food. He had eaten a small amount of something sweet and alien and by evening was famished.

My friend's husband reported in a low voice that Zhong-hua was a disaster as a painter. He pushed the roller so vigorously that paint spattered everywhere, and then, after proper instruction, so slowly that the paint went on triple thick. He held one brush in each hand to paint trim and baseboards. As a last resort, my friend's husband had assigned Zhong-hua to the closet. The good man pressed two hundred dollars into my husband's hand, slapped him on the back, and said he didn't need a helper the next day.

Zhong-hua remained silent after eating two big bowls of noodles. I asked if he was very tired. He looked up, unsmiling. "You think I should be happy? Chinese wife would not send her husband to do this kind of work." He spoke intensely, so low and controlled that I didn't realize at first that he was angry. His body was stiff and his eyes slivers of black ice. I thought I had done what he asked of me: find him work. But I had done wrong. How? I felt waves of nausea. He showered and went out into the spring night. A few hours later, the roving tip of his cigarette still glowed in the darkness.

I later understood that I had caused my husband to lose face but did not entirely understand why. The modern class-conscious urban Chinese shun manual labor, a throwback to prerevolutionary social values. A successful businessman should not get dirty. These complicated emotions were too steeped in the trauma of the Cultural Revolution for me to fully comprehend. In these first days, what people on the other side of the world might think of him, if they could see him, seemed of unbearable significance to my husband. After the long smoke, he came inside and said this kind of job was no problem. He hadn't known that Americans could do this work and not be ashamed. If this were true, he said, then he need not be ashamed either. He wanted to work. Status and image became abstractions associated with a social milieu involving the buying and selling of steel products on the other side of the world.

I didn't know then that my husband had endured labor a hundred times more grueling than painting inside closets. His poverty- and famine-ravaged parents could do little more for him than count his head as safely returned along with the others at night. In his youth he had worked side by side with village farmers, standing bare-legged in an icy winter pond hour after hour, scooping out silt for fertilizer. My husband's first nineteen years of life were years of hardship and deprivation inflicted on him by the policies of political authorities. He had achieved an internal equilibrium that was not easily upset. Taking most things in stride as a coping mechanism for prolonged stress with no end in sight—except, for many people, death—was a skill I respected. My own rugged path had been an upstream battle against raging currents of emotion made even more arduous by choices I myself had made or neglected to make. I sought a peace affected by neither the weather outside nor the storms inside.

That first spring, a friend of a friend gave Zhong-hua a job at a small grocery store. The owner was eager for him to learn English quickly and be able to handle the store in his absence. He had heard that Chinese people work hard. As Zhong-hua had no driver's license, the owner went several miles out of his way, picked him up at the house, and brought him home at night. According to Chinese etiquette, my husband invited him in to drink tea. The owner always accepted, not knowing that the correct Chinese response would be to graciously decline. There they would sit, my husband silent, tight-lipped, and tense, and the owner sipping bitter tea and spitting the leaves out in his hand.

The owner tried to make conversation by boldly asking personal questions, which Zhong-hua found very alarming. The owner ventured to comment that I was a nice lady and asked if I was a good wife. Zhong-hua later told me that only a very, very crazy person would say these things. A man should not compliment another's wife, for this revealed that you had noticed her, were possibly even attracted to her. He told the owner he did not like to talk about these things, to which the man replied that he himself found these things very interesting. On the middle ground arrived at, the owner related conflicts with his wife and struggles with his children in embarrassing detail, and Zhong-hua listened politely while carefully guarding his own privacy, saying only "Oh!" and "Good! Good!" and "Why?" This went on for several months until Zhong-hua got his driver's license.

My husband felt gnawing hunger while at work. The boss, eating an oversized organic cookie, broke off a small piece and offered it to my husband. When Zhong-hua returned home that evening, his face was hard and his eyes glittered coldly. He said a person offering food to another should offer only very good food, not a scrap that he himself had taken a bite of. How insulting! The offering of food to others had a ritualistic importance for Chinese people since the terrible famine in the early 1960s resulting from the sudden collectivization of agriculture and Mao's commitment to massive export of grain. Officials demanded most of the harvest in a desperate effort to fill Mao's production quotas, leaving nothing for the people to eat. Millions of Chinese starved. My husband was still on breast milk at six because there was little other food. His mother finally had to beat him off with a stick and chase him to school. The most common daily greeting in China is still "Chifan le ma?" (Have you eaten yet?).

Zhong-hua's problem of hunger at work was ongoing. Employees were allowed to help themselves to bread and butter and juice, but in moderation. For my husband, the word *moderation* had connotations sloping dangerously into the trough of emptiness. The more he felt the boss's eyes, the bigger his hunger—until an unlimited amount of outdated granola offered a solution. My husband discovered that by eating a saucepan full of granola and milk, he would not be hungry for many hours. He quickly gained ten pounds on the granola diet. Once he brought home two bushels of organic spinach, which the boss had thrown out because it was too dirty. Dirt was no challenge for a Chinese cook in the habit of meticulously scouring all meats and vegetables before using them, scraping off every stubborn hair and routing out the smallest speck of sand. We were also blessed with cases of outdated tofu dogs, soy yogurt, flaxseed, and cod liver oil.

The taboo on saying "good-bye" or "hello" to one's wife ranged from disconcerting to extremely distressing. I routinely thought Zhong-hua was still home when he had actually left, or thought he was out when he had returned. Humming aimlessly while believing myself alone in the kitchen, I would turn to reach for something and bump right into him, yelling in fright. However often it happened, I could not adjust my emotions.

One evening in June, my husband did not return from work. About ten o'clock he appeared at the kitchen door, clothes covered with blood and face bathed in sweat. His eyes danced happily. "You come see!" He had been in the barn skinning a deer that had been hit by a car and left to die. Zhong-hua could not fathom why American people left dead deer by the side of the road. In China, deer were found only in the southern forests, and the meat was a highly prized and expensive commodity. We brought up the seven-gallon tripe-boiling kettle from the cellar and boiled the deer meat.

Zhong-hua carefully skinned the penis and sank it in a bottle of Chinese wine we kept on the shelf. He said it should steep for a few months to increase the medicinal efficacy. The next day he went off to work with two hunks of dark red deer meat the size of fists wrapped in brown paper in his jacket pocket. After that a leg or several vertebrae sufficed as a daily portion. I don't know what the boss made of that. Because it was a New Age health food store and they didn't wish their image tarnished, they bade him smoke in the back alley rather than out in front. Deer meat was organic, but a man sitting at the white wrought iron table by the entrance gnawing on a giant leg bone might still offend the sensibilities of certain customers.

Some months later, Zhong-hua was on the way to work when the motorist in front of him struck and killed a doe but never stopped. Again refusing to see this excellent nourishment go to waste, Zhong-hua put the doe in the trunk and continued on to the grocery store, where he stashed her in the walk-in refrigerator for the day. The boss usually called me if he was upset with my husband, but he never called about finding a deer in the freezer. The guest had escaped his notice.

Zhong-hua reported that moderation was also the rule at the grocery store where the toilet was concerned, and that the boss rapped impatiently on the bathroom door if he were taking too long. This strange behavior disturbed my husband greatly. The grocery store job provided ample opportunity for misunderstandings and inadvertent insult between the boss and my husband. One day we needed to go to an appointment at noon, so I picked my husband up at work. We returned several hours later and were met in front of the store by the boss, red-faced with anger. As I drove away, I saw him gesticulating to Zhong-hua wildly with both arms above his head and jumping into the air.

I got a call from the boss that night. Zhong-hua had never mentioned that he had an appointment and would be gone for a while. Zhong-hua did not understand the upset. He reasoned that since he worked there and had certain things to get done, then obviously he would be returning to do those things. Why would the boss assume anything else? Since he was a grown man, he did not need to ask permission to come and go. After that, the boss insisted on my husband's reporting to him if he needed to go to the bathroom or out in the alley for a smoke. My husband said to me, "I don't think need do this." That incident was the beginning of the end of this job.

Most days left them both feeling at the least vaguely injured and sometimes very upset. The grocer once called me, for instance, to complain that my husband had stacked all the caramel Luna Bars on top of the lemon Luna Bars. "Is he trying to drive me crazy?" I could tell by the man's exasperated whine that he believed he was being deliberately tortured. In fact, my husband had been told by the supervisor in charge to dump all the Luna Bars in one box. He never told this to the boss. When reprimanded for this or any other offense, my husband offered neither explanation nor excuse. He just said, "Sorry, sorry. I make mistake. No problem." I read in my husband's face when he returned home that he wasn't sure whether his boss had been disdainful or congenial, generous or grudging. The more he doubted his surroundings, the harder he worked to erase all doubt, at least in his own mind, that he had done his best.

Based on his years as a manager for a large steel building products company in China, Zhong-hua had his own standards for what constituted fair treatment and what a hard worker was worth. Every day he came home from the health food store unspeakably tired. He was the lowest-paid employee. The others read the newspaper while he mopped up at night and stood by while he moved crates of milk into the cooler and stocked overhead shelves with heavy sacks of rice and flour. The boss called Zhong-hua on his day off to unload truck deliveries. He drove fifty minutes each way and was paid one hour's wage.

Zhong-hua found his boss arrogant, stingy, and uncouth, but also fascinating. "You know, today boss very interesting. He told me I don't need get paid as much as the other workers because I can bring my lunch. Never need eat in restaurant. He said he think seven dollar enough. This boss very crazy, very interesting. Boss want me come his house tomorrow clean out yard, burning some stuff. I say, 'OK, no problem.' I don't ask him if he pay, not pay. Just let him do his way." In English class my husband wrote that this boss man was his best friend, like a brother. This was either Chinese satire or a true expression of love for the cosmic stranger.

Paroda got Zhong-hua another part-time job at Panera Bread Company, a bakery and sandwich shop where she worked as a cashier. They put my husband in the back, slicing meat. Employees were supposed to pay for their food at a discounted rate. This fell under the category of "I don't think need do" in my husband's mind. He had an enormous appetite. He ate roast beef and tomatoes all day as he sliced them. The manager would stroll by and say, "Mr. Lu, you must be very hungry today. You are eating a lot."

"Yes, yes, I am very hungry!"

"OK, OK, you eat more, then." So that was that. When he was not at work and happened to be doing errands in the neighborhood, he would stop in and make himself a big sandwich. Again, the manager would ask, "Mr. Lu, are you working today?"

"No, I just need go Home Depot. Very hungry!"

"You should eat a sandwich. Do you want a soda?"

I don't know how he got away with this, but he often inspired generosity. This did not apply only to food and drink. Whenever we went to a public museum or show for which an admission was charged, I had to pay and my husband walked in free. He would walk up to the ticket taker and say something like, "Do you need me give you money?" Invariably the person would smile kindly and say, "No, no, sir, you can go in," and then look very pleased with himself or herself, having exercised a gatekeeper's prerogative. There were, however, less cosmopolitan venues, like the auto scrap yard and the barbershop, where the gatekeeper could not be won over and Zhong-hua paid full price.

Zhong-hua's reasoning on food matters was very practical: if food is being thrown away by the Dumpsterful, then there surely is no problem with employees taking some little bites to keep their stomachs from rumbling. A bread company must serve freshly baked bread every day. Huge bags of perfectly good gourmet bread are tossed into the Dumpster each night. My husband could not understand this. At first he could not resist and returned home with the car completely full of bread. We ate bread constantly. The dogs ate focaccia. The bull fish and turtles in the pond ate French sourdough boule and seven-grain health bread.

My husband munched on a variety of foods away from home, but deep down he felt that, to be truly nourishing, food had to be prepared and consumed at home. My friend Adrian wanted to meet my husband. She invited us to dinner. I mentioned this to my husband, and he became silent and worried. "Why?"

"Just to be friendly."

"Another person can come here—I give them friendly. I don't think need eat outside the home."

I let it go, but the fifth time she asked, I said yes. Zhong-hua agreed, but with the same look of consternation. Evening came, and it was time to go over the mountain to my friend's house. Zhong-hua was clattering pans and chopping green onions, ginger, and fish.

"What are you doing? Are you coming with me to the dinner party?"

"Coming."

"What are you doing?"

"Need eat some rice. Some fish."

After Zhong-hua's meal, which he ate as solemnly as if preparing to go off to battle, we set out for the party, where he ate daintily. Clearly, Zhong-hua dreaded American cuisine. For many months following that incident, although we occasionally invited others to our house for Chinese food, we avoided dinner invitations or any social functions involving food.

I gradually learned to prepare many Chinese dishes that my husband found edible, if not as hot or salty as he preferred. So I was puzzled why, when friends came over to eat and the conversation turned to food, my husband would rudely disparage my cooking: "Ellen cooks everything not very good. Ellen's sister is good cook, but Ellen not. One time Ellen cooked rice, squash, onion, all mixed together—tastes very, very terrible." He put great emphasis on the *very*. I was not immediately offended, because I knew that my husband greatly preferred Chinese cuisine. However, my sister cooks American food, so that comparison put a different slant on things. He was insulting me, not American food.

When we were with people outside the family, he made blunt, unflattering comments about my ability to cook, clean, dance, and practice Tai Chi. Eventually, I learned that these negative compliments were intended to discourage jealousy and repel wife-snatchers. It worked very well. The friends were stopped short. They opened their mouths but said nothing. They looked at me sympathetically. I shrugged and smiled to reassure them. "It's a Chinese tradition," I said, "to say your wife is not good at various things." They nodded rapidly, smiling tentatively, not sure if they should be smiling or frowning or how to exit the conversation.

From time to time, the older kids came home to visit, Eula, Mavis, and Athan. Zhong-hua put his vocabulary into high gear to entertain them with stories—like the one about ordering noodles in Guangzhou while waiting for a visa. "You want another one, sir? Whaaa, you already had five bowls." The story went on for many bowls but had no point other than that his hunger was very big and made the waitress's eyes big. I think it took great effort for him to tell these stories because he still knew so few words.

Zhong-hua cooked mounds of vegetables, cut hair, massaged shoulders, and hung out on the porch with the kids. He wanted them to know they came first. Children always came first, though the proof of this may not always have been to their liking. Mavis, home visiting from college and whimpering about her aching muscles and clogged nose, promptly received Zhong-hua's super-treatment. It was a kind of death and rebirth: a total-body hand chopping, followed by rigorous stomach kneading. He was especially solicitous of Eula, the oldest, because of her delicate constitution. He taught her Qigong exercises and massaged her back. When she lay in bed with a bad sore throat, he boiled fresh ginger in a saucepan with sesame oil and maple syrup, filled a bowl to the brim, commanded her to drink it, and left the room. After a few swallows, she gagged and thought to hide the bowl under the bed, but just then Zhong-hua returned to check on her progress. He stood over her until the bowl was empty.

Once, after Athan visited for a weekend, he needed to catch a six o'clock bus to get back to college. Zhong-hua rose at four thirty, drove to Price Chopper for hot peppers and chicken, and prepared a breakfast stir-fry with a side of dumplings for Athan, who does not like red-hot food. My son sucked air between every bite. He grinned at Zhong-hua, allowing that he was getting used to the spices and now actually preferred not to be able to feel his tongue while eating. With time he was honest and asked if we could serve Chinese *and* American food—how about pancakes and syrup?

In the summer our food troubles vanished as our beautiful Chinese-American vegetable garden flourished. I had erected an eight-foot fence around my quarter-acre garden and divided it into raised beds mulched heavily with old hay from the neighboring farmer. I came home from a job one day to smoldering fires around the circumference of my beloved garden. "Burning all this junk. This junk no good," my husband said. That junk was all my mulch. He had raked half of the raised beds into one large square and was sifting the soil of nine hundred square feet through a screen of hardware cloth shovelful by shovelful, a job for a small village. Along with the mulch, the border of German chamomile was up in flames. I was horrified and started screeching at him, but my husband just chuckled and shook his head, saying that this chamomile would all come quickly back. It did.

After sifting soil Chinese-style for several hours, he conceded that half of the garden should, in fairness, be tended according to American methods and the other half by Chinese methods. I believe he was confident that I would not be able to ignore the difference in productivity between those plants tended by the ancestral wisdom of forty centuries and those tended by a few decades of New Age foolishness.

By midsummer my end of the garden orgied around a centerpiece of black hollyhocks and purple coneflowers. Outside of that sprang bright fountains of corn in a circle. Another circle of every kind of bristly virulent weed grew up around the corn in a thriving hedge attractive to bees. From the outer circle, red raspberries flung their thorny arms this way and that, and then America ended in compromise with one raised bed of Chinese tomatoes and one tepee of Chinese string beans.

Zhong-hua's side of the garden was neat and regimented. There were no weeds and no rocks. Tall trellises of saplings supported Chinese cucumbers with their foot-long thorny fruit hanging straight down. He had hoed trenches for little waterways between each trellis and every night stood outside spraying into the moonlit vines, holding the hose in one hand and a cigarette in the other. The long-legged shadows cast from the cucumber trellises angled eighty feet across the field, as if they intended to walk back to China, ten thousand leagues at each step. Water beads clung to the darkened jewels of hot peppers, and the patch of Chinese cabbage and lettuce was lush and curly, iridescent green. In the American night, the plants revived, intensified, and shared themselves—human beings could relax without having to justify their existence beyond being waterers of plants. In China the morning watering was already finished, and thousands of simple waterers had gone dutifully into the complications of daylight.

Hustling

MY HUSBAND was having such a hard time with English that we enrolled him in a summer English program at the university. The grocer gave him time off, anticipating a more fluent fellow and greater return on his investment in him. But Zhong-hua and many other students from around the world struggled to understand basic directions and read the blackboard. The immense strain was evident on their faces as they emerged from the building. He said the teacher's explanations sounded like "Wha, wha, wha, wha." I gave him a ride the first few times, and then he drove himself. How to drive to Albany and back was the main thing he learned that summer, and in the process he discovered that many promising streets ended in factory yards by the river and that Interstate 90 west would carry him closer to Buffalo and far from home. I continued to piece together income from sculpture commissions and part-time jobs such as scrubbing frat toilets, frying burgers, and the endless pulling of self-justifying weeds.

Before Zhong-hua arrived I had found myself sweating one Monday up the Statue of Liberty as chaperone to a busload of French teenagers (I don't speak French), and sweating the next Monday in a chair opposite an Episcopal priest to interview for a job choreographing a dance of death and resurrection. The latter task suited me perfectly, and the congregation loved Jesus and the two Marys emoting up the aisles in spandex, but it was a onetime deal. Everyone deserves the satisfaction once of being equal to the task at hand.

Zhong-hua had brought nothing from his business career in China except a business suit, the black shoes, and two meat grinders still in the box from his friend's meat-grinder company. Da Jie was visiting our house with her daughter when Zhong-hua announced that he wished to sell meat grinders at the mall. The admonishing words of my Chinese friend Fanwei came back to me as I perched on the arm of Da Jie's chair: *If your husband has an idea, you should say it is a very good idea, even if you think it is not good. If he has two ideas and wants to know which is the better, you should say both are very good ideas. If your brother-in-law has an idea about what your husband should do, just say, "Very good idea." If your husband has an idea for something he wants to accomplish, even if you know he cannot do it, you should say, "I'll help you!" After two years you can tell your husband what you really think.* I opened my mouth, but nothing came. Da Jie chimed in for me, "Yes, yes, good idea. Try, try, try!"

Da Jie's daughter had come to America at age thirteen and at twenty did not follow traditional etiquette on not contradicting an elder. She said, "Uncle. This is stupid idea. Americans buy their meat already ground up. They don't need this kind of thing." I was both shocked and relieved by my niece's impertinence. Actually, I wanted to hug her.

The tedium of earning money was spiced with spurts of industry that saved money. Zhong-hua showed thrift in unexpected ways. During the Cultural Revolution in China, when Zhong-hua was the village schoolteacher, he did double duty as village barber. With a sharpened wedge of wood, he swiftly shaved each male child's head, leaving only a shock of black hair at the forehead. When I complained that I wished I could visit a beauty parlor because my hair was growing wild and bothering my eyes, Zhong-hua said, "I can do," and sat me down on a stool outdoors. It was all over in less than two minutes. He left roughly an inch of hair everywhere on my head, which, because of its coarse nature, stood straight up like wire. Fortunately, I am not in the habit of looking in the mirror very often.

Zhong-hua looked through the lenses of possibility at everything others had cast by the side of the road. I would have been annoyed had I not associated my husband with Hermes, the Greek god who found a turtle shell on the ground and fashioned it into a lute. Some things Zhong-hua created were not as exotic as a lute, such as the shoe tree he made out of the discarded vitamin display rack found in an alley behind the grocery store. There was also the treadmill with handlebars just right for hanging up the garden hoses. Some of his finds were not as useful, such as the four VCR players dysfunctional for reasons mysterious even when the wiry insides were taken out and splayed on the workbench, or the twelve random hubcaps with no matching wheels. There were microwave ovens, televisions, lawn mowers, electric knives, and computers that refused to work despite the fact that they had "seemed very, very good" sitting on the curb. We soon had a VCR that did sometimes work, a porch glider that glided but clicked loudly and had no cushions, and a moldy office chair that wet the bottom of whoever sat on it from a spongy upholstered reservoir.

Garage sales were exciting to Zhong-hua for the bargaining opportunities. Once, among the hemp rope, sump pumps, and jigsaw puzzles, Zhong-hua found a small black Chinese teapot with gold dragons swimming through blue clouds. In China, an item priced at two hundred yuan can be bargained down to twenty yuan. The teapot with four cups was two dollars.

"One dollar OK, not?"

"No, it's two dollars. The price is marked, sir."

"I think one dollar maybe enough. This teapot small."

"No, I said two dollars."

"This teapot very old. I give you one dollar."

"It's a pretty teapot, and it costs two dollars." The woman stood with her hands on her hips, glaring at him.

47

"Too expensive! I don't need." Zhong-hua turned and strode decisively back to the car. As we drove away, he said, "Very good teapot. I really want, but price no good." He lost out on great deals because he was sure he could cut the already fair price in half with the psychological warfare of skillful bargaining. Just as often he was successful and sped away waving to the bewildered seller, who had just sold a fifty-dollar refrigerator for six dollars or a hundred-dollar table saw for sixteen. One day he picked up a tiny gold pin from the table marked "Free Stuff." I thought it was an angel but on closer inspection saw it was a chubby Cupid aiming his arrow, a flying baby. From then on, he fastened this gold Cupid to his collar before leaving home for any reason.

Zhong-hua said that in China a wife is a man's "left hand." He adjusted to having a willing but unreliable left hand. It washed clothes but didn't fold them, planted seeds but didn't weed, put tools away but not in the right place, crushed garlic but to a lumpy rather than a creamy paste, and strained against big wrenches but rarely could budge them. He was my right hand. When my husband arrived from China, I was working on a commissioned burial urn of solid black wonderstone with a sculpture on the top of the lid. When I agreed to take the job, I had not thought through how I would carve the inside of the bowl without expensive electric tools. So far, I had succeeded only in creating a shallow impression big enough to hold a few cigarette ashes, not the ashes of an important person's bones.

Zhong-hua watched me sitting on the ground holding the stone globe clamped between my feet. I flaked off black slivers with a one-inch chisel. He wore that versatile poker face. There were gradations of the poker face: the don't-bother-me-or-talk-to-me poker face, the irritated poker face, the exhausted poker face, the I-have-no-idea-what-you-just-said poker face, and so forth. This one was the I-think-you-are-in-big-trouble-and-really-need-some-help-from-someone-a-little-smarter poker face. That night he didn't come to bed until three in the morning. I awoke to a

Stone Age bowl just deep enough to inspire a vision of true containment. He had done it with willpower and a regular half-inch electric drill bit, a mallet, and a stone chisel. Tedious hours of chipping and boring remained—and one wrong move could split the thing asunder—but the method had been discovered and proved humanly possible.

My husband thought me as clever as a person paddling a canoe with the wrong end of the paddle. He said I had accepted a job too difficult for too little money and was going at it in the most inefficient and unprofitable way. He communicated as much by asking, "Lady pay how much?" and "You work how much days?" He wasted no more words. We took turns refining the inside with a handheld gouge to avoid cracking the precious vessel. His slender-fingered hands, which had been smooth and elegant when he first came from China, were now as rough-knuckled as mine. He stuck with me until the urn enclosed a pleasing concavity.

Zhong-hua was surprised when I finished the crow on the lid, its round eyes wide open and sleek head tilted forward and down, as if already talking to the future inhabitant of the urn. This grueling task had let us both know that we were equally matched in endurance and skill and could work under pressure in harmonious collaboration. When I think of how many hours went into that job, I am glad that the ashes resting in it are those of a great patron of the arts who had bolstered the careers and morale of many poor artists.

I thanked Zhong-hua for coming to my rescue. He sat me down solemnly. "I am your husband, so I should do these things for you. If you say thank you, it is I not your husband." I didn't get it right away, but from then on I bit my tongue before the phrase escaped again. I gradually learned that appreciation, remorse, and even joy were things one just had to feel in the air over time.

After the urn money paid some back bills, I pondered other ways we could make money together. One of my specialties is hand-built teapots with hand-carved handles. When Zhong-hua saw them, he said at once, "No good." He said they were too heavy and just "No good" in general. To elaborate, he pointed out that the Chinese had perfected the bowl and the teapot four thousand years ago, and these designs had since been working very well. Did I think I could improve upon them? I agreed that my pots were kind of clunky but argued for innovation and a combined vision. After many dummy teapots, we came up with some hybrid designs that I cast in porcelain and he painted. They incorporated my love of nature, making use of twisted roots for handles and spouts, and Zhong-hua's preference for delicacy and tradition, expressed through brush painting and calligraphy. I didn't know much about marketing but managed to sell some to the airport gift galleries in Detroit and Albany. The curators, both lovely ladies, were reverent toward artists and fair.

The grocery store was cutting back Zhong-hua's hours each week because his English was not progressing as the boss had hoped it would from attending summer school. My husband used a Chinese study technique that entailed silently copying words and phrases over and over. He memorized spelling but neither sound nor meaning. This discipline was repeated night after night into the wee hours. One morning I inspected the notebook. In his beautiful penmanship, he had written five pages of "I have an advantage with the doctor. I have an appointment over the slower runners." He copied whole sections from a Toyota repair manual: "The symbol illuminates and chimes sound simultaneously when a fault has occurred in an important vehicle system." Each chosen sentence was written four hundred times. It was hard to see how we were going to move forward at this rate.

I also worried that my husband was very isolated. Our social milieu was a bit thin for someone used to falling asleep to the music of his neighbors bickering and weeping on the other side of thin apartment walls and waking up to their cheery resurrection. He was comfortable in crowds, and I guessed the stillness of our country home stirred feelings of loss. When I suggested he might like to go to the Chinese Community Center to talk with some other people in Mandarin, he said no, he'd already talked with many Chinese people in China. I fretted about making things just right for him even though I didn't know what just right should be. Whenever my heavy thinking got out of hand, my husband said I'd best do some heavy work so that at the end of the day, I would be too tired to think.

One chill day I woke to find my husband already out in the foggy drizzle tying up a gigantic flat rock about five feet by three feet and at least ten inches thick. What must have made a handsome door stone to the house or milk room years ago was about to be used to implement Zhong-hua's brand of geological existentialism. "If you have no thing to do, you can help," he offered. "OK," I said cheerfully. I was always up for doing things that had no apparent purpose and took tremendous effort. The two of us, with ropes, pry bars, wedges, and boards, strategized all day, prying up first one edge and then another, shoving the boards underneath as skids. Sometimes the stone slid half an inch and sometimes a whole foot. Sometimes it slid an inch back uphill, defying the laws of gravity. My husband kept saying "Just try." I never asked why.

We moved the massive piece of granite from somewhat near the house down the bank to the pond's edge, where it platformed into the pond like the dock to a dream. Darkness fell, and the drizzle turned to downpour. In the end we were both covered with mud, his pants were wet to the thigh, and my knuckles dripped blood. I looked back up the hill, where the stone had ripped up the grass as it lurched and slid, and remarked that, actually, the stone would be more useful at the top of the hill as the step to the kitchen door. Zhong-hua said, "Good idea. You want, you do."

Following Zhong-hua's theory of how best to convert worry to aching muscle mass, I decided that it would be best for us to find outdoor work together. Our bodies were not young enough to do heavy labor every day and feel happy about it, but in our situation our bodies were the best resource available to us. We scraped and painted decks, pruned trees, pulled weeds, and shoveled gravel.

Although hauling manure in a wheelbarrow and digging up daylilies was not easy, the hourly pay was good with two people working.

Zhong-hua wore his headphones and listened to English 900 tapes, the ones with monotone voices having a conversation in English devoid of emotion and almost devoid of meaning. "Bob, were you kidding yesterday, because if you were kidding yesterday, then I am leaving next Tuesday afternoon." "Don't leave, Steve. Please don't leave. I was not kidding yesterday afternoon. I will not kid you tomorrow, Steve. I will not kid you next week." Zhong-hua's face grew slack in the shade of his straw hat. His features thickened, and his personality vanished. It was as if he'd summoned some ancestral farmhand to take his place while he listened in on Bob and Steve. The farmhand was an opaque shadow in human form and had a lot more stamina than I did. Zhong-hua spoke once and slapped me on the back in order to prod me into completing the fifth hour. "One more hour. One day, one hundred dollars, is OK. Tonight body very tired, very pain, don't need think anything. Just sleep is OK. Don't need think about terrible things."

Driving and Drinking

IN CHINA, my husband had never driven a car. He was sure he could learn in two hours. He owned a big motorcycle in China. How different could it be? First of all, he had a general irreverence for rules. The centerline had no significance to him. The lanes held no association to restricted sideways movement. Pulling out of a side road onto the main route, oncoming car in view, a hastened version of his motto "Maybe OK. Try!" was put into action, often shortened to "Try!" My teeth clenched, and I felt as if I were swallowing my tongue as the other car roared up on our rear bumper, horn blasting in alarm. Country drivers in big-wheeled pickup trucks sped up and skinned past us, shouting obscenities and flinging the finger. I instructed Zhong-hua that the person on the main road had right-of-way and that a red light meant STOP until the light changed to green.

"I don't think so."

"What do you mean, you don't think so? Red means don't go. You have to wait; that's the law."

"In China, who can go, just go. Is OK. Big road, small road, left turn, right turn—this doesn't matter. Just watch, see, look at. OK—go. Not OK—not go. Also, people drive on any side of the road. Which side open, which side drive."

"What if another car is coming the other way, for God's sake?"

"No problem. Just not hit other car—is OK."

"Watch out! That guy is passing you on the right because you're in the fast lane. You should be in the slow lane. Stay in your lane! Stay in your lane!"

"Another driver say, 'Asshole.' What is *asshole?*"

"It means he's mad. Get over, get over! Holy shit!"

I was gasping and holding on to the ceiling. My feet were braced against the dash. My husband sighed and said I "must be" ride in the backseat because I was making him nervous and this was "very danger." He pulled over on the shoulder, and I got out, took a few deep breaths, and repositioned myself rigidly in the far right side of the backseat, mostly pressing my mouth closed but still involuntarily yelping "Stay in your lane! Signal! Signal! I showed you these words in the dictionary a hundred times! Do you know what a lane is?"

I wasn't in the habit of drinking alcohol, but for several weeks, as soon as we returned home alive from a driving excursion, I sedated myself with Chinese wine, the kind that numbs your mouth like Novocain for a full hour. Zhong-hua must have scared himself, too. He pointed out that our license plate number contained four 4s. This was a very bad thing. *Si,* the word for the number 4, sounds similar and is written identically to the word *si,* meaning death. We had to quickly change this, even though it meant paying extra. He dedicated an evening to playing with number combinations, finally arriving at one that seemed auspicious and contained no 4s.

Barren winter trees allowed our retired neighbors, Dave and Flippy, to better keep a watchful eye on the chain of events at our place, which they greatly enjoyed. Often Dave would telephone after observing us struggling to accomplish some impossible task: "Hey, it's Dave. I wasn't doing anything today and wondered if you want me to bring my tractor up. I can pull that car out of the ditch easy, if you want me to. I mean if you don't want me to, I won't. But no sense you two hurting yourselves." We were very grateful for Dave and the tractor.

They waved each time Zhong-hua drove past to practice driving with me in the backseat. They probably thought this was another Chinese custom, along with setting the garden mulch on fire with a couple of plastic detergent bottles, shooting mourning doves, and chain-smoking while overseeing the wife mixing concrete in a wheelbarrow. Zhong-hua rolled down the window, veering inadvertently toward them, and bellowed, "Hi, hi, hi, how are you?" The rural American custom of waving to everyone whether you know them or not was very alien to Zhong-hua, but he made up for his discomfort by trying extrahard to conform.

Once out on Route 2, we lurched along, first twenty miles under speed, then twenty miles over speed, swerving from side to side as I squawked over and over, "Stay in your lane! Stay in your lane!" At stoplights we looked straight ahead to avoid the glowering faces of other drivers. After a few weeks, their furious looks sobered Zhong-hua to the point that his most common transgression on the road became going too slow in an effort to be extracareful.

We had returned home late at night from Da Jie's house through blackness blossoming spring snowflakes. We pulled up close to the kitchen door. I was so appreciative when Zhong-hua said he would put the car in the garage. All that driving practice was worth it to have help late at night in the cold. He reappeared a few minutes later and just stood in the doorway. "Sorry!" He started quaking in silent laughter, looking down at the floor and shaking his head.

"Sorry?"

"Yessss! Very, very sorry." He started laughing again. "You see!" He pulled me after him into the snow to the garage, which was made of aluminum hoops covered with vinyl. I looked in at where the car should be, but there was nothing there. I lifted my eyes, and there were the still-lit taillights of the car, going west through a gaping hole in the other end of the garage. I ran around the outside of the garage and beheld the front three-fourths of the car hanging out in midair over the stone embankment. The Triple-A tow truck came and pulled the car back into the garage, no questions asked.

The car was not harmed, and we managed to sew the vinyl back together with giant sutures of heavy black thread. I held the pieces edge to edge while Zhong-hua sewed. The next time it happened, a week later, the same Triple-A driver came to the door. "I know what to do, ma'am," he said.

The day arrived in May to take the road test. The testing officer had a crew cut, thick eyebrows, and no waist. She rested a clipboard on her stomach to reference the rules. She didn't crack a smile. I sat in my backseat station. My husband was so nervous that he never exceeded ten miles per hour and stopped dead at every intersection, Stop sign or no Stop sign. He proceeded to the middle of the intersection and stopped again, dead. Brakes squealed behind us. The woman became red-faced and perspiring. "You almost got us killed! Have you ever driven before? You are a horrible driver! Horrible!"

This first failed test was very disappointing, and my husband was determined not to flunk the second test three weeks later. He remarked with some disgust that America was, apparently, not that different from China, in that people judged you according to outward attire. Accordingly, before leaving the house, he gelled his hair, put on the suit jacket, by now two sizes too large, and fastened Cupid to the lapel.

A young man greeted us curtly, clutching his clipboard as if to rein in his natural friendliness. Zhong-hua went to work. They were hardly out of the parking lot before he started inquiring about the young man's love life and offering advice. In the midst of his parallel-parking attempt and with one tire still up on the curb, he offered a 25 percent discount at the natural foods store and explained that he could not learn certain things at his advanced age of forty-four but needed the license in order to support the family. After Zhong-hua failed to signal a lane change and made an incomplete stop, the young man stammered weakly, "Yeah, OK, cool," to Zhong-hua's offer of free Tai Chi lessons and a bushel of Chinese cucumbers with some hot peppers thrown in once they were ripe.

The driver's license opened up a new activity called "goin' 'round." The business suit was kept handy for visits to the Department of Motor Vehicles, the INS, and traffic court, but usually Zhong-hua dressed more comfortably in loose-cut Tai Chi pants, a T-shirt, a light jacket. The gold Cupid pin now went everywhere. I was still not accustomed to my husband's abrupt unannounced arrivals and departures. Working alone in my basement studio on a clay mold for a mask or a batch of new teapots, I often lost track of time. Unaware that Zhong-hua had gone anywhere, I called out but got no answer. I looked in the garage and saw that he had taken the car, perhaps just to the gas station or to the hardware store. But he sometimes did not return until long after dark. By then I was feeling ignored and disrespected. He was supposed to tell me when he left, where he was going, and when he would be back. I soon learned how alarming and peculiar these expectations were to him.

"Where were you?" I said.

"Not where," he said.

"Oh. Really? Not where?"

"Yes."

"Oh."

I was trying to be respectful of what was normal to him, but this new standard of not communicating unsettled me.

"Zhong-hua, can you tell me when you're going out somewhere? I like to know."

"OK, you're welcome. So long. Thank you very much."

Whenever my husband thought something was ridiculous, he would respond with what was, to him, a nonsensical sequence of words.

"And could you call me if you're not coming home before dark? I don't know if you are lost or had an accident or what happened to you."

"Why talk about terrible things? Nothing happen. Just go 'round. Need something, I will call. You think OK, not OK?" Despite my efforts to teach him English sentence structure, my husband translated many phrases literally from Chinese. It was hardwired in his brain. Thus, "OK, not OK?" was a translation of the common Chinese phrase "*Hao, bu hao?*" Literally, this is "Good, not good?"

"OK. It really is OK. But could you call?" I hated that this small request was making him look like a trapped animal and making me feel like a nag and a beggar. Frustrated, my husband became very still. His face hardened, and his lips closed tightly. Frozen in position, he spoke with measured force: "I think no need. In China, no need call. If I want see my friend, I just go. If I need doctor, just go. Never call. No need call. I don't understand why Americans always need call so many times. Why not talk again in the home? Good, not?"

"I like to get a call."

"Do you have another thing?"

"No."

"Uh."

I felt so disregarded that I complained to Da Jie. I didn't know this would cause him to lose face with his relatives and also serve to lower their opinion of me, a wife who could not keep her woes contained. If while goin' 'round he stopped at Da Jie's house and lingered past midnight, she would prompt him, "Must call Ellen. Should be." He did.

"Hello?"

"I am Lu. I tonight late come home. Do you have another thing?"

"No other thing."

"Uh."

He hung up after an *oh* or *uh*. The unceremonious ending at first struck me as an affront, until I heard him end all phone calls to other members of the family in a similar way. I liked the phone calls even though I knew he would not remember if Da Jie did not insist. Paroda said, "Mom, why do you get upset when it's the same thing every time? That's his way." She pointed out that her grandfather, my father, demonstrated similar telephone behavior, unilaterally terminating

the conversation while the other person was in midsentence by saying "We'll see ya" or "Good luck with that" and hanging up. I had
learned to accept this with no judgment and only slightly hurt feelings—but it had taken forty years. I tried another tactic with my husband next time he called. After he came to the part where he said, "Do
you have another thing?" I said tersely, "No other thing," and quickly
hung up before he could. This did not perturb him at all and gave me
the pleasurable feeling of neatly snipping off the conversation.

All summer my husband soothed his displaced spirit with more
focused goin' 'round, such as watching the framing of new houses.
Goin' 'round was by definition unplanned, so I was sometimes in
the car when an outing suddenly took a detour. Frame construction fascinated him and seemed "very easy" compared to the mud
brick or lath and plaster methods used in China. He drove up close
to the construction site as if he were a member of the crew and sat
himself on a cement block with a cigarette, rising from time to
time to stroll from room to room. My husband moved through the
world with no furtiveness, always coolly trespassing. More often
than not, he was provided coffee and a bun or a centralized chair
from which to watch all day. Not sure how to categorize him, people treated him like a long-lost cousin or projected onto him wisdom and mystery, launching into wistful monologues: "You see,
I'm not just a carpenter—I'm an artist. I like to hug trees and shit
like that. I'm real spiritual, you know what I mean?"

Zhong-hua smiled and nodded, "Yes, yes."

"I dig Chinese people. Yeah, I do. Listen, man, can I give you a
hug?"

"Oh, thank you very much, sir."

At used-car lots, construction sites, convenience stores, and
garage sales, my husband demonstrated Tai Chi and taught simple
Qigong exercises. He made lists of people interested in Tai Chi
lessons on the inside of matchbooks and the back of gas receipts.

Da Jie also liked driving around, especially if the promise of mon-
etary reward was attached to the effort. Da Jie was a Wushu master,

trained in traditional Shaolin martial arts from the age of twelve. She was built the same as Zhong-hua—short, thick, and powerful. At home, Da Jie took orders from her husband, but when Da Jie was with her younger brother, she was most definitely in charge.

She told us about a national Kung Fu competition in Cleveland, where vendors could rent a table. Da Jie said that she and my husband should drive to Cleveland and sell the martial arts pants and silk tunics their sister in China had made. Cleveland was very nice, she'd heard. Da Jie said it was a straight line on New York 90 West from Albany to Cleveland, and the tournament was being held right there at the exit. So convenient! I doubted that, but she seemed confident. The straight-line part of the journey went very well, except it took ten hours. They arrived in Cleveland by 11:00 PM and drove around for two hours looking for a cheap hotel. After checking in, they decided to go out for some Chinese food. They became lost on the way back to the hotel and did not find it again until 4:00 AM. Neither of them could decipher the street signs. The tournament registration was at 7:30 AM. They sold one pair of Tai Chi shoes, two T-shirts, and a hot pink silk uniform. It all came to $90. After they paid the hotel bill for two nights, gas, and food on credit, the profit was negative $340.

They were almost home Sunday night, with Da Jie at the wheel and my husband sleeping in the backseat. Da Jie detoured to a casino. Over the next four hours, Zhong-hua snored on, and dollar by dollar, the $90 disappeared into the slot machines. Da Jie was too guilt-ridden to face her husband, Da Ge, so she slept in our big brown chair in front of the cold woodstove with her feet up on the kindling box. The long straight line and disappointing jackpot of the Cleveland trip depressed my husband's driving zeal for several weeks.

In early June, my husband had sown a large bag of lettuce seed from China. The result was enough lettuce to feed the city of Troy. Every seedling that appeared was carefully transplanted and faithfully watered until the garden looked like a dewy green cloud.

Zhong-hua made "lettuce soup" three times a day, which consisted of a few chicken legs plus several armloads of lettuce that wilted down when stir-fried with garlic and scallions. Paroda and I loved the lettuce soup, but we could not eat enough to make a dent in the bushy beds.

One summer evening, my husband suggested we take some lettuce to our neighbor three miles away. We got in the car at dusk with a pile of lettuce. After delivering this offering, we started home down the winding dirt road, our wheels popping gravel into the evening song of birds, crickets, and tree frogs. The road took a bend, but Zhong-hua did not. In slow motion we simply rolled off the side of the road, bumped across a ditch, and jolted into a tree stump. My husband broke out in jolly laughter while I just stared at him in horror. He didn't realize what I already knew—the car was destroyed. I got out and began a grim, brisk climb up the hill to our friend's house for help. Zhong-hua hurried along beside me, his powerful hand pressed into the small of my back, his face stricken.

Our friend towed the car home. We had no collision insurance. Back home, Zhong-hua descended to the dank cellar and ensconced himself in the moldy swivel chair. I knew he was there because the orange moon of his cigarette floated in the darkness, tracking a slow arc at intervals. He didn't speak or move, but apparently the fingers that held the cigarette still worked and his lungs still worked to take a puff.

I had learned not to show sympathy or nurturing affection, such as brushing his hair off his forehead. He did not like that. He told me that a fellow factory worker whose wife was always patting his head and stroking his hair got a lot of trouble because of it. Everyone knows this brings misfortune to a man, but she wouldn't stop. One day at work, his shirt caught in the cogs and he was pulled into the machinery. His internal organs were mangled, and he was in the hospital for three months. When he finally went home, the doctor said to remember one important thing: don't have sex, because it could be fatal. Unfortunately, the wife loved sex very much, and the very first night she seduced him. His penis started shrinking and then developed a permanent crook. A few months showed no improvement, and the wife abandoned him for a virile replacement. This sad story cured me from touching my man's hair.

I left him to his vigil. He spent four nights in the moldy chair, wrapped in a blanket, smoking. During the days, he walked around expressionless or sat on a milk crate by the pond. Eula came home and told him it could happen to anybody, that it was just a car, that at least we were not hurt. She told him that she'd totaled her father's car just two weeks after she got her license, and that was after flunking the driving test four times. He didn't want comfort; he wanted to be left alone. On the fifth day, Zhong-hua took a shower, cooked two pounds of Chinese dumplings with pork and leeks, and ate them noisily. He announced we would fix this car. He estimated it would take three months. We chained the front of the car to a tree. Zhong-hua applied muscle to the come-along until the steel body groaned into alignment. We stayed up late every night pounding the hood flat with sledgehammers. Finally, he bought used parts from the scrap yard and rewired the headlights himself.

Living in the hinterlands as we did, we could not be carless and earn a living. A local low-end used-car dealer had a great little truck on the lot for seven hundred dollars. We had only five hundred dollars. He agreed, a bit too eagerly, and within an hour delivered it himself with two mechanic companions, one of them blind and accompanied by his Seeing Eye dog. One by one, they all jumped out of the tiny cab. The skeletal body sported an intact roof, a truck bed, and a gas tank anchored in air with wire. Jagged, rusty remnants barely hung together around gaping holes, but I was satisfied when it started right up every time and barreled down the highway like a fancy go-cart.

Making the truck "pretty" was imperative to Zhong-hua. He bought a rivet gun and some sheets of aluminum from the heating duct store. He measured, cut, and bent the metal to replace the ravaged body around this brave engine. Every section was an exact replica of the decayed or missing body part. We bought a quart of silver paint and made the whole thing dazzle. When the muffler fell off a few days later, we both descended to a realm of rust and decay, lay on our backs with ants crawling over our faces, and attempted to force into place a muffler made for a different car Zhong-hua had found by the road. Zhong-hua wore the tuxedo pants he had purchased for one dollar at a garage sale. The silk-ribboned cuffs stuck out from under the car above his tattered sneakers. Paroda stood on the grass with her arms folded over her chest, watching in her bemused nonjudgmental way. "Hey, Zhong-hua," she said, "nice pants."

The engine never failed, but everything else did. That year, between the three of us, we used every one of our sixteen Triple-A road service calls and met a lot of other good-hearted people not employed by Triple-A who stopped to help. Zhong-hua quickly advanced from repairing truck parts with a hot glue gun and pouring transmission fluid into the oil tank because he could not read the bottle to being able to properly install alternators, timing belts, fan belts, front and rear brakes, all electrical components, and automatic transmissions. He also fixed electric appliances, vacuums, and cameras and watches. His method required an average of two days sitting in front of the problem, thinking and smoking Old Golds, before he touched anything.

My husband's road troubles continued for a while. He couldn't remember the rule about not turning left from the right-hand lane. He turned in front of a Lincoln Continental. Brakes screamed, and Zhong-hua was looking right into the quivering jowls of the red-faced driver, who jabbed at him with a meaty forefinger. I noticed Zhong-hua noticing the three gold rings and long, curly arm hair. The man stuck his whole face out the window and sputtered, "You almost killed us!"

"Yes."

"I said, you almost killed us, buddy. Do you hear?"

"Yes, yes."

"What do you have to say when I say you almost killed us?"

"Thank you very much!"

"I'm yelling at you. Why do you say thank you?"

"I don't know. I just think, thank you."

"OK, you're welcome." The guy pulled the arm back. Zhonghua waved and thanked him again.

Sometimes I think about the car grinding in slow motion off the washed-out gravel shoulder, totaling itself undramatically against the rotten tree stump. I think about us climbing out of the tilting wreckage, distraught but unhurt, and wonder whether we were pushed off the dirt road by the protective powers of the flying Cupid in order to be saved from some horrible highway fate.

One night at supper, Zhong-hua commented matter-of-factly that it was only because I yelled "Look out!" that he lost control of the car. I do believe in joint responsibility.

Deconstruction

M Y HUSBAND would attempt any task to avoid paying someone else a labor fee. Yet when he had a little money, it jumped out of his pocket. Once, after being paid cash for a Tai Chi class, he sat behind the wheel as if he had forgotten something.

"What?" I asked.

"Nothing. I just think this time have some money. How to make this money all gone?"

Moderation, a value highly regarded by Buddhist monks and Confucian scholars, was a quality my husband did not possess. He was extravagant in habits of food and exertion. The amount of meat he consumed after relocating a small mountain of gravel by wheelbarrow was astounding. Food was to eat; energy was to burn; and money, if we had any, was to buy more bags of cement.

Magnetized by his determination, I willingly cooperated in the most arduous undertakings. Some of these projects clearly saved us money, while others had more obscure inner benefit. My husband never worried about my small body tiring; he expected me to take care of myself. He said, "You want to do—do. You don't want to do—don't do. Every way is OK." I was exhausted but didn't want to miss out after waiting all my life for intensity that matched my own. We made a sidewalk by sifting gravel through a screen and dumping the pea-sized pebbles, together with sand, cement, and water, into the dirt trench we had dug. I thought we should mix it all smoothly in the wheelbarrow first, but Zhong-hua said, "No need." Daylight dimmed to dusk, and dusk slid into twilight. The moon rose, and we worked on. In addition to "One time, eat all gone," my husband's other motto was "One time, make all done."

Our one-car garage made of aluminum hoops and covered with vinyl looked like a small airplane hangar. The dirt floor sloped downward toward the back so that the rain funneled in branching rivers beneath the car. He had an idea that we could take this car hangar apart and flatten it out into a two-car garage with a concrete floor. To be supportive, I said, "Good idea!"

First, the vinyl cover came off the garage. Then my husband told me to climb up on top of each arcing pole and jump up and down. There was a tree branch I could grab onto up there. He steadied the bottom end of one side while I jumped. When the pole had bent enough, he made a sign and I dropped to the ground. We flattened all the poles this way, with me jumping up and down between the spruce branches and my husband holding the bottom of the pole between his legs while smoking a cigarette. It worked. The garage was now wide enough for two cars; however, at three feet high, it was a bit too short to drive into.

We proceeded to frame up five-foot walls with old two-by-fours, which would theoretically give the too-short garage the boost it needed. I actually did know a thing or two about carpentry, but my knowledge was irrelevant to this particular entity. If a board was not long enough, he just spliced it to another two-by-four with a small scrap or a piece of metal, a method slightly better than connecting two boards end to end with Elmer's glue. These spliced two-by-fours wobbled and bent, as one would expect. He said, "No problem."

"No problem?" I asked, trying not to sound frantic.

"No problem!" he said with confidence.

I suspended judgment because I wanted to believe. Finding the pole structure much too heavy for us to lift up onto the wobbling five-foot wall, Zhong-hua sawed the poles that tied the whole structure together in half with a hacksaw. At least before, we had a one-car shelter. Now we had a lot of aluminum poles in pieces, three drunken walls careening in the wind, and a crumpled-up mass of vinyl and rope. I had a bad feeling. He squatted atop the wall, swaying companionably with the spliced-together frame structure. In his field studies of frame construction while goin' 'round, Zhong-hua had observed the overall geometric relationship of the pieces but not the connecting principles. Besides cement, he put much stock in metal. Joints could go anywhere as long as they incorporated a steel plate or an angle iron. A cigarette sticking out the side of his mouth, he held one half of the garage pole apparatus in place with one foot while I stood on the top rung of the ladder and nailed curved brackets over the horizontals to hold them against the wood frame. A stiff autumn wind snapped our clothing like sails, and I thought this must be very like working on a fishing boat in rough seas.

As I wavered fearfully on the ladder, bracing my head against a trembling tree branch for stability, I noticed that my husband was completely relaxed, standing up on the undulating skeleton lighting another cigarette, as if the wind itself were his safety harness. Clouds billowed behind him, gathering speed toward the distant ocean. He was a rakish novice, not as expert as a Baltimore oriole suspending a nest of grass from a forked branch or a beaver slapping mud on sticks, but still worthy of nature's tribe, where ingenuity is the highest value. We managed to get both halves of the garage raised up, one at time, and secured to the sculpture-in-motion that the garage had become.

My friend's husband Mike, a professional carpenter, stopped over to check on our progress. I heard him mutter to himself "Sweet Jesus." He took me aside and said soberly, "You know, when you put the roof on that contraption, the whole thing is going to take off like a giant kite. And the weight of the snow is going to be a problem now that you've widened the arc out." But by this time I was beginning to think, "Maybe OK." I thanked him politely for his warning. The structure stiffened up considerably when we nailed old sheet metal roofing to make walls, and even more when we tightened the laces binding the vinyl over the curved roof poles. By the time my husband had mixed eighty bags of cement one by one with sand and water, encasing the entire bottom edge of the three walls in concrete, we were ready for a hurricane.

As a finishing touch, Zhong-hua installed a motion-sensor light he had purchased at a garage sale. He fed the wires through a crack in the foundation of the house. I held a flashlight while he expertly spliced the wires into the main line outside the fuse box. After that, the light went on every time a deer passed within fifty feet, a skunk ambled by, or Socrates wandered into the garage to check out the garbage.

I had been queasy when our perfectly good one-car shelter was reduced to a scrap pile of wood, metal, and fiber, and I was elated when all this resurrected, as promised, into a two-car garage. We didn't have two cars. We had a seventeen-year-old Nissan truck with a mystery muffler. When I drove down the road and unrolled the window, the glass slid down inside the door, never to emerge again. Winter arrived, and the old truck was cold. Then the toilet backed up. The bathtub wouldn't drain. I asked my neighbor where the septic tank was because he had been born in our bedroom seventy years ago. "Oh, there isn't one," he said. "Me and Pa just used to get in that hole back there once a year and shovel the stuff out."

Snow drifted down. We dug a chest-deep trench and started looking for the six-inch iron pipe that, legend had it, ran underground from the house. Tree roots and boulders thwarted our pick and shovel; I lowered myself down into the muck, grunting and panting to loosen the stones. They made a huge sucking sound on the way out. I heaved one onto the bank, emitting an inhuman sound from my abdomen. "Good," my husband said.

I felt my strength giving out as my mind took in the enormity of the task. He thought I was much stronger than I really was. My knuckles were raw, and my nose was running. Strands of hair blew across my face and stuck there. Sewer sludge piled up in mounds and hardened in the cold, like chocolate cupcakes sprinkled with snow. I wanted to pronounce our efforts futile, sordid, impossible, but my husband never entertained these kinds of self-hexing thoughts. He just kept going and said, "No problem," "Just try," and "Maybe OK." After a few days, we found the end of the iron pipe about six feet down and began ramming the impacted sludge with an iron rod. "One, two, three, ugh! *Yi, er, san*, ugh!" There was a magical moment when we heard a faint rumble. The water gushed through into the trench, and I cheered in joyous relief.

It was still snowing when my husband returned with the Nissan truck. Loaded with bricks, the truck bed swayed alarmingly from side to side as he bounced into the yard over the frozen bumps. He had found a demolition site by the side of the road in the city, where he coveted the heaps of old bricks. The work crew helped him load the truck. I remembered the teeming cities of China, and how the earth regurgitated ancient walls as workers dug foundations for new buildings. Those bricks from the past were neatly stacked, awaiting a present to surround. It appeared to be a continual process everywhere in China, this turning over of the earth that rearranged centuries of time.

On the way home, he was stopped by a policeman who, after following him for some distance observing the swaying of the truck bed, concluded that he was drunk. He satisfied the officer that he had not been drinking and completed the mission. Before dark we had mixed more concrete, dug a deep hole with a pickax, and constructed a septic tank. It was like a brick troll house in the side of the hill topped with a slab of stone for a roof. That night I lay in bed with a sharp pain in my left shoulder, Band-Aids on three fingers, and an Ace bandage around my knee. But I was beginning to think I had married a genius.

Marriage Is Sacred

WHILE STILL IN CHINA, my husband confessed that it took him many hours over three or four days to write a one-page letter to me in English. I finally told him to write in Chinese and I would find someone to help me read it. I could not decipher the five pages of Chinese characters that arrived, except for "I," "you," "see same moon," "together." I took the letter to my friend who translated from the tissuey pages of rice paper. I still remember one part:

In my imagination I see your slim figure buffeted by icy gusts of wind, and I want to cross the street and stand next to you. I long to shield you from the cold. But I am across the world, not across the street. We must both be patient. I will come, and I will be with you forever. In the meantime, remember to put on your heavy coat. The greatest wealth is health. We are not so young, after all. Please trust me. Marriage is a sacred thing.

Here in America, my husband never used such words; it was as if precious things could be endangered by being named. His deep appreciation was expressed spontaneously under cover of darkness, preferably interrupting my sleep. It was sufficient. Yet sometimes I felt abstractly disgruntled and took the opportunity to get peevish about the lack of clichéd romance. I found reasons to indulge in feelings of deprivation—one sore point being the lack of dancing opportunities, another the lack of a symbolic wedding ring. I looked at other women's smooth, pretty hands with diamond rings on them, and I wanted one.

I am an artist, and my hands are rough, red, and arthritic; they wouldn't look good even if you covered them in rubies and emeralds and glued long designer fingernails on them. I can't wear a ring for ten minutes without getting it clogged with clay, papier-mâché, concrete, or bread dough. But for a while I became obsessed with the idea that I had no glittery ring to let everyone know. Know what? That I was not trying to pick them up; that I was married, for God's sake; that my husband thought my hands were good enough for an expensive ring? I tried not to examine this list too carefully.

In China, I had a soft gold wedding ring that bent and fell off every time I caught it on my hair or the buttons on Zhong-hua's shirt cuffs. Upon arriving in America, Zhong-hua had given me a stoic, geometric nickel-colored ring. Its squareness hurt my fingers, so I often took it off and placed it to the side if I needed to work with my hands. One day I thought I heard it on its way up the vacuum pipe while I was cleaning the windowsill. I cut open the bag and dumped everything out, but couldn't find it. Even though I was the careless one, I brought the subject up as if someone else had wronged me and should make it right. I was annoying even myself, but my husband took it in silent amusement. I could hear him thinking, "This woman is very interesting. I give her two rings, and she throws them away like garbage. Now she wants another one." I couldn't rid myself of this irritating craving for something people considered sacred to marriage, even though whenever I owned one, it proved nothing but a nuisance. My neighbor Flippy had lost the ring Dave gave her fifty years ago. She had been hanging out laundry, and it disappeared in the long grass. She said she didn't miss it one bit. "They say diamonds are a girl's best friend, but they're not mine. I have no use for 'em."

What exactly makes a thing sacred? At our house, it seemed

that all the things I thought I held sacred meant nothing to my husband. When he took over the kitchen, my favorite cup disappeared; I found it in the shed behind the house with some coffee cans full of hinges and screws. Before he came, I had spent days preparing the house, intending to make a clean, airy sacred space, and the first item my husband added to this space had been the vitamin rack shoe tree. This metal high-rise quickly overflowed with gagging garage sale shoes with their tongues hanging at all angles. Next came a black metal shield with two gold British knights, an eagle on the center medallion, and two lethal-looking daggers crossed behind. A loud neon wall clock, twelve crystal punch cups, and glass end tables resting on gold chrome bullhorns took their places when I wasn't home and gave me a shock, as I've always had a visceral aversion to shiny, bright, or ticking things. I kept looking away and then back to see if maybe they were not as ugly as I thought.

Zhong-hua's favorite color was an unearthly blue, the blue of plastic cemetery flowers. Mine was brown. He replaced the handmade crazy quilt on our bed that my sister had labored over for three years with a green plaid comforter from Wal-Mart. He found a gigantic framed painting of the Swiss Alps in someone's curbside garbage and put that up in the bedroom. He would take it outside sometimes, lean it on a tree, and sit on a milk crate, leisurely observing it through a cloud of cigarette smoke.

Da Jie's aesthetic also migrated into our home. Every time she cleaned house, she loaded her car with things she no longer wanted: an eight-by-eleven white rug stained with dog poop, an old kitchen table with loose legs, a large blue and white porcelain urn, four mattresses, and all the old food in the freezer. It was taboo to refuse these offerings and, with the exception of the expired food, taboo to dispose of them; however, with them came a smaller rug, all wool with only a tiny spot of dog poop; two sturdy kitchen chairs; one good mattress; and eleven boxes of chocolates, each one opened with only a few pieces missing.

By our second winter together, my sculpture studio had become Zhong-hua's late-night study grotto, where he would torture himself with *Speak English As You Wish*. My chisels, planes, and files I found angling out helter-skelter between the slats of an apple crate. I protested that I needed to have a workspace. "No problem. You need do something, just do. I move." I pictured him moving the study grotto into our tiny kitchen, where the headlight of the car was being reassembled, or the cramped living room, where he was growing tomatoes and peppers from seed sent from China. Nothing was sacred anymore. No, that wasn't it: nothing was more sacred than anything else. As Zhong-hua passed through space, he changed it to a chartless no-man's-land where anything could happen.

My old surroundings winked and shifted as Zhong-hua made himself comfortable. I did a double take at the unexpected sight of a big garish purple poster on the wall called "Iris Joy." I did another when the ceramic mask of Obatala, an African god of creativity and wisdom, on our living room wall began wearing a woven Chinese hat. I removed it several times and placed it respectfully on the table, but always the next day Obatala's mouth remained serene under the straw brim. Since this recurrent placement was obviously deliberate and Obatala seemed unperturbed, I decided to leave it alone.

I was poking around an antiques store where Zhong-hua and I sold some of our teapots when my eye caught a dirty little wooden statue. Being a sculptor, I recognized that the maker had succeeded in creating a piece in which the spirit of the subject had agreed to reside. I loved the vitality of the full-bellied immortal sitting on a tiger, one foot firmly on the ground and one foot jauntily subduing the tiger's head. I asked the owner how much. He said it was $375. He saw my face fall and, to my surprise, handed me the statue. "Make me a very excellent teapot for my wife. You can scrub that thing off with soapy water and make the colors shiny again." I promised to do this and took my treasure home, where I proudly unwrapped it for my husband to admire. He looked troubled. He said ordinary people should not have such things in their home. This was a very sacred statue to live in a community shrine. People could go there to offer their prayers and incense, but this energy was too great to live in the home. "You need take this back to another man. We cannot keep this statue. Also, you must not wash. The dirt needs to stay. Dirt protect power." I was disappointed, but I understood. The home is not a shrine.

Meanwhile, our native speech patterns jarred each other's nervous systems. My usually quiet husband spoke English in harshly sectioned and powerfully expelled monosyllables. This is the sound of northern Chinese. Americans listening in on a conversation between a Chinese couple might assume they are angrily berating each other when in fact they are saying something like "I think the flyswatter is over there behind the door." Zhong-hua used this frightening tone of voice to say things like "You can go to the garage and find the jumper cables!" The way he commandeered words alarmed me. Why was he so emotional and bossy about the jumper cables?

"Why are you mad?"

"What?"

"Are you mad at me?"

"Mad what? Not mad."

"I don't know. You were yelling."

"Not yelling. Just talk. Just think maybe find jump cables very good. Maybe need these things today. *Should be* find." This machine-gun talk was used for definite communications about things that needed to be done the right way—like how to cut squid, how to pick out the right length screws at Home Depot, or how to clean out a dog's nose.

The rest of the time my husband spoke very softly. According to Chinese etiquette, I was told, the woman should always talk in a soft voice. I had trouble remembering this. My uninhibited squealing and bellowing frequently caused my husband to flinch. "Zhong-hua, Zhong-hua, quickly come. Oh my God. Hurry up!

There's a hummingbird!" My husband came, but looking stricken, as if I had just streaked naked across the road and he needed to throw a blanket over me. "No need loudly. Softly is OK."

My husband found the word *ardent* in the English-Chinese dictionary and said, "You are very this word." He did not seem entirely displeased. The paradox of my husband's loyalty to four-thousand-year-old standards was that he took their correctness for granted even as he embraced contrary standards. He thought it best for me to talk little and in low volume but found it refreshing not to have to guess what I was thinking or feeling. My husband did, however, take strong exception to my unconscious habit of deeply sighing.

"I think this for lady not good."

"Sighing is not good?"

"For lady not good. For man maybe OK."

"Oh." This one made no sense to me. I could not control my sighs. Then I told myself, "Be yourself." But clearly myself was cloaked in layers of culturally woven clothing. Take "good morning," for instance. In my family, this was acknowledgment of the other person, a form of respect. To my husband, it was an irksome, unnecessary, stupid utterance. In place of the signposts of respect, a familial forbearance reigned that was, I had to admit, comforting. Within a family, many times a person feels tired, disagreeable, or disinclined to socialize, and having to perpetuate niceties can be a strain. I appreciated being able to be out of sorts without someone's trying to cheer me up. When I became locked in petulant affect, my husband never judged or took offense. He either totally ignored this or commented neutrally, "You looks not happy." Having to claim ownership of a bad mood or justify it with explanation usually felt undignified enough for me to either chase it away or corral it for private reflection. "Family just like this. Let time. Person's bad weather will pass over."

Involuntarily loyal to my inborn nature, I never resembled a suitable Chinese wife, except when we were actually in China—and that was only because I couldn't have spoken my mind if I wanted to. By now I had torpedoed that resemblance by talking too loudly, expressing too much, complaining, crying, and emoting in ten thousand other ways.

Once, while backing up to the shed in the car to unload some wood, Zhong-hua ran over some masks that I had drying on the grass and crushed them. I ran around gathering the remains and shrieking, "I hate you. I hate you. This is money, don't you know? My work is not real to you? You just drive over it?" His calm non-response allowed my hysteria to play itself out at a pitch so high that Dave and Flippy probably thought I had run the lawn mower into a hornets' nest. He observed my fuming face with absolutely no visible response, then turned slowly and walked more slowly toward the corner of the house. Once he was safely out of sight, my deranged mind rearranged itself. Of course he hadn't known that the masks were drying on the ground. I should not have screamed at him. What a shrew. What a bitch. I felt terrible. Ten minutes later my husband reappeared and asked me where the Phillips-head screwdriver was. The whole incident was erased by that question.

He performed this magic erasing trick countless times, whenever I was escalating into argument or had let slip an inexcusable comment that we both knew I would prefer to retract. "Zhong-hua, I think your sister wants to be in charge here. Why don't we just marry her?"

A long, electric pause as my husband attempted to process this insult, which he took literally. He said only, "How about beans? You today want to eat beans, not?"

"OK. Let's eat beans."

This timely intervention obviated the need for saying "I'm sorry." I'm not sure, but it seemed this phrase offended my husband's familial sensibilities because he considered husband and wife as one being and the family one organism. So besides the obvious silliness of apologizing or excusing part of yourself to yourself, decreasing the number of obligatory words eased the everyday tension of knowing you were to spend the rest of your life with someone. Unsavory moments were treated like foul breezes that would soon be gone and did not deserve notice. A few days after my territorial remark, he took time to clear up any misconceptions I might have. "In the China," he said, "you should know, sister and brother cannot marry."

My husband was also averse to all habitual perfunctory inquiries such as "How did you sleep?" and "How was your day?" as well as remarks such as "You look nice." He said he did not like to say these things because they were "not from the heart."

That unfortunate phrase clowned clumsily about in my mind in the face of every nice thing my husband did, causing me to suspect it was "not from the heart" and done only to placate expectation. I collected a miserable burden of words and gestures that had become suspect due to my pained awareness that they did not hold the same significance for my husband as they did for me. I would say something commonplace and natural to me, like "Thanks for the good dinner," and he would look at me as if I had completely lost my mind.

I could not deny that overuse hollowed out daily platitudes and made insincerity inevitable, yet their omission wreaked havoc with my emotions. The utopia of our time together in China faded into a new landscape booby-trapped with blurry communications in the guise of familiar phrases. If I had remembered that we knew how to talk mind to mind in that perfect language of no words, I would have found peace again, but in the bright daylight, I could not remember this. Only at night, when my husband took me in his arms, did I feel the signifiers stop vying for position and recede to wherever they had come from. We had no use for them where we lay pressed together, my slow breaths and his quick ones mingling, thought and feeling passing back and forth, unaltered by expression.

In the morning I again insisted on making conversation. "Hi. Oooooh, it's very windy."

"Uh."

"Did you sleep well?"

"Um."

"How about noodles?"

"Uh." He did not open his mouth to make this sound.

We circled through recurring dawns to arrive at a third way: me trying out the silent method but feeling as if something was missing, him conceding a formal "Good morning," definitely not from the heart; me brushing past his body as he dressed but not looking up, him mauling my face with his palm before getting out of bed in a gesture of tenderness disguised by comic affront. Through weeks of experimental morning rituals, a mutually acceptable exchange evolved: eye contact was made—just barely, no words, no grunts; he nodded imperceptibly, I smiled imperceptibly. Both creators were content to let the world start turning.

When words or words' absence confounded, I summoned the memory of our time in China, which had taught me another way of being based on letting things alone and paying attention. It was much easier to do this in China, where I had only to follow the leader, than it was now that I felt in charge of the universe. But if I reflected on our first days together, it usually helped me remember how to relax. Knowing that nothing was spoken for the sake of politeness allowed a calm silence at the dinner table within which we munched, letting out small Chinese monosyllables that meant, variously, "no thanks," "yum," "have some," and "that's enough." Conversation was simply absent or spontaneous, the air charged with tacit acknowledgment. By the time my husband had begun to pointedly sing out "good morning" and "thank you," I had stopped even saying "hi." I felt myself cringing from friends' booming hellos and Paroda's slobbery good-bye kisses.

Zhong-hua continued to observe the strict unwritten Chinese law against hugging, kissing, or holding hands with one's wife in public and stiffened in embarrassment if I moved to embrace him. In my husband's case, the embarrassment had more to do with daylight than with other people. He would glance around, as if the walls had eyes. "No need. No need. Nighttime is OK. In the bed enough. Daytime no need." He stoically tolerated my impulsive bursts of affection. It felt like hugging a tree.

My husband adapted good-naturedly to hugging my kids, my friends, my sisters, his coworkers, and any strangers who threw open their arms, as his homage to American culture. He always laughed while hugging. Massage, on the other hand, came naturally and carried with it no self-consciousness. Zhong-hua frequently rubbed Paroda's feet when she got home from school and would offer a deep pressure-point massage to anyone he came across who was in pain, including a used-car salesman in the middle of the hard sell. He had an aversion to overt expressiveness and affection, but invasive nonerotic physical contact for healing purposes raised no inhibitions.

It had been ten months since Zhong-hua arrived, and I still wasn't used to the omission of "hello" and "good-bye." I stood there in the middle of the kitchen as if hit with a stun gun on many occasions because my husband had abruptly walked out without saying a word. Even after I knew that this behavior was the norm and signified that all was well, it stopped me short. The world was not right. This person whom I had waited so long for and summoned all my powers to bring here now appeared and disappeared at whim, according to private motivations. "Where's Zhong-hua?" became the most frequent question in the house: Paroda asked it nonchalantly; I asked anxiously. She said, "Mom, why do you even worry? He goes away, and he comes back."

Then Zhong-hua went missing. We were going into his second winter in America. The leaves had fallen, and the ground had frozen several inches downward. All day the wind blew, and toward dusk frozen bullets of snow pelted the metal roof. A winter storm warning was in effect, and I didn't know where he was. I played Paroda's precocious insight in my head: "Mom, this is just his way." More than once he had not returned, and it turned out that he really was lost, driving east through the state of Massachusetts, having overshot home by fifty miles, or winding his way north on Vermont

Route 7 thinking he was on New York Route 7. A blizzard gathered force. Paroda was at her girlfriend's house. The thin old window glass shook, and I paced anxiously through the darkening house, finally coming to rest on the big armchair in front of the woodstove, where blue flames quivered over the bed of coals. Ice pinged down the metal chimney pipe. I hugged my knees. What if he hit a telephone pole? What if he slid off the road on the black ice? What if he was lost in Connecticut or New Hampshire or on his way to Canada?

I called Da Jie's husband, Da Ge. He told me to call the police. The police told me that because my husband had been gone only eight hours, he could not be considered a missing person. He must be missing forty-eight hours. That is, unless he was suicidal. Was he suicidal? Could he in any way, shape, or form or by any stretch of the imagination be deemed suicidal? I hesitated, considered how frozen a person might become in forty-eight hours, then answered, "Maybe." They agreed to look for him. A few more hours went by.

An officer came to the house and asked me more questions. He said he had almost not made it up the mountain to our house, that no sane person would be out in this blizzard by choice. His mustache unthawed and dripped as he took notes. I told him my husband had recently come from China and was having a lot of trouble with English. I said he might be depressed. Actually, anytime I had asked my husband if he felt depressed, he knit his brow and blew air, "Puhhh," at this ludicrous possibility, then forcefully added, "Not! Never this way." The officer left out the kitchen door and in four strides vanished into the howling whiteness.

I sat in the dark until the phone rang. "I have your husband here. His car was under a snowdrift at the bottom of the mountain, and he was inside sleeping. He says he wants to come home. If I can get back up the hill, I'll bring him on home."

Zhong-hua had been at the movie theater. Being money-conscious, he had entered for the four o'clock shows and stayed in the ten-screen theater until closing to get as much value as possible from one ticket. From the final James Bond scene on a tropical island beach, he emerged to the upstate blizzard. It took him an hour to locate the car in the parking lot, because he exited on the wrong side of the theater. Then he began the long journey homeward.

I stood in the garage staring at him in disbelief that he would stay out in this weather and not let me know where he was. I couldn't even speak, I was so angry. I put up my hands in surrender. "Look, I can't even talk to you. I don't want to hear stupid words. I don't want to see your face." I turned away and clomped back into the house. He came in and climbed the stairs to bed, looking thoughtful. I slept in the brown chair with my self-righteous rage spilling over the edge with my feet. Resorting to the brown chair turned out to be just the right communicative gesture. The next morning my husband said, "This time I wrong!"

Before the blizzard, I had been working on internally dissolving the distress I experienced when my husband stayed away from home and did not call. Afterward, more anxious than ever and wishing to put myself out of misery, I repeatedly determined to discuss the importance of calling home. At first, my husband's standard answer to such invitations was "I think no need talk" or "Not talk is OK." Or he looked at me curiously and said, "This for you very important thing? You have free time think about this?" He did not persist with this tactic once he saw that it resulted in my becoming more and more agitated and unhappy and less and less like a good Chinese lady. "Why your eyes jumping out of your head?" he would ask, visibly shaken. He must have thought carefully about a new strategy because, instead of refusing to talk, he began to say, "Yes, yes, go ahead, you talk. I will listen." He positioned himself dutifully beside me, usually with a pillow, indicating that he was there for the duration. He listened; indeed, he said it was "like music," even though sometimes I was screaming and crying, but he did not say a word and maintained excellent composure. When I finished, he said that yes, it was best for me to talk, healthy for the body, and then got up and left the room.

When I was growing up, birthdays were low-key and presents very small. Paroda, however, loved celebrations of every kind, expensive presents, and shows of affection. In Zhong-hua's first year, she had been distracted by high school graduation, and both of our May birthdays slid by with a new shirt for Zhong-hua and flowers for me. The second May, she was home from her first year of college and able to focus on instigating: "What are you getting Mom for her birthday?"

Zhong-hua was taken aback and then distressed. "You think I should do what?" he asked her. He hated the idea of buying anything that had no purpose other than sentiment, like flowers. One cannot eat flowers, he pointed out. When my birthday came, I made no mention of it. In China, birthdays are celebrated only for the very young and the very old. Old age is considered an accomplishment, and one is allowed to gather all descendants together and gloat happily. But it was not good luck to celebrate prematurely, unnecessarily calling attention to oneself that could invite jealousy. Middle-aged people should just carry on as usual. I was doing that. It was eleven thirty at night, and I had my pajamas on. He came into the bedroom more animated than I had ever seen him.

"We should need to go dancing! It is your birthday!" I knew very well he didn't think my birthday was an event, and anyway it was Sunday—all the dance clubs were closed.

"Come on! It's your birthday. Let's go to the mountain." I saw he was determined to honor this birthday idea one way or another, so I put on a coat and boots over my pajamas and off we went. At the top of the pass between New York and Massachusetts, we got out of the car. It was pitch-black, and a stiff May wind blew from the northwest.

"Go on. I think you love the mountain. I'll wait for you." He got back in the car and smoked cigarettes while I walked around the blustery parking lot in my pajamas. We were not done yet. Next he drove to the lake, which he knew I also loved. We got out and took some tiny blind steps onto the tilted fishing dock. The water lapped against the shore rocks. Owls called one another. The air smelled of pine needles, Old Gold 100s, and fish. After that we went to the place where the road crosses over the Little Hoosick River. A steep trail leads down the bank to the underpass, where the water runs swift and deep, full of speckled trout. Upstream is a secret waterfall: secret because it is so difficult to get there. One must step in shoe-sucking mud, scramble up slippery rocks while grabbing at branches to keep from falling into the rushing water, jump an abyss between two boulders, and crawl on hands and knees to the base of a falls that crashes through bowels and chest and takes the breath away. Icy spray wet our faces and put out Zhong-hua's cigarette. The water fell to a deafening maw of foam. We crouched on the churning edge, where I felt both a terror of being swallowed whole and the safety of containment in thunderous calm. Zhong-hua lit another cigarette. On the way home, he said with an indignant air that in China dance clubs were always open, especially Sunday.

The next year some friends stopped by to wish me happy birthday, which startled Zhong-hua into action. He had a talent for making visual feasts out of anything we had on hand, however scanty. Our cupboards were bare that day, but on the counter sat a salty growth of fungus that had grown in the rock crevices of Szechuan Province. This gray, amorphous lump had brooded undisturbed for months, looking like a human cerebrum. He sliced this fungus into flowery cross sections and served it embellished with even saltier homemade pickles, made by drying long finger-thin cucumbers in the sun and dropping them into a vat of salt and vinegar, where they sank and reappeared months later, like immortals who could hold their breath for up to two years. Chinese wine was served on the side. My friends' facial expressions ranged from curiosity to puckered concern to outright alarm as the 100-proof flower "wine" scorched their throats. This was the famous mao-tai wine that the medical staff had used to disinfect wounds and sterilize instruments on the Red Army's Long March during the Communist revolution. Our guests made efforts to be polite

84

and appreciative: "Oh, this is diiifferent!" "Zhong-hua, you're so taaalented," "Very, very interesting ...," and then, "Oh, dear God, DEAR GOD!"

On Independence Day, Zhong-hua invited our friend Kathy for supper. He filleted shrimp with minced ginger and vinegar; heaped a bean-thread noodle mountain with chopped cucumber and sesame oil; sautéed squid with scallions, garlic, and hot red peppers; and boiled a savory cabbage, pork, and sweet-potato noodle stew. Preparing so much food reminded Zhong-hua that he was a bit fat. "You can cut some of my fat off and cook it while I am sleeping."

"What?" I thought I had not heard correctly.

"You can cut some of my fat and cook it when I am in sleeping time."

I had no answer. What was the answer?

"You can make a delicious meal from my side."

Still I was speechless. Was this supposed to be funny?

"Long-ago times, there was a wife and husband, and they had little to eat. The wife very loved meat. While her husband slept, she cut off some of his shoulder and some of his thigh and cooked it. When he woke up, he walked a crooked way. He said, 'What have you done, wife?' She told him what she had done. 'Oh, well, wife, next time you must cut meat from both of my sides so I can walk straight and do not fall to one side, OK?' From that day on, the two never saw the full moon again, only the sliced moon, and that is why every month the woman feels the man's pain, where she sliced his flesh."

Until he was nineteen years old, my husband never had enough to eat. People stripped trees of their leaves to stay alive. The boiled leaves had some nutritional value but caused the children's legs to break out in blisters. After supper, they would run outside to pop the blisters. Zhong-hua laughed as he told this story. This was "just so" laughter, not joyful mirth. My husband was born in 1958, the first year of Chairman Mao's Great Leap Forward. At the core of Mao's plan was the forced communal agriculture implemented on thousands of state collective farms resembling feudal manors. The villagers were encouraged to smelt their own steel to further industrialization. The homemade steel furnaces produced brittle, unusable steel and took manpower away from food production.

The Chinese government wanted citizens to believe that the new commune system would bring China out of poverty. Officials grossly exaggerated harvest statistics while continuing to collect the grain falsely reported as excess from the starving peasants— grain that was then exported, most of it sent to Russia to repay China's debt. An estimated 30 million people died between 1958 and 1962, in the largest famine in human history. My husband's insatiable appetite and inability to drive past a Price Chopper without veering into the parking lot undoubtedly comes from his having barely survived this terrible tragedy, the magnitude of which the rest of the world did not discover until decades later.

Even years later, when he was a sixteen-year-old sent by Mao to work in a village as a farmhand and schoolteacher, food was scarce. Mao's revolutionary scientists had developed hybrid field corn that produced ears twenty inches long. It was so dry and tasteless that even the chickens refused to peck it. Zhong-hua ate nothing but this corn for two of the three years he lived in the village, three meals a day of pounded kernels shaped into flat cakes and heated on sheet metal without oil. The hybrid corn caused constipation, and the people squatted moaning over the latrines using small pointed sticks to dig their own feces out. I cringed when someone mentioned corn in any context, since it always prompted Zhong-hua to retell this story.

With more stories, Zhong-hua let me know that forbearance, otherwise known as long-suffering, was the cultural norm in the face of marriage difficulties. He told the story of Zhou Enlai, whose devoted wife, Deng Yingchao, was a buck-toothed and homely woman who had not given him a son. When Zhou became premier of the People's Republic, she entreated him to find a prettier wife who would be an asset to his new global image. He flatly refused and kept her by his side until his death. Zhong-hua also told me a story of one of his colleagues at the factory. This forty-five-year-old man had never married. Finally, he had married a very friendly thirty-five-year-old woman. After the wedding, his friends took him out drinking. He seemed morose and declined the toasts. He didn't eat the steamed fish, the garlic with oysters, or the spicy cabbage. My husband took him aside and coaxed it out of him:

"I'm not happy," he admitted.

"You just got married! What do you mean you are not happy? Is your wife not good?"

"Good."

"What, then?"

"She has everything."

"That's great! What woman has everything? You are very fortunate!"

"No, I mean she has everything—she has balls, a penis like a pencil, and a small hole."

"You cannot have sex together?"

"Can, but the hole is small, and my wife has pain. I am depressed, very, very depressed."

I asked Zhong-hua if the man would divorce this wife who had everything. He said no, because the woman was a good woman whom everyone liked. She had done nothing wrong. Marriage calls for acceptance. Marriage is sacred.

Sweet Sweet

H ER NAME TRANSLATED TO ENGLISH was Sweet Sweet, and she was Zhong-hua's daughter. Eighteen months after my husband arrived, I finally succeeded in bringing her through the immigration maze from China. There is an expression in Chinese that means that although something may be such and such, this suchness is not pure and simple. The expression is a qualifying one. For example, *Hao shi hao* means "Good is good," and *Congming shi congming* means "Smart is smart," but such phrasing invited contextual inference on why a good thing is not entirely good and why a smart man is in some way foolish. There was a book called *Honey Bunch* that I had found in my grandmother's attic when I was a child. The little-girl character Honey Bunch, consistently loving, obedient, and helpful, so nauseated my mother that she finally threw the book in the backyard incinerator. I thought it unfair to name anyone Sweet Sweet and did not intend to hold my stepdaughter to her name.

I soon realized with dismay that my husband had no clue how to raise a girl into a young woman or to parent in any way other than to nurture and coddle as one would a very young and helpless child. Sweet Sweet, at sixteen, did not know how to go about the most basic daily chores. No one had taught her how to wash a dish, make a bed, hold a broom, or squeeze a sponge. I showed her how to use the washer and dryer, run the vacuum in her room, and wash her woolen sweaters by hand so they wouldn't shrink. Then I assigned her the simple task of wiping the bathroom sink every day. She did this, once. I was more puzzled than annoyed. My other four children had always helped with communal chores, either willingly or with prodding. Not helping was not an option. Sweet Sweet seemed to have no awareness of responsibility, no desire to please others, and no natural inclination to reciprocate their help. Her father hovered about her anxiously. He even brushed her hair, while she acquiesced. I gently pointed out that he might need to prepare her for the rough road ahead. He replied, "You already raise four children. Why not this one?" I was just dumb enough to have a go at it.

I opened her bedroom door that first day. She was standing there in the middle of the low-ceilinged room, having finished folding all her clothes and putting her things in the drawers. The look on her face said she would like to fold herself up, too. She had ordered her few belongings with startling precision: colored markers, pencils, and erasers lined up with the bottom ends flush, largest to smallest. Identical plastic pencil sharpeners queued up in a progression of hues from lightest to darkest, according to the spectrum of visible light. Inside the desk drawer, gum was neatly stacked next to candy bars and small foil packages of gelatinous Chinese confections. One drawer was completely full of miniature pink origami cranes, another of hearts. Nothing migrated out of its own category. It was as if the hermetic room had been shipped intact from China.

The contents and inhabitant revealed themselves with frank innocence. I say "revealed themselves" because Sweet Sweet never tried to conceal or reveal. She was matter-of-fact where most people would be secretive, ashamed, or at least evasive. I sat on the floor and talked to her in my bad Chinese. I asked her about her grandfather, my husband's father. She said flatly, "I hate him a little. He only likes grandsons, not granddaughters." When I told her to call her mother whenever she liked, she replied, "I don't like talking to my mother. She has nothing to say to me." When

I questioned Zhong-hua, he said her mother never took time for her. This unforgivable shortcoming was the only reason he ever gave for his divorce. He told me his first wife constantly bickered with his father and disliked his siblings but seemed not to consider contentiousness a serious flaw compared to a dearth of maternal impulse.

I showed Sweet Sweet pictures and maps and pointed around the room speaking the English names for things. She had the slightest of reactions, just a half nod or a small noise, "Hmm." She cultivated the art of being indifferent to the world, though not unobtrusively. Her very stillness cast an electric shadow. It was impossible for me to know if this was the shadow of her life in China or if she had been born this way, with a crackling moat around her where forces of attraction and repulsion canceled each other and left a void.

School would not begin for three weeks. It did not take long to figure out that Sweet Sweet preferred her room to the outdoors, where bumpy country terrain buzzed with blackflies and bees that left swelling welts on her thin arms. She was from a city in northern China where people moved down the road by bicycle in slow, wide rivers, each so closely pressed from all sides that it was impossible to fall down. Sometimes there was a quarrel and someone got shoved; then a hundred people would topple over. My husband had described his windy city, where plastic bags billowed and tacked high in air so thick with pollutants that people went about their business with masks covering their noses and mouths. Sweet Sweet told me she hated the smells of sweat and urine that steamed from the stone steps and walkways of Linyi City. She loathed stepping on slimy garbage and getting her white clothes smudged with soot. She preferred a clean solitude to crowded anonymity.

Short on things we could do that skirted the insect world, I thought to invite her for a ride in our pickup truck. The truck had no muffler, and the windows rattled inside the door casings when we hit the bumps. It was kind of fun hurtling downhill on Route 2, making tremendous noise, with a green blur of wind rushing past on either side—at least I thought so. Sweet Sweet sat looking straight ahead, not having fun. She wouldn't give me a glance, a smile, a question. Sweet Sweet had no interest in playing the simple game of give-and-take that was human relationship, not with me.

Then the noise took a turn for the worse. It wasn't just the rattle of the truck's improvised sheet metal body. It was more like gunshots. I pulled over, and the engine died. We had to hitchhike to a friend's house and call Triple-A. He drove us back to the truck. I opened the hood and peered in. To get a better look, my friend thrust his baby into Sweet Sweet's arms. She held the gurgling baby with awkward impassivity until it was time to go. When the tow truck arrived, we crowded together in the front seat with the husky driver and towed our silver spray-painted gem back home. I was used to this kind of adventure, but all the way home, my stepdaughter's pretty mouth pursed in a tightly closed porthole, then let out an exasperated sigh as her eyes rolled skyward. She seemed to wish her surroundings would all go away, especially the people.

I decided that Sweet Sweet's apparent apathy was a result of culture shock that manifested in a generalized lack of interest in interacting with other people for any reason, except to ask for something. She asked without hesitation as soon as she had the words: "I have homework, need you help," "I want get hair cut," or, to her father, in Chinese, "Give me a massage." It was always matter-of-fact: "I want," "I need," "Give me."

When well-meaning neighbors brought their teenage daughters to meet her, she endured their advances politely, never responding with warmth or interest. When classmates from school called and invited her to gatherings, she made excuses not to go. When Paroda stopped over, Sweet Sweet was loath to rise from the floor in front of the TV to greet her but just a few days later asked if Paroda might take her shopping. This seemed a most peculiar way of relating. Paroda could not help feeling disheartened when Sweet Sweet did not respond to her efforts at conversation during the three hours that it took to hunt down jeans and bras. She wanted to be a good big sister. Sweet Sweet even refused to come downstairs when her aunt visited. Da Jie whispered to me, "Sweet Sweet don't like talk to me. I try, but she don't like. She come to my house, don't say 'Hello,' just walk in and sit on couch. Ignore me! I decide: 'You not baby. You don't care me, I don't care you.'" This formula could not work for me.

Sweet Sweet asked me if she could join the school's soccer team. I bought soccer shoes, socks, and shin guards. My husband frowned when I told him. "You don't know Sweet Sweet. My daughter only do something new one day, two day. After three day, she already want to stop. Not interesting anymore." At the school, Sweet Sweet was the only Chinese student. Besides two French patois—speaking orphans recently adopted by a local farmer and his wife, the student body was overwhelmingly born and raised in our rural village. The first day of practice, Sweet Sweet jogged behind the other laughing girls. They turned and motioned her to catch up. Not being mean-spirited, they asked her all about herself, but when she could not understand, they fell silent. I felt a mother's helplessness as I watched her cross the playing field by herself. After the season began, she sat on the bench alone for most of the games. The other girls had gotten tired of trying to reach her and often neglected to let her know when the schedule had been changed. She would find herself alone in an empty locker room or running after the team bus as it left the parking lot. When the coach motioned her, she set out on her gangling legs chasing an elusive ball. If she got close enough to kick, she invariably missed. After two weeks, she wanted to quit.

My husband fed her as if she were a toddler, watching her chew each bite. At home or at her aunt's house, she sat hunched at the table, her sullen face hidden behind a silky cascade of black hair, while the extended family bustled around bumping into one another, chopping, peeling, mashing, stirring, chatting in Chinese. They sounded as if they were taking turns hitting each other with flyswatters. That's just how northern Chinese usually sounds—it's not gentle. The sounds are pushed from the deep chest with great gusts of air and fly like arrows to a bull's-eye. My husband picked out the best morsels of food and placed them in Sweet Sweet's bowl. He murmured, as if he did not want his sister to hear him coaxing her, "Ni xiang chifan ma?" (Do you wish to eat?). Da Jie and her daughter exchanged disapproving frowns. Behind my husband's back, they called Sweet Sweet "the big baby."

Once, in the middle of the night, Sweet Sweet appeared by our bed, a willowy wraith in cotton pajamas. "Bu neng shuijiao." My husband sat up and fumbled hurriedly for his shirt, as if the house were on fire. He followed her to her bed and crawled in beside her so that she could more easily fall to sleep. He did this whenever she had a cramp, a headache, or fear of lightning. I considered the possibility this might be customary in China, but my husband's sister did not consider his way of dealing with his daughter normal Chinese behavior. She said, "My brother do wrong way. He stupid!" But then, back in China, my sister-in-law had sucked the phlegm from her daughter's nose whenever she had a bad cold. "And that's love!" her daughter told me.

Not knowing what to do with a child who did not wish to leave her room, I applied the boot-camp tactics I had used on my first four children to instill in them the principle of common effort. I asked her to help me split wood. She shrugged. "OK." Stepping outside, she squinted and reeled on her long, just-straightened legs. It appeared to be an inconvenience to have to stand up. In my mind, I heard the Taoist Lao-tzu's words: "Neither seek to help nor hurt. Each thing will of itself transform." I believed this, and yet this approach required an inhuman amount of patience. I suppressed an urge to shout at her: "You are the most helpless, clueless sixteen-year-old I ever met."

Sweet Sweet followed me in her bright white sneakers, the skin of her bare arms and legs fragile and pale as leaves kept from light or the thin, translucent skin of caterpillar larvae. She looked exactly like the grim, wispy teenagers in the manga cartoons she loved. Her black eyes were perfect half-moons behind long icicles of black hair. She wore a tiny, little-girl shirt and spotless white cotton pants. She could stand perfectly motionless, as though she were a hologram and not a real body with intestines and bones and blood. She watched me balance a log on end and crack it in two with one blow on the splitting maul.

"Have a try," I said, passing her the handle. She lifted the heavy maul above her head. It wavered in the air, held in her childlike arms, and thudded into the soft ground. She spaced her feet apart and tried once more to lift the maul. On the third try, she brought it up over her head and let it fall on the log. It bounced off, and she shrugged, looking up at me. "You don't have to have big muscles," I said, touching my biceps. "Do it with your mind. It's not about muscles." I pointed to my head. She focused her eyes on the log and lifted the maul in the air with both hands gripping the hickory handle. Her face remained placid and calm. She lowered the blade in her flimsy arms, halving the oak log. I grinned. "Yeah, like that." She let out an exhausted sigh. I now possessed what would prove to be the most useful information about my stepdaughter that I had to date. She had true grit, and if she felt like it, she could use it.

Though the true grit of Sweet Sweet did not daily manifest itself, I tried not to forget it was there and to let go of useless judgments. "Sweet like an onion" was the one thought I couldn't erase. Otherwise, we were only a displaced girl in an orderly room painted with the fluorescent green she had picked out herself, a disquieted stepmom, and an overcompensating father on an out-of-focus topography of values and expectations. I felt I had half stumbled out of my body and was watching myself try to walk and talk. My husband and stepdaughter held themselves in, which made me too aware of myself. My small gestures felt invasive and my speech garrulous. We were pieces of a puzzle that couldn't find how to fit together.

I asked my husband why he did not just teach his daughter all the things his parents had taught him about how to behave. He sighed heavily and shook his head. "You don't understand. Every day family think one thing: 'Today we can find what food? Can eat what?' No food! No food! Teach what? Kids need go outside look for leaves or try to kill small bird. Parents no time teach kids, no energy care kids. Also, mother have bound feet, almost cannot walk. Father lose job because government say he think wrong way. He need clean garbage, push big broom, sweep street. Father can teach what?"

I didn't know what to do, and when I recalled what I had learned from the other kids, it didn't apply to this one. Mavis was eight when she confessed that she had no idea how to write a poem for school. I told her this was very easy—just climb a tree and wait there until one came. To my surprise, it worked. Trial and error was always an acceptable way to proceed, better than giving up. I rewired lights by looking at how the guy before me had done it and, when the pipes under the sink fell apart, put them back together with hardly any leaks. Gradually, I gained authority. I thought being able to tell a Phillips screwdriver from a regular one made the world more hospitable; held securely in the hand, the way the star-shaped tool fits the star-shaped groove is an antidote to anxiety. By the time my son wondered how he could learn to do something with his hands besides catch a ball, I had the answer: "Honey, you just have to be willing to be bad at it for a while." I had mastered other things by first being terrible at them, and now I wondered how long I would have to be a terrible stepmother before I learned how to do it.

Sweet Sweet's cousin Xiou Mei brought over her old computer so that Sweet Sweet could talk in chat rooms with other enthusiasts of Japanese anime cartoons. Despite this global competition, I resumed reaching out to Sweet Sweet with as much detachment as I could muster. I got used to "No" and sometimes, amazingly, "No thanks." If I was going somewhere, I opened the door to her room. She would be there, all right, hunkered down over the computer with bloodshot eyes. "Sweet Sweet, I'm going to an African dance party. It's cool music. You might like it. Want to come with me?"

"OK."

"OK" always surprised the hell out of me. Off we went to the riverfront warehouse where a Senegalese dance troupe was performing. People were already dancing. I spotted some old friends and eagerly joined them, towing Sweet Sweet by the hand. We were in the middle of the happy dancers. A young African woman bumped up against Sweet Sweet, who was making minuscule hip movements and twitching her shoulders in her own shorthand version of dancing. The woman said "Hi" and smiled warmly, looking directly into Sweet Sweet's eyes. Sweet Sweet kept up her understated swaying; her lips curled up just a little, accepting that a stranger was dancing with her, just inches from her face. We danced until we were hot and sweaty and the drummer's hands disappeared into the final frenzy of sound.

Every night we bumped heads in the center of the table over the family bowl. Together we slurped, smacked, belched, and spat fish bones on the table. Before school, after school, all weekend, and on vacations, Sweet Sweet sat immobile in front of a computer screen. The neat stockpiles of candy in her drawer could keep her going in the Chinese chat rooms for twelve hours at a stretch. When she got tired of that, she played solitaire. She came out to eat, use the toilet, and once in a while ask me for help with English essays. Those evenings would begin with the question "Did you read the story?" No, she had not read the story. "OK, let's read the story together." At the end, I asked, "What do you think?" Shrug. When I asked, "Do you like this story?" her answer was, "I never think about." Her English class was reading *The Great Gatsby*. The assignment was to find a place where Nick is suspicious that Gatsby is not what he says he is. Her response: "Gatsby really love Daisy with true love." That's what grabbed her, so I had no choice but to abandon the teacher's agenda and follow her lead.

"Really? OK. How do you know that? Do you think he loved her or his perfect idea of her?"

She cocked her head and thought. "No. I think he really love. He know Daisy do some bad thing, but he never tell."

Homework took us hours. We read *The Great Gatsby* from front to back and back to front. We read Langston Hughes's "One Friday Morning," about a girl who has a scholarship taken from her because she is black. The teacher wanted the students to talk about irony. Why was the author emphasizing the flag and the Pledge of Allegiance? What was he showing the reader? The hesitation was long enough for me to gaze out the window at the pond. The heron rose from the darkening reeds, his long legs streaming with silver strands of water. "Incomplete America," she said.

Da Jie

D A JIE COULD DISPERSE OUR GLOOM whenever we succumbed to bicultural fatigue. We had only one technique for dealing with this, which was basically to cease talking altogether until our communicating faculties recharged. Da Jie was a traveling party. Instead of walking to the door, she pulled her car up on the grass as close to the door as possible and honked loudly until someone ran out to carry her bag and her little shih tzu dog inside. My own dogs, not allowed in the house, pressed their noses to the glass door to observe this imperial brat, who was shaped like a small keg of whiskey.

Before sitting down, Da Jie unwrapped a pork bone for her dog-child to munch on. Soon the bone spun around on the floor with the dog prancing happily in the grease. She tracked it into the living room and then bounded upstairs to leave a turd on our bedroom floor.

Da Jie's first concern was that her brother not perish from my cooking. To prevent that, she tried to educate me. She brought three chickens, dead but not beheaded, plucked but not really. Old chickens were best for soup, she said. "Small feathers around pee-pee part you need pull out. You need cut up-ah." She laughed uproariously at my efforts. "Oh, you cut like that. He-he-he! Maybe OK. He-he-he. You kill me! Now you need boil short time. Now you need take out, wash again. Now you need boil again. Now you need take off dirty. Now you need boil one more time. OK-ah. Now you need put green onion. Put ginger. Now you need cut daikon. Small piece no good eat. Cut big piece. I show you-ah. No, no, Ellen-ah. You need not cook too little. Not cook too long. I remind you later make sure, OK-ah."

Da Jie lay down sideways in our one plush chair, her feet hanging over one arm and her head pillowed on the other. I hastened to get the woodstove blazing for her pleasure while Zhong-hua made tea and peeled some fruit to place before her. By now the brat was back, crawling backward dragging the pork bone and growling through clenched teeth. Zhong-hua unwrapped the remaining packages of meat and fish while I peeled garlic, chopped ginger, and dashed outside to dig scallions in the dark. One would think we had a host of visiting dignitaries rather than just one.

Zhong-hua drew up a kitchen chair next to his sister, and the tea party began in earnest. The talking became more and more excited and loud, the teacups emptied and refilled, steaming water replenished the tea leaves in the pot, the mountain of cubed papaya shrank, crisp winter melon replaced the papaya, and pork knuckles and fish heads bubbled furiously on the stove. Brother and sister read their way through the mint green and hot pink pages of the Chinese newspaper, crumpled them up, and strewed them about like big paper flowers. The wood floor creaked as Da Jie rolled her weight around in the big chair. Such evenings always passed in a cacophony of abundance. I sat on the arm of Da Jie's chair and followed as best I could the deep-throated speech that sparred and thrust about the low-ceilinged room propelled by a tireless recycling of air.

Da Jie brought over some "very, very special" tea that cost one hundred dollars per pound made from the first leaves gathered in the mist on Tai Mountain in the two hours before dawn. I brewed the tea in a tall light green pot with old monks and flying cranes painted on it that Zhong-hua had made under my tutelage when he first arrived. He was very proud of it. Da Jie sat sideways in her favorite chair, and Zhong-hua pulled up one of the folding metal chairs from the kitchen. I set the teapot carefully on the floor between them, and the dainty cups Zhong-hua had painted with cucumber vines and ducklings on a trembling TV table. They took turns leaning forward to fill and refill the cups. Da Jie's voice became more and more shrill, and she poured the tea right up over the rims, paying no mind to the puddles on the table, which turned into a lake and sloshed onto the floor.

They had drained five pots of tea, eaten both platters of fruit cubes, and were gnawing on boiled pork knuckles. Then Da Jie had to pee. When Da Jie's feet felt around for the floor, they struck the teapot and broke off the spout. A split second of dismay stilled his face, then Zhong-hua said emphatically that this teapot was no good in the first place. His sister agreed, and we all laughed from the belly now that the beautiful pot was no more. Da Jie clapped her hands. "Ellen-ah, I tell you: I believe I lose something, must mean my luck change. Maybe whole life get better now. I this time break teapot is good thing! Good!"

As conversation gained speed, I understood less and less. My Chinese relatives did not usually bother to translate, but once in a while Da Jie patted my leg. "Ellen-ah, you know we talk about what? We talk about my mother after Chairman Mao times get very fat. Very fat. Oh my God! Fat! You know, Ellen-ah, my mother have small feet, lotus flower feet. Cannot walk far. Cannot walk fast. My mother have best heart. Before she get fat, long time family have not enough food. My mother just drink water, chew small piece dry, flat bread. Food she all give to husband and children. Two hands can fit around my waist like this because nothing to eat. Also, mother worry about my brother—he cannot run after she because he feet lotus flower feet." The Chinese language is not gendered. There is just one word for *he*, *she*, and *it*, which is why many Chinese people, when speaking English, sometimes use *he* and *she* interchangeably. Chinese also does not use different tenses to indicate past, present, and future. The present tense usually does triple duty, with the context clarifying time frame. Grammatical differences, added to the inverted sentence structure of English, make it a mind-twisting challenge, as is Chinese for the English speaker. Personally, I think English is harder to learn.

"Zhong-hua love running along top of rooftop. Rooftop not flat, so very dangerous. Some neighbor look up and see my brother running on roof. He tell my mother. Mother say, 'Son, you want to fall off rooftop and die? Don't bother. Instead, I beat you dead right now with this stick!' Zhong-hua like to swim in the river. Every year some children dying in river because river very deep, water too quickly. Mother hold Zhong-hua's arm when he come home; with her fingernail scrape off river dirt and know Zhong-hua go swimming. She say, 'Oh, you want to die in the river? No need! I beat you dead.' She beat him so hard he cannot sit down in school for a week. Teacher say, 'Sit down! Sit down!' but he cannot sit. My God! You know, Ellen-ah, my father's mother don't like my brother. Zhong-hua is only son of oldest son. Tradition say he is number one, most important grandson, but grandmother say she don't believe this old stuff. Instead, she give special food to our cousin, younger than my brother, also taller, more handsome. Grandmother little bit mean. She tell Zhong-hua, 'You don't need eat my food.' He every time very hungry, walk six miles home."

They lapsed back into Chinese, and Zhong-hua brought out more pork knuckles and cold, spicy chicken feet. Da Jie smacked my leg. "Ellen-ah, we talk about my father very smart. He oldest of eight brothers. Uncle pay money send just my father to special school learn old culture stuff. He seven brothers cannot go to school because family too poor-ah. My father is special person: he can same time read two books, write down something with left hand, same time write down something with right hand. His brain both sides same time working.

"When Chairman Mao become number one man in 1949, he decide make country perfect. He say things like 'More and more people makc China stronger.' Some people say no, this is wrong. They say Chairman Mao should make plan so China not get too many people. Chairman Mao said, OK, anybody can disagree, but they need write down their suggestion. He say people having ideas is like One Hundred Flowers Blooming. He say government really want to read all people's good suggestion. But when so many smart people talk, Chairman Mao get worried. He don't like. He say we need to find all these bad people and make them learn how to be good. When father twenty-two years old, he was accountant. Some government people asked him, 'If a person borrow $100 from bank, should she pay back $110?' They ask him, 'This fair? This way good for people?' Father think about, but he not sure because his brain think from both sides. He say, on the one hand maybe this way; on the other hand could be that way. Government people wrote down she name on bad people list.

"Chairman Mao say all the people who criticized should be punished so they can learn. He say father need go three years country do farmwork, wear piece of wood on she neck say she very bad. Anybody can throw stones, shout, spit in father's face. Chairman Mao say this fine. Zhong-hua just small baby. This 1958.

"Then Chairman Mao make Cultural Revolution. Old idea, old art, Confucius, Buddha, he say all no good. Taoist person no good, too. Young people from city need go to country work hard. Never know how long need stay, how long not see family. Terrible. We don't like talk about."

Chairman Mao's Cultural Revolution lasted officially from 1967 to 1977, but according to Zhong-hua, it included all the years of Mao's reign of power. The government demanded that people inform on others who showed any interest in things foreign, exhibited bourgeois tendencies, or seemed less than enthusiastic about the revolution. Mao said, "All erroneous ideas, all poisonous weeds, all ghosts and monsters, must be subject to criticism; in no circumstance should they be left unchecked. However, the criticism should be fully reasoned, analytical and convincing, and not rough." The last part was ignored.

Zhong-hua told me that his favorite teacher in grade school was removed from the classroom and forced to walk around the perimeter of the school every day for months, wearing around her neck a pair of high-heeled shoes found in her desk drawer. High heels were a bourgeois symbol. At the marketplace, a person needed to hold Mao's Red Book to his heart and recite from memory if he wanted to buy something. If he could not remember, he was turned away with verbal abuse hurled at his back and would quickly be reported to authorities. Even at the dinner table, every family member had to hold the Red Book up and recite or risk being reported by his or her own kin.

"Ellen-ah, father all the time not happy. Zhong-hua talk about he remember time he head only high as tabletop. He say father call him come, then hit his head with wood. Father say, 'Hurt, not hurt?' Zhong-hua say, 'Not.' Father hit harder. 'Hurt, not hurt?' 'Not.' father hit again and again until Zhong-hua say, 'Hurt!' Then father say, 'Good. You can go.' Father mean because father not happy. Now I want stop talk terrible things. Talk about happy things."

Da Jie slapped my leg extrahard. "OK, Ellen-ah, I tell you what. Zhong-hua and I say probably gas station for you very nice job. Sit down on chair, take some people's money, very easy for you. You early come, work half day. Three o'clock my brother come, twelve o'clock come home."

I was caught off guard, but my instinct for self-preservation prompted me to say, "Da Jie, I don't know. I'm an artist. That's a job."

"Really? You have job? Artist? Okaaaaay. No problem. You can change. Artist no good for money."

"I know, Da Jie, but money is not the only thing important."

"Really? I think important. Ellen-ah, you listen me. You need change. Wintertime again, need eat, buy a lot of food. This time Zhong-hua already come America two year. You need quickly change."

I loved my sister-in-law and would let her do almost anything to me—except completely change who I was. In the beginning, she thought I was good enough for her beloved only brother, but now I sensed she was doubtful of my intellect and meant to have a try at fixing me. According to Confucian family hierarchy and its implicit obligations, it was her duty to take charge of her younger brother's life and his place not to openly oppose her. The implications of this for our future set me on edge. I said, "Zhong-hua? How do you feel? Do you want a gas station?"

"Very love gas station. Really, really want!" He was serious. *Really* came rumbling up from deep in his throat. "I just think whole family can every day eat at gas station. No need go home eat. Also, I think maybe sell my wife's teapots, my wife's art. A lot of stuff can sell in gas station, like Tai Chi shoes."

I knew this was my cue to say "Good idea!" like a good Chinese wife. I wasn't practiced at repressing what I really thought; and besides, I had a poor Chinese poker face, and mine was already betraying alarm at the prospect of selling Lucky Strikes and Lotto tickets and breathing gasoline vapors for the rest of my working days. I wanted to give a hysterical, impassioned rebuttal to this stupid idea, but I knew they would only think me touched in the head. So I played along.

"I'll look into it. We can check in the paper and see if there are any gas stations for sale." I did this and reported to looks of thoughtful consternation that the price of a gas station was upward of $160,000. I spent hours more elaborating on the concept of franchising, but when I answered negatively the question of whether the owner of a Stewart's convenience store franchise could sell Chinese dumplings and handmade teapots, my husband frowned and said, "No good." I was not confident that I had killed the gas station idea, but the immediate threat to my well-being had passed.

There was nothing Da Jie wouldn't try to do. She got her driver's license after two hours' practice in a parking lot. She drove for two years believing that the correct positioning of the car was astraddle the centerline. She bought an electric drill and a screwdriver set and put in shelving all over her house. She said, "Very easy. I can do. Everything I can do." She was genuinely shocked when the brackets fell out of the wall. She had power-drilled the screws effortlessly into the chalk wallboard without hitting one solid stud. Da Jie also landscaped her own yard. The soil was pure sand, and only a few tufts of crabgrass thrived. Not to be defeated, Da Jie went out and bought full-grown flowering plants and lined them up staggered at equal distance along the top of the bank sloping toward the house. They looked like garish nomads about to charge the house. She looked out the back window clapping in satisfaction at her blooming militia. "Red one. White one. Blue one. Yellow one. Pretty!"

For someone who could throw most large men across the room, Da Jie had a tender, vulnerable heart. She wanted everyone around her to be contented and happy. I was visiting her house when her mother-in-law called from China, and I watched Da Jie grow pale. Her eye twitched and her hands shook as she hung up the phone and sank into a kitchen chair. "Now I get big trouble. Mother-in-law want to come live here with my husband and me. Ellen-ah, I a-fraid. Her voice make my heart want to stop. I cannot breathe. She want to control my husband, my family. She want be number one boss. I think she want kill me. I a-fraid this lady." This was a very difficult problem for Da Jie because she came from a traditional family, and for them the Cultural Revolution's slandering of Confucius had not toppled the sacred edifice of family ethics. A wife was the keeper of harmony in the family.

The mother-in-law arrived from China. She had a huge color photo of herself framed and marched it right into her son's bedroom, where she set it on the shelf facing her son's bed. Da Jie complained to me that she could not sleep with her mother-in-law staring at her like Chairman Mao. She said her heart beat too fast and her throat closed up. "I told my husband, 'Your mommy cannot be in this room. How about the living room, OK?' He very angry and ask me, 'Why Mommy cannot be in our bedroom?'" When her husband went out of town, Da Jie put the picture in the hamper under the dirty clothes. Da Jie said, "Happy family always same way happy. Unhappy family have own unhappy. This traditional Chinese saying." Tolstoy, actually, and I hope he took the compliment.

Da Jie tried to do her duty by her mother-in-law, cooking for her, cleaning up after her, driving her around to sales, and doling out a generous allowance, but the woman always wanted more. The mother-in-law trundled about with a benign smile on her face preparing herbal remedies for her granddaughter while conspiring to divert the family bank account into a secret one. One especially brazen cash transfer emboldened Da Jie to threaten divorce if the mother-in-law were not transferred out of the house. The missing money reappeared, and the mother-in-law was removed to her daughter's house a few miles away. At the New Year's dinner, she was back, presiding at the head of the table, a diminutive autocrat, toasting everyone and saying how happy it made her to see everyone together. Then everybody drove to Montreal, ate together in Chinatown, and lost the disputed money at the casino.

The old woman resided in exile at her daughter's house but managed to trouble Da Jie's life from there. Da Jie's protest ranged from not answering the old woman's telephone calls to disappearing for a few days, usually reappearing by the third day, rumpled and listing, having sacrificed a few hundred dollars to a marathon game of mah-jongg in the back room of the Chinese grocery store. She dragged us to a casino with her. As she hustled us along like children across the parking lot, her black eyes got blacker and her high voice got higher. Inside the door, she thrust ten-dollar bills at us and careened limping around the corner alone, her big black pocketbook bouncing off her hip. We lost our seed money in the first five minutes and retreated to the car, where we huddled together and waited for her to come out. She did not come out. She never came out. We had to go back in and escort her forcibly, one of us at each elbow. That summer, she took us to the racetracks and gave us each a twenty-dollar bill. There were thirteen horses in the first race. Zhong-hua bet on twelve. The thirteenth horse won.

Nice, and Loving

I OFTEN WISHED Sweet Sweet could have grown up with the rest of my kids—in a small herd instead of alone. Besides pulling one another's hair, punching, biting, and stabbing with pencils, the four of them did a good job of chastising one another for not doing chores, not being nice to Mom, eating someone else's share of chicken tenders, and not doing homework. They taught one another a lot of the hard lessons of life. I recall Mavis pushing Athan up against the wall and saying between locked teeth "Don't you *ever* call me a bitch again!" He never did.

According to Zhong-hua, there were three kinds of children. The first kind were smart and did not need to be taught anything. They looked around and figured everything out. The second kind could be reasoned with. You could tell them "If this, then that." The third kind had to hit their head against the wall until the pain made them stop. He said it was no use to tell this third kind anything at all. For them, the best rule is no rule, he said. The world will teach this kind of person. "My daughter is third kind. Let her do herself. She will sometime think, 'Oh, this way no good. Let me change.'"

If I had gazed into her newborn face and had the privilege of viewing her undisguised nature, would that memory help me now? I could have fallen back on honest infant revelations. As it was, the past was shrouded, and so my mother's path. I reminded myself of what I had learned from raising children: to grant others authority over their experience and over their own kind of reason. Growing up, my son wanted to listen only to mythic tales and at breakfast insisted his dead grandpa was standing behind his chair. Mavis requested only "true" stories but left notes for fairies in the potted plants and kept Kleenexes in her pocket into which she had twisted waists and appendages and to which she had given names. The oldest, Eula, determined the existence of God by throwing her ring into a wild meadow. "I'll pray to God to help me find it." She did and concluded, "Yep, there's a god." Paroda was the most materially grounded, and her room was full of pinecones, rocks, and dollies. But at four and feeling unhappy, she had stood in front of her trinket shelf and lamented, "What good is it to have all these things when you feel like this?" I have found it impossible to sum up other people, as each abides by a private, fantastical configuring of living and logic, his or her own sovereign sense.

I had a scary vision of Sweet Sweet with gray hair and gallstones, sitting in her room on the same chair, staring at the computer. I made doctor and dentist appointments for her just to get her out. "We have to do something, Zhong-hua. She cannot stay in a room like a small lapdog, just coming out to be fed or have her back rubbed. You make it so comfy for her, she has no reason to come out."

"You think room is comfortable? I don't think so. Just like jail. She will herself decide this way is no good. Not speak English—no good. Always very poor because not have job—no good. Not because you say no good. Let herself feel. She will sometime know—no good!"

"I am not as patient as you. If I were her real mother, I would hound her to clean the toilet and take out the compost. I'd swat her butt sometimes and kiss her on the cheek, but she would be washing the car and running the vacuum. That's how I got my kids out in the world. They couldn't wait to go. Well, except Paroda. She loves cleaning."

"American way and Chinese way different. This is not urgent. You don't worry about this kind of thing. Urgent thing is our family have food to eat. Another thing not urgent. Let me do."

I looked for signs that he was doing but could not detect any. Finally, I asked him what exactly he was doing and according to what plan. "I have no idea," he said. He told me that in China, the parents banked on the world's being able to teach the child what the child had failed to learn at home. But I was not Chinese. I was unequipped with the level of patience needed for this long-term child-rearing strategy and unacquainted with the level of faith in the world needed to be reasonably sure that it would not crush a child as unprepared as she.

Sweet Sweet went with Zhong-hua, Da Jie, and her cousin Xiou Mei to a Tai Chi convention to sell Tai Chi clothes—a budding family business. Zhong-hua had been suffering pains in his stomach, which we attributed to too much heavy lifting at the grocery store. Friday they drove eight hours and arrived in Pennsylvania after midnight. Xiou Mei later told me: "Uncle was dead-tired. We all carry suitcases and heavy boxes of videotapes and Tai Chi swords to the car. Only Sweet Sweet carry nothing. When we return to hotel room, Uncle start rubbing her feet." Xiou Mei turned her palms up and opened her eyes wide. "I could not believe! I said, 'What? This so wrong! Right way is just the opposite: you need rub father's feet.'"

Da Jie chimed in: "Sweet Sweet don't care you, don't care me, don't care anyone. She not respect other people. I tell you, Ellen-ah, let she get job. She need get job, help family. Ellen-ah, this age girl you don't need care. Just let her care herself. Don't worry about. She have roof, that's enough. Let her learn: money not easy get."

Sweet Sweet was on the Internet from morning until midnight. What I had assumed to be a reaction to the shock of a strange land turned out to be a long-established way of life. My husband described the closed bedroom door, the days and weeks and summer months of sedentary solitude, and her unpleasant snapping tone when disturbed. Since many modern Chinese parents work seven days a week from early morning to late at night, Sweet Sweet, like many other children, had often been alone—neglected, in fact—when she wasn't being spoiled. Before she arrived, I asked my husband what his daughter liked to do. He said he didn't know—he had never asked her about her interests and likes. "No time," he said.

"Do you think that is good?" I asked.

"I never think about good or not good. This is just 'must-be' things. Everybody need work."

The computer became a real problem. We had a dial-up Internet connection and only one phone line, so my husband was unable to receive calls from new Tai Chi students and I missed calls from customers, gallery owners, or art professors needing models. I firmly explained to my stepdaughter that she must not tie up the phone line like this. How about after 9:00 PM? How about two or three hours a day? She nodded, looking into the distance, unsmiling and bored. My husband seemed paralyzed. He never said no to his daughter, made demands, or enforced a rule. Da Jie told me that as a baby and toddler, Sweet Sweet had suffered fever seizures. The seizures left her by the time she was five, but afterward the adults were afraid to deny her anything for fear her eyes might roll back in her head. They didn't, but when crossed, Sweet Sweet threw fits of rage, held her breath, and turned blue. The mystique of this historical drama subdued my approach from what it would have been had one of my own children thoughtlessly undermined the well-being of the family. I said softly, "You need to remember, you are part of a family. Everyone needs to think of the other people."

She threw me an icy look, her lips pressed into a tight bud. "Family?" she spat out. She spun around in her chair to face me. "This is family? Puh! This is stupid family. I don't like. I don't need. Just myself! My own life! Myself! You not my mother. Get out!" Her rag-doll persona was gone, and her whole body tensed like a viper. I left a space between us longer than a sword blade. This was the most words in English that Sweet Sweet had ever spoken. Actually,

I was relieved to see the fiery side of Sweet Sweet. Ice baffled me, but I could work with fire.

She had singed me, but my head quickly cleared. I had already raised four children. "That's right, I'm not your mother. I am the mother of this house. If you cannot respect this family, then you need to lose this computer."

Her lips trembled. "But this is my computer. My cousin gave to me."

"Yes, and your cousin can take it away."

Sweet Sweet fell silent and stared miserably at the computer screen. I understood that everything outside, everything and everybody not accessed through that screen, was unreal to her. She was an addict who needed a fix. I tried another tactic. "Everyone has reached out to you, but you do not reach to them. Others do for you, but you do not do for others."

The light sliced her eyes. "I like my aunt. I like Paroda and my cousin. I like my teachers. Just you I don't like. Because you are liar."

I fell right into the trap. "A liar?"

"Yes, you are liar!"

"How? What lie?"

"You take time, think about!"

I recovered my balance somewhat as I realized the absurdity of this accusation, at the same time considering the possibility—had I lied? Not intentionally, of course, but I was capable of lying, certainly. Wow, I thought to myself, with her fifty words of English, she could already work black magic. "Hmm. OK, I will think about that," I told her, as if she had just mentioned the title of a good book. "But you need to know one thing: I don't need you to like me."

She pulled back as if I had thrown cold water in her face. She had been struck. Then she played her last card: "I don't care."

"I also don't care," I said firmly. And that was a lie. If I was anything, I was a mother. I would always care, because mother-caring was autonomous. How many times had Paroda or Athan shouted at me "I hate you, Mom"? I had answered "And I hate you" with conviction, but that was different. Where there is certain love, people can talk like this. Zhong-hua couldn't bear for Sweet Sweet to be angry with him. I would have to be different in order to do my job. I had never been unable to relate to a teenager, but could I be a worthy opponent to her nastiness? I thought not, but I had to try. It would mean being outwardly stern while remaining inwardly fiercely resolved in her favor. Sweet Sweet was in a strange land without her mother. She had an eccentric stepmom and a culture-shocked father. I couldn't let myself give up on learning the enigmatic language that was Sweet Sweet. I wasn't her real mother, but she was my real daughter and I didn't want to lose her. "Good night," I said, and closed the door.

Stumped, I related my dilemma to a Chinese friend. She explained that my stepdaughter, like other urban Chinese children, was the only child of parents who had themselves grown up through two decades of starvation and deprivation under Chairman Mao. The parents cherished abundance. They came home at night, arms laden with groceries—always first for her, to share with no brother or sister and with nothing expected in return. Even my husband admitted that she would often take one bite of an apple and discard the rest. She ate only the freshest, best food, never leftovers. He noticed this all the more because, when he was a child, his stomach was always grumbling and his skin blistering from a diet of boiled tree leaves and wild roots. My friend said that spoiling the only child happened in so many Chinese families that it was now considered a national disaster.

The next day Sweet Sweet had an appointment for immunization shots. This meant I needed to pick her up from school. I did not relish the thought and tried to push the appointment off on her father. He reminded me curtly that he did not know where the Health Department was and could not fill out the forms, which were all in English. "She need understand," he said, "she not like you, but she need."

"Great," I said, "just great. Put the computer in the trunk of the car, please. I'm taking it back to Xiou Mei."

I waited in front of the school. Sweet Sweet got in the backseat, and neither of us spoke. I took her downtown to the Health Department, and we walked up the two flights of stairs to the clinic. Sweet Sweet followed a few steps behind me, hanging her head. We sat in the waiting room, and I pretended to read the brochures on sexually transmitted disease. I didn't try to talk with her as I usually did.

On the way home, I stopped at the Department of Motor Vehicles to get a permit application for Sweet Sweet. I had to wait ten minutes. I stopped at the pharmacy, the grocery, and the hardware store. Then I stopped at an outpatient office for internal medicine to make an initial appointment for my husband, who had been inexplicably weary and had begun having night sweats. He always said, "This small problem will quickly pass. Not big deal." He probably would refuse to go because he was wary of Western doctors with their arsenal of pharmaceuticals, but I made an appointment anyway. I waited in line for another fifteen minutes. Each time I spoke to Sweet Sweet with flat affect, "Wait here," and left her sitting in the car. It felt better to be acting exactly the way I felt inside. I had my husband as a role model: never fake nice, fake polite, fake apologetic, or fake chatty. We arrived home, and my stepdaughter rushed upstairs to get on the computer. I wasn't there to see her face register the space in which it was not.

She should apologize. That's what I believed. I always insisted my kids apologize if one hurt another's feelings, called a bad name, or threw a punch. Usually, the victim was not satisfied with the apology: "It's not sincere" was the usual complaint. The one who had blurted out "asshole," swatted, punched, or stolen invariably moved to make it right. It might be a few days or a week later, but the two parties made their own perfect peace without me. This oft-repeated scenario replayed in my consciousness but didn't release me from indignant expectation. "Sweet Sweet should say she is sorry for disrespecting me," I told myself, and then Zhong-hua.

This contradicted Lu family protocol, which deems spoken apologies inappropriate, even insulting, to another family member because everyone knows that, within the family, all is forgiven. My husband studied my face solemnly. "You think this way?"

"Yes! This is the American way."

"This is family. Inside family, no need say 'Sorry.'"

"This is family, but this is not China."

"Why not take short time—let herself understand she this time make big mistake, let herself think about how to fix?"

"Hfuh." I had no actual answer to this. It was a novel idea, and I would allow the possibility of its efficacy just because it piqued my curiosity. Yes, let her think about that. Good. He was offering to take the burden of correction from me, a burden I carried as ungracefully as the burden of patience and disengaged inaction.

For her part, Sweet Sweet demanded to be allowed to go and live with her aunt, Da Jie, whose house contained candy, Klondike bars, computers, and Chinese cable TV, just forty minutes away from our sugarless cupboard and dilapidated farmhouse at the end of a dirt road. Horrified at the prospect, Da Jie told me how she scolded my husband when he relayed this request: "No! Why you teach your daughter this way—teach her she is princess and don't need do anything? Don't need? Really? I don't think so. Whole family rake leaf—just Sweet Sweet sit on couch, watch cartoons. Whole family carry heavy things—just Sweet Sweet carry hanging-down hands. This good way? You think? I don't want princess! I don't like! You want take care baby. This not baby. This woman. Brother, you forget: when I sixteen-year-old, I take care of you; take care of mommy, daddy; take care three sisters. Every day I go to factory, bring home money for feed family. Your daughter is big baby. No good. This not her fault. This your fault. Little Brother, you do wrong way." My husband hung his head.

Life went on almost as usual. Every night the three of us sat down to a single bowl of food placed in the center of the table. Proper etiquette dictated that each person capture small mouthfuls with chopsticks from his or her own side of the bowl, never digging into the center of the food, and never rooting around for the biggest piece of meat. Also proper was the spitting out of bones and skin onto the table, occasionally corralling them into localized refuse heaps, or not. I observed this through my mother's eyes and never got used to it. Chewing with your mouth open while making loud smacking noises, slurping broth noisily, and burping were also not frowned upon. Our three heads almost touched over the family bowl. Silence was a great equalizer. Since Sweet Sweet's blowout, she and her father hadn't been talking much in Mandarin, and that did make me feel less paranoid, even though I had learned enough of the Shandong dialect to know that they only exchanged such comments as "too much pepper" or "this tastes no good." They never talked about ideas or events or people or anything other than the food in the bowl.

Sweet Sweet mostly stayed behind her curtain of hair and maneuvered the chopsticks through a narrow slit to her mouth; I didn't engage in my usual routine of telling funny stories to Sweet Sweet, asking her questions, and talking slowly to her father so that she could catch the meaning. No. The hell with the little bitch. I soberly contemplated four more years of high school and beyond. I even went to a counselor to try to get a grip on my emotions. He suggested I tap my collarbone and sternum while imagining my stepdaughter far away and no more than two inches high. This was not helpful, and I didn't go back. My dread of being ruled by a surly, demanding giantess was incongruous with the lonely, helpless, hunched-over teen at my kitchen table. I surprised myself by handing her the thickest, most buttery slice of toasted bread. Who did that? I was more surprised when I sent the check to school for her school photograph and even felt excited to see how it would come out. Apparently, I had a mother on automatic pilot inside me that strove to nurture, even while my hurt feelings held out for recompense. Apparently, I loved her, and it was OK that she didn't love me.

I began to take note that, despite the nastiness in the air, whenever I engaged Sweet Sweet, she was either faintly sweet or neutral.

The nastiness I felt like many small daggers in my chest wasn't coming from her. I told my husband I felt unsafe in my own home, as if I could not breathe. I felt as if someone wanted me dead.

"I might be crazy, but I feel this is coming from China."

"Yes. Not one person want you dead. Three people want you dead."

"Who?"

"Sweet Sweet's mother, grandmother, grandmother's sister."

"My God, what should I do?"

"Don't think about."

I practiced not thinking about the Chinese juju trio, and gradually the pressure on my chest subsided.

Christmas was coming, and I wanted to make my grandmother's recipe for coffee cake. I rolled the soft dough on the wooden counter, inhaling the yeasty fragrance. I had prepared a bowl of chopped walnuts and another of brown sugar for the filling. I was patting the dough with my hands and sprinkling handfuls of nuts on top when the sound of the sliding door behind me signaled that Sweet Sweet was home from school. The next thing I knew, she was beside me, her whole right side pressed up against my left side. Her book bag had dropped to the floor. Looking down at the dough and following my example, she reached for a handful of nuts and sprinkled them over the dough. Next she sprinkled the sugar.

"This is my mother's mother's coffee cake," I said softly. "It's French."

Sweet Sweet nodded, still looking down. She stood with the whole side of her body pressed against me until the sugar and nuts were all spread on the dough. Her beautiful impassive face was both relaxed and intent. My heart submitted to this somatic apology.

It was spring before Sweet Sweet said "OK" again and went adventuring with me into the roar of the Little Hoosick River where it rushes toward a cement bridge on Route 2. The river crashes down the giant slanted cliffs and sluices into natural channels it has carved for itself. At one side it thunders straight into a deep pool it is eternally drilling into a deeper, rounder hole in the rock. The waterfall was very difficult to approach. First we had to descend the sheer riverbank facing backward and leaning into the steep slope while grabbing onto tree roots. At the bottom of the gorge, we worked our way between jagged rocks, bracing ourselves on the dripping graffiti wall of the underpass, then crawling on hands and knees over boulders until we reached the river's edge.

We stood together gazing at the pine tree lying a foot above the rushing torrent. The waterfall was on the other side of the river. We would have to balance on the tree trunk to reach a ridge of rock that offered diagonal passage across the middle of the river to the waterfall. I acted as if this were an ordinary activity, except that I put a life jacket on Sweet Sweet. She looked doubtfully into the treacherous channel. The water was dark green, swift, and deep. It was impossible not to imagine being carried away. I didn't know how sure-footed she was, so I sat down on the slippery tree and inched myself along. "It's OK," I said. "You can do it like this. Come on, hurry up before the spray makes you cold." She did it. We jumped into the foaming din beneath the waterfall, where liquid thunder churned with air. It couldn't be called swimming, this thrashing around in the maelstrom, and our gasping for breath couldn't be called anything as ordinary as breathing. The excitement made our hearts pound, and we laughed and screamed while paddling furiously against the current to keep our heads above the frigid froth. We shared at most five minutes of an exponential awareness of being alive and potentially dead.

Sweet Sweet asked me to help her find a job. We filled out a dozen applications, but only Dunkin' Donuts offered an interview. Zhong-hua and I went with her and slipped discreetly into a booth while she met with the manager. She was on her own. We strained to hear the conversation. The manager was saying that her poor English was a big concern. Perhaps she should come back next year. Then he said, "If you could only have one word to describe yourself, what would that be?"

"Nice, and loving," she said decisively. She got the job.

Master Lu

MY HUSBAND WAS GIFTED with natural grace, usually unnoticeable because it belonged to the sparkling he kept concealed. More often he appeared absent, even depressed—visible, but not to be looked into. I first noticed his superb memory for complex footwork while stepping on his feet at the outdoor dances in China. Every evening loudspeakers in public squares blared out music, both Chinese and Western. Punctually at seven o'clock, fountains of water spurted high into the air. Hundreds of people did the cha-cha, fox trot, waltz, and other ballroom dances, despite temperatures above ninety degrees. Husbands danced with wives, ladies danced with ladies, and long lines of ladies danced a Chinese version of the country line dance. The first time Zhong-hua saw my freestyle dancing, arms flinging over my head and feet skipping in every direction, he set his jaw and determined to steer me around despite the impossibility. He was the most skilled dancer in the park and drew wistful glances from ladies of all ages. He pretended not to notice the eyes of curious people all around us but before long herded me off the dance floor to a bench.

Da Jie was visiting our house, sideways as usual in her favorite chair while the little dog greased the kitchen floor and Zhong-hua's wok sizzled with hot oil and crushed pepper hulls.

"*Gemer, lai! Zuo gei wo kan ni de Tai Chi quan ba!*" (Pal, come here! Show me your Tai Chi form!)

"*Ni mei kan wo xianzai zhengzai zuofan?*" (Can't you see I'm cooking?)

"*Ni kuai yidiar ba. Lai!*" (Hurry up and come here!)

Zhong-hua sighed and wiped his forehead with the dishrag. He shoved the chair laden with Da Jie to the wall and tucked the piano bench under the old upright to clear a six-foot-square space. He centered himself, inhaled as he drew up the energy of the earth with his hands, and exhaled, pulling down the energy of heaven as his body sank into bent-knee "Horse Stance." No pans clattered. Da Jie shut up. Even the small dog sat on her haunches and watched with bulbous round eyes. Each time Zhong-hua shifted weight, the floorboards creaked. My mind wandered to the crawl space underneath the house, where I had recently ventured to check the condition of the joists with a screwdriver. It plunged in two inches to the heartwood of the two-hundred-year-old timbers. Zhong-hua was moving in a slow-motion dance, perfectly paced and perfectly balanced, his knees deeply bent and his weight first on one leg, then shifting through the center to the other. The voices of chanting monks rose from the small boom box. Da Jie was watching intently.

I watched, too, but the creaking floor kept pulling my thoughts under the boards, where spiderwebs had tickled my face as I examined the calligraphy of the adze marks on the hand-hewn beams. Those rugged sheep farmers must not have expected boulders when they started swinging pickaxes to dig a foundation hole. In the end, they capitulated to the gray-green bones that turned out to be only the shoulders, hips, and knees of sleeping giants. Entranced, I dreamed myself one of the ancestor builders: *The weight of the tool swung in my hands and bit off a good, satisfying chip. I heard the other men shouting and laughing, passing a bucket of water and ladle in the bright fall air. The water dripped off our chins, salt splash drying on the tangy oak.*

Da Jie's left eye twitched. A seagull spread its wings in the center of the house built by sweaty, gruff men, all dead now. A flower opened and closed. A middle-aged man became an old man and then a young woman. My husband, whose legs were as heavy as concrete pillars, now flowed like air between cattails or water over small pebbles. Da Jie clapped her hands. "You better than my husband! Brother better than husband. Yes! I think so!" She laughed with glee. Da Jie's high-pitched laughter came in explosive bursts, settling a wealth of silvery particles over the room. I could relax and enjoy these fireworks now that the Gas Station Idea had been placed on hold.

"I cannot believe! Ellen-ah, you listen me. Zhong-hua do Tai Chi very perfect. I think now he can teach Tai Chi make money. You talk English. My brother do Tai Chi form. Teach all old people. This easy way. Old people cannot do. Oh my God, old lady all cannot remember. One week learn—next week he mind empty, Tai Chi form all forget. I tell you, Ellen-ah, need teach same thing long time. Long time you can make money."

Da Jie showed up to observe her brother teaching his first Tai Chi for seniors class at the Community Center. She sat on the side bench with her thermos of green tea, firing criticism in Chinese as if the students could not decipher a scolding tone: "No, no, no. You wrong. You teach wrong. Don't need break down one-two-three. Just one and two is OK. You teach terrible.... Brother, you no good." Zhong-hua was mortified but said nothing to her. This was his big sister. Later, he lay in bed staring at the ceiling.

"How to talk to Da Jie? I don't know how to say. She need stop talking, stop telling me how to do. I am grown man. But how to talk? I need think how to talk very nice way." I don't believe he ever had this conversation with Da Jie. He just grunted in noncommittal acknowledgment of her dictates and continued to teach in his own way when she wasn't around.

Da Jie tried to bolster her authority over her brother by convincing me of her superior knowledge, not realizing that I had no influence over whether he listened to her or not. "Ellen-ah, I tell you: I know how to teach best way. At Qufu University, I was not just Ping-Pong professor. I was top Tai Chi teacher. I teach Tai Chi, Qigong, Kung Fu, and also Chinese energy stuff. Energy come from where into body, how go through body, how make more energy— all special things. In America I cannot teach thee-o-ree, right? Because my English no good." She shook her head, chuckling, and then the contagious silver laugh erupted. "My God, my English terrible!" Da Jie eventually stopped supervising Zhong-hua's class, which freed up another night for her to play mah-jongg.

We asked Da Jie to substitute-teach our largest Tai Chi class at the YMCA while we were out of town at a Tai Chi convention. When we returned the following week, only one lady out of twenty had not fled. She told us that Da Jie had commanded them to hold their hands behind their backs and watch her feet. They practiced the first step over and over for one hour. She told them next time they could learn the second step. Zhong-hua had told me that in China young students just starting out with Tai Chi masters had to do nothing but stand in Horse Stance for the first two years until they could hold this wide bent-knee standing pose for several hours without pain. When not standing in Horse Stance, they could carry water, fetch wood, and cook rice for the master. American students expected to make swift progress from the beginning to the end of a form; otherwise, they thought they were no good and became dejected, or decided the teacher was no good and became disgruntled.

Zhong-hua had been an exceptionally strong and athletic youngster. His elementary school teacher wanted him to stay after school so that he could coach him for the Shandong Province tumbling competitions. He did go one time, but after that he always made the excuse that he had to study. The real reason he could not continue was hunger. There was nothing at home to eat for breakfast. After a morning of classes, he curled up in a ball in the sandy schoolyard and slept with his head on his books. There was no point in going home for lunch. After five more hours of class, Zhong-hua was too weak to spend three hours doing flips and cartwheels. Dinner was a thin broth made from boiled sweet-potato vines his mother was able to get for a penny a bundle. He said black beans floated in that water "like a few stars in the sky."

On the street, bullies abounded. Once a fellow five years older and a foot taller than Zhong-hua kicked him in passing as he played in a sand pile. Zhong-hua sprang up to tackle the boy, but the big fellow sat on his chest and, with two forefingers, spread his mouth wide open. One cheek ripped in a straight tear from the corner of his mouth to his ear. The big boy then swung a metal pipe at Zhong-hua's head. The wound stayed open for many weeks. This boy was the son and grandson of beggars who had been made factory supervisors according to Mao's new social reorganization.

Mao categorized businessmen, along with landlords and intellectuals, as the worst enemies of the revolution. A poor peddler could be classified as a businessman, and the owner of a half-acre vegetable garden could be classified as a landlord. During this time, the only "good" families were those who had nothing of their own and no education. Zhong-hua came from a family disgraced by having very little of both. Zhong-hua's grandfather had been a peddler with his own business carried out from a large pack on his back as he walked from village to village selling needles, thread, elastic bands, and fabric dye. Zhong-hua's father, the eldest of this peddler's eight sons, was sent by a benefacting uncle to a *shushi* school, where he studied traditional cultural arts for one year. This single year of education proved a liability under Mao's rigid categorization because it led to the accounting job that classified him an "intellectual" with potentially dangerous opinions. The bully received no reprimand because all insult and harm inflicted on the "bad" people and their relatives were condoned by the authorities. Thousands more innocent people were accused and punished as officials carried out Mao's orders to fill regional quotas of "Rightist Deviationists." Since the time of One Hundred Flowers Blooming, Zhong-hua's father lived as a cast-aside man whose formidable skills were no longer made use of by society. He was given the job of street cleaner and ditch digger and wore a wooden plaque about his neck that said "Enemy of the People."

Zhong-hua remembers only that his father cuffed him on the head whenever he came near him and that whenever there was a piece of meat in the house, his father ate it.

During the Cultural Revolution, Mao sent many urban youths to the countryside to be reeducated. They lived in the villages and toiled together with the village people. Capable young minds like Zhong-hua's were made use of. In 1974, Lu Zhong-hua, just sixteen years old, was appointed the only teacher of a village middle school. His parents had no money to pay his bus fare, so he walked forty miles to this appointed village. On the way, his feet burned and his stomach growled. He rested against a tree, where an old toothless farmer with a cartload of watermelons took pity on him. He cracked open the largest fruit and set the two halves to sparkle before the hungry boy. Ever since that day, watermelons held a numinous power for Zhong-hua.

The students sat on the ground outdoors, where Zhong-hua hung a small chalkboard from a tree. Many of the boys outsized him by two heads and were five or six years older. Their families needed their help in the fields, and they fell more and more behind, never completing the year's studies in order to graduate to the next grade. They mockingly called Zhong-hua "Small Teacher" and set out to thwart his efforts by guffawing loudly in class, belching, falling asleep, or shooting flying objects at his head. Small Teacher cleared his throat and trembled behind the lesson book he held in front of his still-beardless chin. He knew he didn't have much time to solve this problem before mayhem would rule. Thrusting the book to the ground, he folded his arms across his chest and challenged the worst offender to knock him down. Iron roots grew downward through Zhong-hua's short, powerful legs, anchoring him to the center of the earth. The big farm boy could not budge him. Each ruffian charged him in turn, red-faced and panting, only to be lifted off his feet with the force of his own bluster, inverted, and dumped unceremoniously to the ground. After that, few boys risked an uneven match with Small Teacher.

Tai Chi derives from the fighting forms of Kung Fu. In the West, many people think of Tai Chi as a very soft and peaceful pastime. It is relaxed but not soft. The body is supple and ready at any second to mobilize internal power that emanates from the center of the body out through the trunk and limbs. The knees are bent in Horse Stance so that one moves on a low plane and cannot be knocked off balance. My husband maintained a Horse Stance so low that his head was a foot lower than his students'. They often complained that their legs burned after a few seconds. Zhong-hua reassured them: "Legs burning is no problem."

After Da Jie frightened our students away from the YMCA, a nursing home hired us to give an introductory Tai Chi and Qigong class. The residents seemed heavily drugged, judging from their half-closed eyes and dreamlike movements. Most had to be wheeled into the room, while those on foot stood facing a wall or staring down at their stomachs. Zhong-hua took in the scene in a split-second glance and clapped his hands. "Follow me!" he commanded in military posture. "You follow me. In one week you can get out of your wheelchair and run everywhere outside. OK? Let's go!" I couldn't believe he was saying that. I realized he had never seen such a scene as this and was thrown off by it. In China, the elderly rise at five o'clock and migrate to the parks and underpasses to practice Tai Chi.

Zhong-hua forged on in an effort to counteract the powerful drugs. The folks squinted at him in the fluorescent light. When he moved his left arm, they moved their right arms. When he bent, they stiffened. When he exhaled, they inhaled. Some nodded off, drooling, and then snored loudly. Zhong-hua panicked and began to stride briskly from one inmate to the next, taking their hands in his and pulling each finger with a loud *pop. Pop. Pop. Pop. Pop.* "This very good for you," he said. The snapping sound came from the expulsion of air between Zhong-hua's thumb and forefinger, but they thought it was their own knuckles breaking, and he left looks of horror in his wake as they examined their bones for breakage. Some cried out, "No, no, don't touch me, you devil!" Others laughed, "Do it again! Do it again!" The remainder of class was tense, as those who hadn't mutinied feigned follow-the-leader: they clapped their hands with no clap, slapped their knees with no slap, and exhaled with no air. Once outside the door, Zhong-hua leaned to my ear. "I don't think we are can go back there. I did something wrong."

"No I don't think we can."

We got another job at a home for retired nuns. These keen-minded and less heavily drugged ladies initially demanded to know the definitions of yin, yang, and qi; see xeroxed charts showing the pathways of energy through numbered meridians; and hear explanations of the metaphysics of breath. It was not unusual for a whole room of Sisters of the Sacred Heart performing the Tai Chi form "White Crane Spread Its Wing" to be stopped in their tracks by one of them piping loudly: "Master Lu, what is the symbolic spiritual meaning of this movement we are doing? Can you talk about that for a few minutes, please?"

"Yes, this-ah mean another person try to hit you, you need bring right arm up. This another person have power too big, so you don't need push. Let another person make his power all gone, then your stomach turn like this way, make stomach energy out through your shoulder—this easy way make another person fall down."

Zhong-hua was very traditional in this way of teaching the precise martial application of every form. The poetic name of one Yang-style form, "Parting the Wild Horse's Mane," carried this explanation: "If some person punch you, grab his arm like this and pulla. With left hand, pusha he hand off. He fall down, no problem." The explanation for "Looking for a Needle on the Sea's Bottom" involved the opponent's genitals coming to a bad end. The nuns' faces registered silent consternation at Chen-style forms, such as "The Ape Presents Fruits," or smiling nods at "Stepping Up into Seven Stars."

Zhong-hua broke them down further by talking about the philosophy of Chinese medicine in unintelligible English punctuated with Chinese. "Yes-ah, you see, in China we call this *chenrou* (wind up), and this we call *liuliu* (save and store). In Tai Chi you need think circle, circle, all the time circle. Bring qi from under belly button—China call *dantien*. With your breath, move qi through your body. Blood follow qi. Where qi stops, blood stop. If qi stop in your *beihui* (energy point at top and center of head), then blood stop in your *beihui*. This is called 'Big Problem.' Maybe have something grow up in there, like cancer something, on-the-bone something."

The class stood on shaky legs until their eyes glazed over and they begged for chairs. The director intervened crossly with the order that no explanations were necessary and that if Mr. Lu didn't want to get fired, he must give no lectures. The next time, he curtailed his speech to directives and body parts: bend your elbow meant bend your knee, turn your wrist meant turn your waist, and circle your ankle meant circle your shoulder. The sisters, ranging in age from late eighties to one hundred years old, adapted to this language of interchangeable joints and followed along in happy confusion.

There is a Tai Chi form called "Wind Brushes Emerald Willows." There is also a private girls school near our home called Emma Willard. My husband had once visited this school, and thereafter, in every Tai Chi class, announced this form as "Wind Brushes Emma Willard." Many such pathways were made in his brain that could never be redirected. Encouraging the nuns to feel the qi energy moving through their bodies and out their palms, my husband would say, "Feel your hands warm and tingle." Then he would look over at me and ask in a low voice, "What means warm and tingle?"

One sister quipped every few minutes, "I don't get it. Why are we doing this? Why are we here?" These questions, repeated many times a day, seemed to refer to life on earth in general. Another sister said testily, to me this time, "So what is this qi?" I explained that qi is breath energy and one could bring it into the body from the universe.

"Like God?"

"Well, yes, maybe like God."

"Oh, well, He can come in whenever He wants anyway. I don't need this foolishness." She stood frowning skeptically in the doorway for several classes, then one day marched in and planted herself in the prime spot right in front of Mr. Lu, giving him her rapt attention from then on.

The "I don't get it" sister had been a trial lawyer. Her name was Barbara, and she was ninety-six years old. Dementia had touched her mind but left her sense of humor intact. She was usually muttering under her breath: things like "I'm still a lawyer, but a lot of good it does me here. What's the point?" She greeted the nurse with "Hi there, Useless." But from the very first class, Sister Barbara took to Zhong-hua and faithfully attempted her version of the exercises, or at the very least gazed lovingly at Mr. Lu. For the Qigong exercise "Ten Dragons Climbing the Mountain," all ten fingers are crooked to rake the head from hairline to the base of the skull. Barbara's wig would slip off first, and the dentures would soon follow as the dragon fingers stretched the skin on her face.

"This ain't right, teacher."

"No problem." Zhong-hua bent to swoop up the hair. "No hair no problem. No need."

After that, wig and teeth were gleefully discarded at the beginning of class, much to the disgust of another sister whose hair still grew from her head. "Put that back on! Who wants to see that bald eagle's head? I'll never do that. When I go bald, I'll keep my wig on like I should."

Now that she had Mr. Lu on her side, Barbara told her to shut her trap. The final Qigong exercise for those still standing required inhaling deeply in Horse Stance and then grabbing both buttocks in big handfuls with a guttural exhale from the *dantien*, the energy center of the body, three fingers below the belly button. The students were never guttural enough and had to repeat three or four times until my husband heard the right kind of grunt. Satisfied, he grinned, said "Thank you very much," and bowed.

The last ten minutes of class were reserved for neck and shoulder massage. At first, the sisters squeaked and shrank fearfully in their chairs.

"Mercy! You're hurting me."

"Oh. Oh. Ah. Uh."

"Oh, thank you, Mr. Lu. You're so kind."

"God bless you."

Barbara especially loved the massage part. When she was too confused to keep up in class, she came anyway to interrupt at random times throughout the hour. "Hey, teacher, my shoulder hurts, you know." After class, Barbara's teeth remained behind, unmissed until mealtime. A few times the nurses caught her waiting slyly behind the door, sans wig, hoping to follow Mr. Lu home.

I gave several workshops at the convent in mask making, dragging Sweet Sweet along as my assistant to get her legs unfolded for a while. She was annoyed and wouldn't talk to me in the car but rose to the occasion once we were there. She helped one sister mix colors for a fish mask and another whittle a beak for a dove that looked kind of like a blowfish. One sister made a mask of Puerto Rico, including native flowers, mountains, and streams. When it was dry, she put it on and began to sway and bend, singing a song of praise to her beloved land. Another sister made a dachshund mask. Her eyes brightened when she spied a tiny LEGO monkey that had fallen into my box of beads and buttons. She reverently glued the monkey on the dachshund's head, then put it on and told me this story of the year she turned eighteen: Her twin brother had a small monkey he carried inside his jacket everywhere he went. The monkey went with them as they traveled together across Germany by train. For her birthday, her brother surprised her with a dachshund puppy. The same year she resolved to join the convent and had to say good-bye to her two loves, her brother and her puppy.

On Chinese New Year 2004, we made dumplings at the convent with the sisters, who helped roll the dough by hand and spoon in the fillings of shrimp or pork with ginger and leeks. The director had admonished us that the sisters had little appetite and one dumpling each would suffice. The sisters slurped down their firsts and stood in line elbowing and nudging one another for seconds and thirds. Those in wheelchairs sent couriers to refill their plates. Da Jie had come along to help roll the dough. She soon felt herself in safe company, and her laughter, as always, rang like silver bells. Rather than sustain the effort to make her broken English understood, she cleared herself a space in the corner by the window, closed her eyes, and danced with outstretched arms while humming along loudly to the Chinese folk tunes that played over the speakers.

One sister, whom I had told of my husband's singing ability, requested a song. Not able to refuse an old woman, he burst forth with a traditional Chinese song in his booming Pavarotti voice. The sisters clutched their napkins to their hearts, and the dumpling line stopped moving as they all turned to listen. This was the first time I had heard his arresting voice since he sang the Chinese national anthem at a karaoke bar in China. In his youth Zhong-hua often hiked with a friend from the village where he taught school to a secluded riverbank five miles away. There Zhong-hua belted out the classic opera melodies while the friend coached him. "Keep going, buddy! You will be famous. Who has this kind of voice? One in a million, that's who. Keep going! Don't you care about the government." This traditional music was banned as reactionary. Chairman Mao's government had ordered six brand-new operas composed and performed all over China. These were the official operas of the revolution. If caught singing the old classics, a person could be beaten, jailed, or even killed. The singing sessions were very secret.

I cannot sing, and Zhong-hua's voice seemed the most enviable of his gifts. I would have traded all my capabilities for that one. But whenever I asked Zhong-hua to sing, he just shook his head emphatically: "No need. These things all in the past. Sing song is in the past."

The Power of Destruction

A PERSON HAS A FORCE FIELD. Things happen there. I noticed that when my husband passed through a room, glass objects that had collected dust on the shelf for years quaked and shattered. Legs fell off chairs, handles dropped off pots, and the china Dalmatian toppled onto the German shepherd and cracked off his hind leg. Maybe the goblet on the shelf had been walking toward the edge since it was used last Thanksgiving. Maybe I didn't put enough glue in the hole when I made the stool. By the time he had been here about eighteen months, the breaking objects got bigger and of greater significance to daily life. He could break things that were far away and not in line with his intent. One day, while splitting wood, he made an unlucky swing with the iron maul; it struck the plastic wedge askew and sent it spinning end over end through the air. The wedge crashed through the kitchen window forty-five feet away.

One bad week shortly after the Chinese New Year started with the tape player incident. Zhong-hua set it on the trunk of the car and forgot to place it inside before we drove away to teach Tai Chi class. I wasn't paying attention. Fifteen miles later he remembered the player. We drove back and found the black plastic fragments and colored wires by the bridge where Route 2 crosses the Quaken Kill. Zhong-hua pawed around in the snow and rescued several cassettes of soothing music, the casings all cracked and the ribbons tangled like linguini. He found the two halves of an uncashed check from a student along with a paycheck from the grocery from four months earlier that he had stashed in the tape box. Money dealings in China are almost always in cash, and he could not get in the habit of regarding checks as actual money.

Soon after this, he was loading the woodstove and forced the door closed on a stick of wood with a pointy end, shattering the hundred-dollar fireproof glass. He drove our reconstituted silver spray-painted Nissan pickup to the barn to unload some boards and parked it on the slope, forgetting that the emergency brake didn't work. When he turned his back, it drove away by itself in reverse, coming to rest a few hundred yards away against a tree in our neighbors' woodlot. The door fell off. He wired it back on but afterward was obliged to climb in and out the passenger side.

The wind howled and rattled the glass of the old farmhouse windows. A massive ash tree crashed to the ground across the frozen dirt drive. Zhong-hua filled the chainsaw with gas and drove it into the massive trunk. The engine seized, and within the hour the saw was pronounced dead by Earnie, the local chainsaw expert. Zhong-hua had filled it with pure gas and neglected to add the special oil ingredient. He thought the oil additive was optional. He replaced the saw with a cheap electric one, designed for occasional bush trimming in the suburbs. He ran it all day. The engine was still moaning and sputtering in the moonlight until it started spewing black smoke. This one was pronounced dead under warranty. Number three made it through two days and then expired. The store manager was unhappy but gave him a new one and told him not to come back. By this time, only small branches of the great ash remained to be sectioned, but darkness descended on the rising and falling of cut after cut. I refrained several times from running out to stop him. He was convinced that the leaves falling from the trees were choking the pond—maybe he was acting on this belief. I wanted to trust his good sense but didn't, actually. It was my reluctance to be the one always taking charge mingling with a manic sadness in the air that turned my mind from asking aloud, "Have you lost your mind?" In the morning I looked out, and all the small trees surrounding the frog pond lay on the ground. The pond, just freezing around the edges, looked as startling as an eye plucked of lashes.

The razing of the pond left an unsettling carnage, severed tree trunks with sap dripping, and toppled branches clawing at the blue sky. Burning rituals ensued. Zhong-hua spent long hours tending the fires. Dense smoke billowed from the wet branches. One fire was directly above our buried telephone line, which melted, cutting off our connection. Our alarmed neighbor saw the smoke and rumbled down on his tractor to make sure no disaster had befallen us. He cast a disturbed glance at the pond's nakedness but didn't say anything.

Zhong-hua kept vigil into the night. From the kitchen I could see the orange embers and small flames around which Zhong-hua's dim form stepped trancelike as he raked. The lit end of his cigarette floated back and forth. I knew he liked to take a process to the end, "make all done," so I went to bed. He didn't need me in that dream space between the sawed-off world and the new one.

Soon he was shaking me awake. "Ellen, Ellen, come! Quickly come! You see what! You know, not?" Crooked twigs caught in his hair, and his black eyes were liquid and shining. Something had shrieked at him, he said, something very close but invisible.

"Was it an owl? *Who, who, who-who-who-who?*"

"Not."

"Was it coyotes?"

"No. Not. Not animal. Not bird. Terrible! Don't talk about."

"You mean a demon?"

"No. Enough! Don't talk about." He wanted me to go out there and look, because, he said, this thing that was neither animal, bird, nor demon was not after me, just him. There was another thing.

It had spoken very clearly: "You are de-strepped. De-strepped!"
Then he had rushed terrified to the house. All the next day he
kept asking, "What you mean, *de-strepped*?" I assured him this was
not a word, but he could not accept that he could be attacked by
a nonexistent word screeched in the night. He was sure the unknown entity had let fly a real word that had struck him like an
arrow.

Chinese demons could appear disguised as pious monks; old,
frail men; or lovely, seductive maidens. This not-a-demon impos-
tor took the form of a word that seemed to be English and seemed to
have meaning, but was not in the dictionary. We called our friend
Michael, who speaks three languages, in New York to see if the
word was German. It was not. The word had no nationality, nor
could it be categorized in any manner. This gave it fearsome power.
I wondered what I could do to get us disentoiled from its influence.
I had read once about a small flying creature in Manchuria that
the indigenous people avoided because it belonged to no category.
It was neither bird nor mouse. With its enormous nocturnal eyes
and strange webbed legs, it was believed to be the lost spirit of a
dead child. If accidentally encountered, it must be helped along on
its journey to the land beyond the sunset.

I didn't know how to help our visitor along, so it stayed with us.
Every few days he asked again, "What do you mean, *de-strepped*?"

"Well, *de* means 'not' or 'un,' like 'untied.' It means 'separate,'
like in 'depart,' *fengkai*."

"*Fengkai*? Oh, this not so good."

"Zhong-hua, that's just *de*. The other part, *strepped*, doesn't mean
anything."

That thought drew his worry tighter. *De-strepped* harassed my
mind. I returned to the Funk and Wagnalls dictionary. *De* means
"down," as in *descent* and *decline*; *de* means "completely," "utterly,"
as in *derelict* and *denude*; *de* means "the undoing, reversing, or rid-
ding of." *De* was certainly sounding relevant to our situation, but
just what was being reversed? *Strepped*? What was *strepped*?

I found *strephosymbolia,* "a condition in which objects, letters, etc., are seen in reverse, as in a mirror." The roots were *strephein,* "to twist," and *symbolon,* "to sign."

There was *streptococcus,* the virus, from the Greek word *streptos,* "twisted." I paused. If *strepped* was *streptos,* then *de-streptos* could mean "untwisted." In the context of physics, *twist* meant "torsional strain." *Torsion* meant "a state of being twisted." The two words bumped heads, signifying each other. But wait—in mechanics a synonym for *torsion* was *stress. Stress* is the measure of a mechanical force acting upon a body. I had to stop and lie flat on the floor with the Funk and Wagnalls upside down and open on my forehead. If *strepped* was *streptos* was *twisted* was *torsion* was *stress* was the measure of mechanical force acting on a body, and *de* was the reversal of this measure, then *de-strepped* was the process by which the body rid itself of the effects of external forces upon it.

The week culminated in a car crash. It was sleeting. A woman driving the car in front of Zhong-hua suddenly stopped. He said she was reading a book while driving. Our car was totaled, and the policeman's comment was, "I don't know what you are saying, sir. I don't understand you, sir. Stop talking and sit down. You were behind, so you are in the wrong." Triple-A's tow truck deposited the car back in our driveway. I felt that our life was imploding, but I didn't want to say anything to make my husband feel worse than he already did.

That night he dreamed that his dead uncle, aunt, and sister were sitting together at a table playing a game of mah-jongg. They saw him and beckoned, "Come here, come here. Play with us, nephew. Play with us, brother."

"This kind of dream is very bad, I know." He held me tightly, uncharacteristically straightforward: "I can live two years. Then probably I need dead. In my young times, I very strong. Factory have four thousand employees. We have competition to lift heavy iron thing. A lot of people try, but only me could do. A person in young times very strong, very crazy—I know—cannot live a long time. Is OK. Every person need sometime die. Die young, die old, doesn't matter. I not afraid die. Eh-lin, I want you take care of my daughter."

"Of course I will do that. But, Zhong-hua, this kind of dream can have another meaning. Maybe your relatives are trying to help you before it's too late. Maybe they are telling you to quickly pay attention. Let me make an appointment with a doctor."

"No! I don't want doctor. If I need, I will tell you. I already saw Chinese doctor in China. He say gallbladder no good; he say if not cut out, I need eat special herbs. I decide I don't want cutting. This gallbladder no big deal. Just sometime hurt a lot. Nobody can change what time he need go dead. You know, in China we have a kind of person can tell you exactly when you will die. Chairman Mao one time say, 'Bring me to this person. I want to know future. I want to know who will try to stop me from making a new China. How much can I do in my life?' People lead Mao down many small streets until he don't know where he is. Chairman Mao sit at small table and listen. This know-future person tell Chairman Mao he in danger. Chiang Kai-shek's people want cutting his head. But, he say, Chiang cannot catch Mao. Mao could do this work of changing China for forty-one years and then die. Chairman Mao believed this fortune-teller, but when he went back to search for him later, he could never find him again. Chairman Mao told the Chinese people they cannot believe in this kind of superstitious thing. He want them be modern people. But *he* believed. *He* believed. Chairman Mao ruled China for forty-one years, then dead."

"But, Zhong-hua, everything around you lately is breaking—this means something is very wrong. I don't think some bad thing *must* happen to you. There has to be some part you can change."

My comments disappeared into his expressionless face. This is how his face looked when he listened hard to things he did not wish to discuss.

A few days later, we drove up the mountain to teach Tai Chi at the church on the other side. Zhong-hua pulled over and asked me to drive. He slumped in the seat beside me, and before we got over the mountain pass, he was bent over retching into some newspaper. He greeted the students apologizing with small bows of the head, saying his wife would be teaching the class. He remained standing, facing me behind the students. I could hear my instructor voice disembodied, echoing in the rafters as I was thinking how badly he must be hurting to step back.

He spiked a fever of 105 at two o'clock in the morning, clutching his side. He said, "No problem, wait short time, maybe OK." I drove him to the emergency room in Troy and told them my husband's gallbladder was inflamed. The doctors could not decide what was wrong because they said test results did not show that the gallbladder was bad enough to be causing such a high fever. Four specialists hovered until morning, when they concurred that he had malaria, a novel idea suggested by the gastroenterologist. The others said they wished they had thought of that and started an IV with medication for malaria. The next day a general practitioner joined the team and ordered another test that proved that bile was backing up from the gallbladder into the liver because the gallbladder was inflamed. They stopped treating him for malaria, and the surgeon took out his gallbladder. When he woke up, he asked the nurse to please bring him his gallbladder, that he wished to take it home. She said she was sorry to say it went out in yesterday's trash.

Washing the Dog

ACK AT HOME, Zhong-hua lay on a floor mattress all day,
rolled up in a cocoon of blankets. He was always cold. The
old dog Socrates lay around, too. When I came home, I
poked my husband quizzically. "Give me get hot water" or "I feel
very, very tired" was all he ever said. My heart contracted when I
drove up the mountain and saw my dog's limp body in the middle
of the driveway. I jumped out of the car and ran to him, thinking he
was dead, but he rolled over and showed his impressive grinning
fangs. Every time I arrived home, he was playing dead in a different
spot. He had abandoned his usual place in front of the door for random spots in the middle of the field or in the driveway.

Instead of getting better, my husband continued to worsen
until he was sleeping most of the day. When I expressed worry,
he said, "No problem," "Nothing," "Pffff," and "Don't talk about
bad things. Short time rest, probably OK." The more he lay still,
the more I worried. It turned out that the antibiotic prescribed
upon discharge for the gallbladder surgery caused a virulent case
of Clostridium difficile, a bacterial infection that sometimes results
when prescribed antibiotics destroy the body's natural intestinal
bacteria. The doctor prescribed more antibiotics to cure this infection, and I was in the unenviable middleman position of insisting
that Zhong-hua take more antibiotics while explaining that the

cause of his misery was antibiotics. By this time, Zhong-hua was profoundly distrustful. In annoyance he said, "You want to fix me like a teapot." That hurt my feelings, even though I didn't understand the metaphor. Like a teapot? I knew that in China people called a small boy's penis a tea spout, but what about the handle? This puzzled me much longer than it should have considering that we were teapot makers and *teapot* was one of the few English words that held no ambiguity in my husband's mind. It should have been obvious that he referred directly to my fixing compulsion and was not obscuring a metaphor in the anatomy of the teapot.

The biopsy of the gallbladder's cystic duct, leading from the gallbladder to the common bile duct, had come back as precancerous. The doctor told us that when he removed the gallbladder, he had not suspected it of being precancerous and therefore had left the small cystic duct inside my husband's body. Now he feared this duct might also be a source of cancerous cells. He said he could never find this wandering sentinel again because by now it would be tiny and shriveled and far away from where he had seen it last. He referred us to a radiologist and an oncologist.

Zhong-hua never spoke of sickness, death, or fear in the light of day. Only under the protection of darkness and lying next to me in bed would he speak sparingly of such things. Around this time, he told me that the sister he had dreamed of had died of colon cancer and another still-living sister had just had her colon removed due to colon cancer. I turned on the light and fetched the fat red Chinese-English dictionary. He hadn't used the word *colon* or the word *cancer* but had said the *dachang,* the "large intestine," "grew many small fingers." By this he meant the precancerous growths growing inward from the lining of the intestine. Once they rooted outward through the intestinal wall, this was cancer.

My eyes opened wide in alarm, but I still couldn't see my husband's face. "All those times the doctors and nurses asked you about your family's health history, you said everybody was fine. Now you say that two sisters had colon cancer and one is dead? Dead is not fine!"

"Yes, I know."

"Why didn't you tell me this before?"

"I don't know."

I remembered that the general practitioner had mentioned that my husband was anemic, but this had been forgotten during the malaria scare. If my husband did have polyps in his colon, these could be bleeding and causing anemia. I called the general practitioner and got a referral for a colonoscopy. She said she had been meaning to call about that. The local gastroenterologist did a colonoscopy and found hundreds of polyps in Zhong-hua's colon, indicating a genetic disease called FAP (familial adenomatous polyposis), which predisposes a person to colon cancer. This man was not comforting. He said, "Mr. Lu, if you are going to die of cancer of the cystic duct, then there is no point in doing surgery to remove your colon."

Tests led to more tests. The radiologist said to give him a week to call Japan and India, where two other cases involving the gallbladder had been reported. The oncologist in Troy told us he had never seen this particular variation of FAP—with the involvement of the gallbladder. He conceded that he was over his head and felt an obligation to send us to the Dana-Farber Cancer Institute. This was in Boston, three hours away, and the insurance company reluctantly approved this one visit, for consultation only.

I drove to Boston with my husband in the backseat buried in blankets. We had an appointment with Dr. Mayer, an esteemed doctor of gastroenterology and oncology, and his young assistant, Dr. Ngoyen. They appeared to us like two gods in white coats, the taller with white mustache and the shorter with jet-black hair. The two moved as one, at once relaxed, warm, and gently humorous. Dr. Mayer seated himself on a stool so as not to tower over us, and Dr. Ngoyen took notes. Dr. Mayer spoke slowly and concisely, giving each word time to travel through space and translation. He kept looking at my husband's face to see if the words had arrived.

He told us: "Mr. Lu, you have a very rare condition. It is a genetic disease called familial adenomatous polyposis, or FAP, and it causes precancerous polyps in the lining of the colon and abdominal ducts and sometimes stomach and small intestine. We need to take out your colon and rectum. If we do this, you will live. If we do not do this, you will soon have cancer. We don't know if your polyps will become cancerous in one month or one year; however, we are 100 percent certain that they will become cancerous." Dr. Mayer paused, again waiting for the words to make their crossing. "You did not have cancer of the gallbladder. You had cancer cells in the duct that leads out of your gallbladder to the common bile duct, which empties into your small intestine. We believe that these cancer cells started in the place where your bile duct joins your pancreatic duct and enters the small intestine. This place is like a traffic intersection. It is called the ampulla of Vater. The ampulla of Vater is often the source of cancer cells that migrate to other abdominal organs besides the colon in people, like you, who have FAP. We want to go in and look at this place. If we can find the source of this cancer, then we can stop it from spreading. We're going to help you, Mr. Lu. It will be very rough for a while, but we are going to take care of you. Do you understand?"

"Understand."

Dr. Ngoyen was a gentle young man who shared that he had been born in Korea but raised in America. His smooth face was boyish except that it never showed impatience or distraction. We had a Mandarin translator named Mr. Ng. Zhong-hua and I sat on plastic chairs leaning forward while Mr. Ng followed the doctors into the besieged tunnel of my husband's colon. It was as if the three of them—the tall one, the medium one, and the compact, hyperalert Mr. Ng—walked into this tunnel, pointing and peering around the corners and finally crawling on their bellies in the narrowing culverts hung with precancerous stalactites and stalagmites. With their powers of abstraction for headlamps, they reached the ampulla of Vater, the sphincter muscle at the junction where the ducts from the liver and the pancreas converge to enter the small intestine. There Dr. Mayer motioned and continued liverward. Ng translated everything Mayer said into Mandarin. They focused on the task as if there were no place in the world they'd rather be.

Dr. Mayer felt my husband should be treated at Dana-Farber, since his condition was uncommon and might require a complex surgery with a higher survival rate at experienced medical centers than at hospitals where few of these operations had been performed. Our local surgeon who had performed the gallbladder surgery insisted that there was no need to go to Boston. The primary doctor concurred. I made dozens of phone calls and wrote letters to the insurance company but could not penetrate the system. I begged and then I threatened, but this only encouraged them to dismiss me as hysterical. They refused to approve any treatment in Boston. Dr. Mayer tried calling our local surgeon to explain his point of view and was rudely contradicted. In the meantime, Dr. Mayer had ordered a second colonoscopy in Troy to examine the ampulla of Vater, where he suspected the abnormal cells had originated. The local gastroenterologist came forty minutes late eating a Danish. He wiped his fingers on his gown and performed the procedure. Afterward he came to the waiting room and told me my husband was ready and was cured. He quickly walked away. I ran after him: "Doctor, what did you find? How about my husband's ampulla?"

He waved me away and continued walking. "It's gone. There's nothing there. I took it all out. Your husband has no problem now." I didn't understand why he was showing me his back as he talked, forcing me to scuttle after him. He lost my trust completely.

At home we lay in bed in the dark, not sleeping, not talking. Whispered words required less effort, but even those felt like unnecessary leaks of energy. I said only, "Are you warm?" Zhong-hua said only, "You comfortable, not?"

Zhong-hua was forced to quit the bread company and the natural food grocery because he could neither stand on his feet all day chopping nor lift heavy juice boxes to shelves above his head. The grocer missed him for his strong back and fastidious floor mopping. The bread company manager said nobody could chop so many tomatoes in an hour. My husband was pleased that his worth was noted.

Between appointments I continued to support us with small jobs modeling, gardening, and cleaning. Sometimes I worked side by side with others who had more experience and counseled me to slow down, hold back, take longer breaks. My nature is never to hold back, but they were wiser; aware of the toll the manual work was taking on their muscles, tendons, and ligaments, they projected the fortitude needed for a lifetime. People helped us through this time, including Da Jie, my parents, and friends who bought multiple teapots even though they probably could not use more than one. Landscaping work we had done together I found I could not do without my strong partner and reluctantly left a small mountain of stones and five cubic yards of mulch right where the truck had dumped them on one employer's driveway, saying only, "I'm so sorry, but I cannot do this." She was very displeased.

I posed for painting classes at Bard College as a collapsed heap of bones and felt gratitude for the first-year students who turned my naked exhaustion into lovely penciled sand dunes. The professor urged them to pay attention to the "geometry of Ellen." This was in contrast to the "fluidity of Sara," the other model. Where was my fluidity? I used to lie under the Norway spruce and gaze into the blowing branches. I used to swim in the river with my kids and climb onto the ridge in back of the waterfall, gasping in awe behind the heavy veil of water. I used to be a part of what moved and dreamed, but now had crystallized into geometry. I was like angled rocks on a scree slope. Down underneath there was still audible a thin tinkle of water on its way to the ocean.

We lived inland, and I longed for the ocean, but when I thought of its frigid saltiness and wounding debris, I asked myself what this longing was really for. I envisioned each wave rolling in, thinning out into foam upon the sand, and sliding back to the deep. The ocean never forgot to breathe. I forgot. At the modeling job, I remembered, not who I was or what I was doing on earth—those questions seemed irrelevant—but how to breathe. I lay with an empty mind like a piece of driftwood on the beach or stood like a tree in the pasture. The scratch-scratching of charcoal on paper, the small sniffling and coughing and shuffle of feet, was as relaxing as wind in the trees and small birds jumping branch to branch. It was hard to imagine how a person could be an outcast at Bard. The students adhered to a peculiar fashion fad. They looked as if a Salvation Army plane had dumped rejected thrift store donations on the common and each student had donned whatever fell on or near his or her person. They wore slips on top of trousers and sweaters two sizes too small. They maintained serious, stony looks of concentration that I deeply appreciated.

Every day I called the insurance company and was transferred to a different office in the bureaucracy, only to be snidely rebuffed. Armed with statistics and medical jargon, I must have sounded like a possessed madwoman. Then, at last, from one of the dozens of offices where I had left messages, a person named Sherri called me back. She listened and said she would try her best. Sherri arranged for Dr. Mayer to conference by phone with the medical director of the insurance company, who quickly agreed with Dr. Mayer that my husband must be treated at Dana-Farber Cancer Institute. Dr. Mayer was a great man willing to use his power to save a life. I will never forget Sherri, whose face I never saw, as the person who was the crucial link in the communication that furthered my husband's treatment.

We traveled to Boston for a third colonoscopy, and the doctors found a precancerous polyp on the ampulla, exactly where the local gastroenterologist had assured me there was nothing. This was removed, and now Zhong-hua was ready for a dual surgery. A team of surgeons would remove my husband's colon, his rectum, and the vagabond cystic duct. I told Dr. Mayer that the Troy doctor had said this small thing could never be found. He smiled wryly. "Believe me, we will find it." The surgery was scheduled for the end of the summer, and we returned home to plant our garden.

Zhong-hua was frightened of surgery. It wasn't the Chinese way. It particularly bothered him that the surgery would cut from the breastbone down, all the way through the seat of his body's qi energy to stop a few inches below the navel. He said if this energy center were cut through, he could never be well again. It had to be just as disturbing to envision clusters of headless polyps wagging from the walls of his entrails. I read surgical statistics on the Johns Hopkins Web site. What did it mean that a given surgical procedure had a 50 percent survival rate if 80 percent of those 50 percent died within five years of the surgery? Only one certainty emerged from the statistics: patients had a far better chance of not dying in or around the time of surgery if they were able to go to a medical center that frequently performed the complicated surgery my husband needed.

We each tried to keep our balance in our own way. A qi master breathed in through the heels, moving energy with his mind into the body's center, where it collected. When needed, it was moved from there swiftly back out the hands and feet or mind. Outside in the moonlight, my husband did Tai Chi, then stood holding the qi ball to his stomach. I read the Taoist philosopher's praise for the master who lives in such a way that there is no place for the rhinoceros to sink his horn:

> Appearing means life
> Disappearing means death
> Thirteen are the followers of life
> Thirteen are the followers of death
> But people living to live
> Join the land of death's thirteen
> And why
> Because they live to live
> It's said that those who guard life well

Aren't injured by soldiers in battle
Or harmed by rhinos or tigers in the wild
For rhinos have nowhere to sink their horns
Tigers have nowhere to sink their claws
And soldiers have nowhere to sink their blades
And why
Because for them there is no land of death

—LAO-TZU, TRANSLATED BY RED PINE

I wanted to find this land of no death, but everywhere I looked, I saw life slumbering unguarded and exposed to danger. The burdocks grew up by the kitchen door as high as a man, prompting our old dog Socrates to pee on them as invading species. His tail gathered so many burrs it looked like a beaver tail and threw him off balance. He tottered past the kitchen window and lay down in the dewy grass belly up, exposing gigantic black balls. Zhong-hua and I both stared.

"My God."

"In China, this dog already eat. When somebody's dog get old, he invite his friends: 'Come over. Let's eat meat and drink together!'"

"That's not our way."

"Dog old. Why not eat?"

"I don't know. I don't know. We just don't do that."

Socrates' tail got bigger and bigger, and he spent more and more time turning around and around attempting to bite the burdock seeds, which then stuck between his teeth. Socrates' tail upset the ecosystem. I followed him around and tried to pry the outermost burrs loose, but Socrates eluded me by heading deep into his honeysuckle grotto to a hollow of cool earth, where I couldn't reach him. I had adopted this dog from some people who had kept him on a short chain for six years, and he didn't appreciate being restrained for any reason less urgent than having porcupine quills removed from his nose.

At midnight I sat upright in bed. Something horrible was happening in the pasture by the barn. A demonic chorus sent chills up my spine, like a hundred dogs being thrown on a bonfire—coyotes. Socrates barked hoarsely and unceasingly, but when I went downstairs, he and his beaver tail were pressed against the screen door. He was entreating me to silence the eerie cries, which he had no intention of investigating himself. If the screaming coyotes hadn't already awakened our neighbors, then the barking dog would. I got in the car and coasted down the grassy hill to the barn. The headlights shone on a half dozen tails disappearing into the dark pitch. I returned to bed.

After a short time, the howling roused me again. I jumped up again and this time started for the barn on foot. As I waded through the thick mist of dawn, I saw a row of people sitting on the old wooden benches and on hay bales along the west wall. They looked at me with disinterest from under languid, oily eyelids. They wore farm clothes but were oddly misshapen. Their skin had a damp pallor, and their sneering lips curled back over small, sharp teeth.

"What do you think you are doing?" I demanded. "You can't have a meeting here."

"Oh, I think you are wrong," said one man, stepping forward off his hay bale. He grabbed for my throat, and I kicked him. His bloated overalls popped like a water balloon, and sickly green smoke exploded in my face. A coyote ran for the woods. I awoke in the bed.

"Zhong-hua, wake up. Wake up! There were coyote spirits gathered in the barn. Come on, do something! They're not friendly. They are not really coyotes. They are not people. They are like demons or something. What should we do?" I was shaking him, but his sleep had been behind the thinnest veil. He was lucidly awake.

"You don't understand this kind of thing. Do nothing. Don't talk about. Don't say anything. No word. These things already pass. Nothing."

"Don't talk?"

"Don't talk."

It was a Sunday that Da Jie roared up in her Toyota, braking just in time to avoid mounting the back steps. I was never so happy to see her. She clapped her hands and announced: "Today we need wash old dog. Too dirty! Give me get some water, some soap, some scissor, some rope." Our sixteen-year-old wolfy mongrel had never had a bath in his life and hated water. He had slept out in the elements through so many starry nights, snowstorms, and foggy hours that he had become one with nature, like an old Taoist monk who disappeared into the landscape whenever he wanted. In the morning he shook off what had settled atop his fur, but the residue of time contributed to his impenetrable thatch.

Socrates had a reputation for snapping if touched around the neck. When the children played ball in the yard, he threw himself into the air in wild-eyed ecstasy, snapping at shirttails on the way down. In the winter, he pulled off their mittens and scarves and ran to the woods with them. He barked all night, knocked over the garbage can and tore the bags open, lunged at glass windows trying to get the cat, and rammed through two layers of chicken wire to nab a hen.

Da Jie grabbed him by the collar and tied him to the porch rail. After a few halfhearted snaps at her hand, he remained docile for the entire two-hour haircut. Three people snipped. Da Jie clipped all around his balls, anus, and the tip of his penis. Her high-pitched singsong English put the wolf in him under a spell. "OK, boeey, no problem, right? Clean poo-poo part, clean pee-pee part, clean sexy part, OK?" Zhong-hua twisted a wet cloth and cleaned out inside his nostrils. He scrubbed his tongue and teeth and clipped his toenails. I trimmed the hair guarding the hot, deaf labyrinths of his ears.

The hair underneath the top layer was matted into a two-inch layer of foul-smelling felt, which accounted for his being able to snore through blizzards without even shivering. He liked to sleep right outside the kitchen door. The old dog's eyelids began to droop as he relaxed into the bliss of being fondled all over by thirty fingers. When we were done, he was shorn like a sheep and there was a golden brown haystack of hair, small sticks, and burdock seeds. Socrates blinked like the Heavenly Worthy that he was and waited to see what was next. The shampoo and water came next. Da Jie barked orders while I carried bucket after bucket of suds and my husband lathered and rinsed, lathered and rinsed. Every vertebra on the dog's spine stuck up, and his long, shaved tail hung down like a rudder from a boat. I towel-dried his bones, and he swayed back and forth, drunk with sensual pleasure, afterward tottering a few dozen feet clear of the scissors to lie in the grass. Big Sister was satisfied, but I had an uneasy feeling that we had stripped Socrates of his armor.

No Place of Death

ZHONG-HUA HAD SEEDS SENT every year from north
ern China for foot-long green beans, thorny cucumbers,
Chinese chives, and pungent Shandong celery. The cherished cucumbers are named *huanggua*, or yellow squash, for their
pale, translucent interior rather than deep green skin, and nothing was more eagerly anticipated. Zhong-hua and Da Jie stood in
the garden and ate the supercrunchy vegetables right off the vine,
spikes and all. The cucumber plants were very demanding. Each
tender baby required a sturdy hardwood sapling to wind itself
around on its way skyward. The tops of one row of slanted poles
crossed the tops of another parallel row eight feet in the air, where
hemp twine lashed the intersection to a ridgepole that held everything to the sky. We had to tie the weak necks to the pole as
they grew. Every day they determined upward until their necks
drooped again, and we rescued them with bits of rag or string.
They spiraled up the poles, spreading handlike leaves and blossoming yellow goblets for the bees. The fruits grew like infant fingers.
By moonlight the poles cast ghost legs running to the dark wood.

Zhong-hua wanted Da Jie to come with us to Boston. I arranged
for Sweet Sweet to spend three weeks at a camp in the Adirondacks.
The social worker at Dana-Farber Institute reserved a room for us
at the nearby Holiday Inn at a special rate for families of patients,

but the hospitality was limited to three nights; after that we would have to give our room to the next family in need and move to the more expensive Best Western. Da Jie brought a trunkful of snacks, including two shopping bags of tomatoes, a bag of cucumbers, sweet and salty dried fish, bean cakes, pumpkin seeds, and a large slatted crate of peaches. The pumpkin seeds had a hard shell, which she was expert at spitting out while holding on to the soft, edible kernel with her tongue. She could eat vast quantities of seeds at one sitting. While Zhong-hua was in surgery, we waited in a room of family-sized cubicles provided by the hospital. Sweet Sweet called from camp to plead for Chinese food. Da Jie was unsympathetic as she set up our own camp in the cubicle with soda and a balance of healthy and unhealthy snacks. "I think don't need send the big baby food. She father sick, and she just think about she own stomach. Ellen-ah, how about you? Eat, eat, eat!"

I wasn't hungry. "No, Ellen-ah, you not understand. This one you don't need hungry—eat anyway, is OK. Don't need hungry! Go ahead!" She took another handful of seeds. "This one I eat a lot. Hungry, not hungry, doesn't matter." I left her at the carpeted campsite and escaped out the revolving glass door to bustling Brookline.

The alleys between the Dana-Farber Institute and Brigham and Women's Hospital navigated canyons cacophonous with hissing steam and the humming silver turbines that diced the sunlight on the multileveled roofs. Sirens rose in precise vertical screams from ambulances as they crept clumsily into congested emergency ports. Plastic pipes traveled the concrete walls like giant opaque vessels. Outside the immense revolving doors, women sat in wheelchairs with newborn babies in their laps waiting for their rides home while cancer patients in hospital gowns leaned on the cool wall and smoked.

Clusters of crisply dressed people holding cell phones to their ears proceeded across the intersections with the green light. Women clipped along in high heels that rang out on the pavement so loudly

I could hear them for two blocks. The electronically connected coiffed heads struck me as novel, and the secure strides bespoke a strength of purpose far removed from what I felt. Two ladies in blossoming skirts sipped Frappuccinos and flashed the chartreuse and fuchsia soles of flip-flops while ducking into a taxi, which sped off without hesitation. They had a destination. I thought of my husband's large intestines and of the doctors lifting them out of his body, revealing what is ordinarily hidden. They took out his entrails, all six feet of them, bejeweled with polyps too numerous to count, the kind that have the power to transform themselves a hundredfold. They saved this wizardly organ for science. Tall, pretty Dr. Beecher reached inside him again and, with the free end of the small intestine, folded a loop like the letter J that would become his substitute rectum. While this healed, my husband's excrement would squeeze out a hole in his side into a plastic pouch. I decided not to think anymore about this for the time being.

They cut my husband from breastbone to groin, stuck their hands inside his body, and rearranged everything. After six hours, Da Jie was still spitting hulls and watching the national poker tournament on TV. Dr. Beecher came in smiling. She said her team was done taking out the colon and rectum. There had been too many polyps to count. She had fashioned the J-loop into a new rectum, sewed it to Zhong-hua's anus, and poked a penny-sized hole in his side for the colostomy bag. The wayward cystic duct had its own surgeon, Dr. Swan, assigned to locate and remove it. That night in the darkened recovery room, Zhong-hua looked dead. The skin on his face was taut like a mummy's face, and he couldn't speak or turn his head. A whispered gust escaped his cracked and barely parted lips: "Cold."

When the sisters in Zhong-hua's Tai Chi class at the Sacred Heart Convent had voiced their curiosity about what lay behind their belly buttons, my husband tried to enlighten them, but his English was not up to the task. He wanted to say that in the area around and behind the navel lies the Sanctuary of Spirits. The point corresponding to the navel on the spine is called the Vital Gate. The Vital Gate is the point where physical vitality is generated. On both sides of the Vital Gate, deeper in the body, are the kidneys. Between these four landmarks—the Vital Gate, the Sanctuary of Spirits, and the left and right kidneys—about two inches below the navel, is the Golden Stove, where internal energy is cooked and stored. Instead, he said, "Below belly button area is factory, and you is factory worker." The sisters had nodded.

The first few nights, I sat in a chair by Zhong-hua, and Da Jie went to the hotel. Her ankles pained her when she walked as a result of injuries sustained long ago when another Kung Fu expert threw her against a wall. Both ankles and a hip had fractured. It was no small hardship for her to walk from the hotel room to the car and from the car down the hospital corridors. Evenings when I drove to the hotel and asked, "How would you like to take a little walk to see your brother?" she always said, "Sure! Yes! Yes! Yes! You rest." In the room her willingness was soon dampened because Zhong-hua could stand neither the nervous light nor the babble of television. The globes of Zhong-hua's swollen eyelids glistened, reflecting light as flesh should not. He looked like a miserable owl except when he opened his eyes enough to release an accusatory gaze. He didn't move a muscle. If he wanted a drink, he touched his lips once. If he wanted the bed raised, he brushed the sheets with his fingertips. If he wanted not to be conversed with, he showed the heel of his hand.

Eventually, Zhong-hua consented to the silent hospital TV station that played close-ups of leaves quivering with raindrops and sandpipers on rapid legs like needles stitching and unstitching land to ocean. Flocks of shorebirds lifted into the sunset, the undersides of wings flashing white against a blue and orange eternity all at the same instant. Keeping vigil in the dark, unable even to read a newspaper, Da Jie had little to distract her from her own aching bones. She could not relieve me for long.

Once I opened the hotel room door into the blue light of the Las Vegas poker game on TV and found Da Jie sitting cross-legged on the bed like the Happy Buddha, with peach juice dripping down her breasts and an almost empty bag of dried fish on the pillow. Another time she had fallen against the tub while trying to scrub it to meet her standards. One whole side of her body was badly bruised. Making a home away from home was not easy for her.

My husband held up first six, then seven, eight, and nine fingers against a visual pain scale that ranges from a smiley face to an agonized grimace. The doctors started him on intravenous morphine. Zhong-hua became nauseous, agitated, and paranoid. His eyes glittered in icy alienation, first from the doctors, then from the nurses, and finally from me, too. He was terrified to be left alone in the hospital room. Even my short absences to fetch food upset him. The hospital had a rule that family could not stay overnight in rooms shared by two patients. They bent the rule for me but would not provide a cot. I made a bed out of two chairs padded with pillows, but my bottom always ended up sagging into the crack. The crack had a jokester personality, always gaping suddenly wider just as I was falling asleep.

A dozen times a night my toes blindly searched out my shoes. My feet shuffled into the overilluminated halls of polished tile, stainless-steel cabinets, and monitors that never stopped beeping and flashing red warnings. A shadow creeping along the wall and into the storage room, I fetched clean pajamas, dry bedclothes, hot washcloths, and extra blankets, sleepwalking back and forth so many times that the nurses ceased to see me. Gradually, I lost all self-consciousness, existing at the edge of even my own perception. Teams of brisk doctors arrived at 5:00 AM to find me in a T-shirt and underwear, which conveniently concealed themselves, along with the center section of my body, deep in the seam of my makeshift bed.

Mother Nature had been banished and replaced by a well-intended but awkward substitute. Instead of warm arms and breasts, there were electrically heated blankets that lost their comforting power in ten minutes. Instead of flowing brooks and dripping trees, there were hooks hung with plastic bags leaking fluid into the veins of patients. The coffeehouse fifteen floors down had day-old buns at half price. I chewed these buns outside, sitting in the half-light of dawn or dusk on the pebbled concrete rim of a raised garden. On one side, ambulances sped to the emergency room; on the other, speckled sparrows hopped close along the hospital wall on a carpet of myrtle and cedar chips. Red flowers trembled on long green stems, and dwarf trees with shiny heart-shaped leaves made dappled shade. I never saw the people who tended these healing gardens to thank them.

Through a haze of pain and paranoid delusions, Zhong-hua perceived my exhaustion and urged that I go to a hotel. I was reluctant because it seemed to me that the bag stuck to his side was not filling up with waste as it had started to do the first days after surgery. I feared that the morphine might have stunned his small intestine, preventing it from contracting normally. The doctors said this could happen. Zhong-hua still insisted that I get one night of rest. Our Holiday Inn time was expired, so Da Jie set out to scout for another room, planning to return for me that evening. When she didn't appear by ten, I called her cell phone. It was not in service. The Foxwoods Casino billboard flashed in my mind. That was one hundred miles west of Boston, wasn't it?

When I returned to the hospital room and sat down, Zhong-hua made no sign of being awake. His head was propped up, and his eyes were closed. The man in the bed next to Zhong-hua was scheduled for triple bypass surgery the next morning. Just a few feet away and separated by a curtain, he was talking on the phone:

"Hey, Little Brother, this is Joe. I'm going to have triple bypass surgery on my heart."

Zhong-hua turned his face to the curtain and responded with concern: "Oh!"

"Yeah, they're going to take my heart out and put it on the table."

Zhong-hua raised his eyebrows and asked the curtain incredulously, "Why?"

"Oh, you can't understand. None of you understand how hard it is. I've smoked for forty years. Now the doctors say I can't. It's a bummer."

"Yeah, bummer." Zhong-hua looked momentarily confused but pleased to have a new friend. He leaned a few inches toward the curtain, as much as his condition allowed. "I understand!"

"Thanks, I'm going to need it. You're the man. Bye, Little Brother." He hung up.

Zhong-hua was still leaning toward the curtain after a long silence. He said, "Bye, Joe. Nice-to-meet-you-Joe." When there was no answer, Zhong-hua settled back on the pillow and sighed.

The morphine had indeed paralyzed my husband's small intestine. His stitched-up belly stretched bigger and bigger against the sutures as fluids built up inside him. The nurses were very busy with the bypass patient. Every few minutes someone came in to bolster the man's confidence with jokes and allay his fears. Zhong-hua's call button brought no response, and the overworked nurses ignored the messages I left at the desk that my husband was vomiting, that he was alarmingly distended. They did not heed my restrained "Excuse me. Excuse me, nurse." Nobody expected my husband to have serious problems—the surgeons had done such an excellent job. I put a hand on his belly and felt it hard. His face was a mask of utter misery. His stomach filled with fluid but could not empty. He gagged, and I grabbed a basin. He vomited a full gallon of green fluid. I yelled. A very annoyed nurse tipped her head into the doorframe, then immediately shifted into wide-eyed action. A doctor appeared to hold one side of the basin somberly while I held the other, supporting my husband's head with my free hand while he vomited volumes more of fluid.

The doctor placed a nasogastric tube down Zhong-hua's nose and through his esophagus to his stomach in order to drain the fluid. Because of the NG tube, Zhong-hua could not move his head an inch to the right or left without stinging pain. Because of the catheter in his penis, he could not move his legs without more stinging pain. He glared at me, and I realized that his morphine-induced paranoia was intensifying. He thought I had conspired with the strange doctor on the other side of the basin. He was certain I had given the go-ahead to force the plastic tube in through his nose. I knew better than to deny it.

We sat morosely through a day and half a night. I dozed off to the intermittent sucking of the NG tube as bile soup climbed jerkily toward a canister fastened to the wall. I awoke to an unmistakable absence of tension. My eyes adjusted in the darkness, and there was Zhong-hua, looking less tortured, even relaxed, sans NG tube.

"You took it out?"

"Right."

The nurse chose this moment to lift the curtain, and the next thing we knew there was a frantic doctor, white coat flying, accompanied by a sleepy Chinese translator.

"Mr. Lu, we must place this tube back in your nose."

"No."

"Mr. Lu, you don't understand. Sign this paper. You must. You must. If you don't, your belly will blow up again. Does he understand? Make him understand, will you! Sign this release giving me permission to reinsert the NG tube, Mr. Lu. I need to quickly put this tube back." The poor fellow's face was red, and he looked anxiously over his shoulder, as if expecting a rescue squad. There was no rescue from the small, glum translator truthfully conveying a negative. After more pleading, the doctor left angrily with the translator in tow. It was my turn.

"Zhong-hua, if you don't want to follow the doctor's way, then we have to think of another way. Your body isn't working. Do you want to explode like a balloon? Sit up. What do you think? We are going to walk. Can you? I don't care how much you don't want to move or how tired you are. We have to do something. We'll bring everything with us—the IV and the pee bag. Come on! We have to get your intestines to wake up. No more narcotics. Can you take the pain?" He nodded.

Somehow, with my help, he got to his feet; then we hung the catheter and IV on the rolling pole to take with us into the hall. He took small, stiff steps, as though walking on nails. We made it to the elevator of the fifteenth floor, where there was a wide window seat. I sat down sideways on the bench, and Zhong-hua sat between my legs, leaning back against my ribs. I looked through my own reflection down upon the gravel roof of a lower section of the hospital, with its whirling vents, puffing stacks, and lonely seagulls, an unaccommodating heaven that I imagined inhabiting, the same way I had laid on the floor as a child and imagined an upside-down life on the ceiling. People waiting for the elevator seemed unable to see us. I identified more with the seagull pecking sky pebbles. Zhong-hua grew heavier and heavier in my arms, but I murmured that it was no problem. He shuddered and closed his eyes. I felt as if a mountain were dying against my chest.

We continued this walking and resting pattern for forty-eight hours, with many half-hour rests by the window. Slowly, the bag stuck to his side began to fill up, a sign that his small intestine was contracting and moving waste through. We kept on walking. The doctors were very pleased to see the brownish green debris emerge from the detoured plumbing in Zhong-hua's abdomen. I was so relieved, I clapped and cheered. Then Da Jie called.

"Da Jie, where are you? I thought you were coming back."

"What? Oh, I forget come. Come now, OK?" She appeared two hours later with puffy eyes, rumpled clothes, and her hair flattened to one side of her head and flying up statically on the other. She had spent the last two nights sleeping in the backseat of her car in the parking lot of the casino between gambling sprees. The social worker was able to get us a few more nights in the Holiday Inn. We could pay later.

I went to inform Da Jie we might be able to go home the next day. The Holiday Inn room was hot and noisy because it was right next to the pool. The carpet was damp and smelled like feet and chlorine. Da Jie leaned forward toward the TV poker table as if she were right there with the players, the only one without clothes.

There was one more problem: an abscess had formed deep beneath the suture line. The surgeons decided to remove a few inches of sutures in order to drain the pus. The hole needed to be left open so that infection could continue to drain. The nurse brought saline solution, gauze, tape, and tweezers and showed me how to clean and bandage the big hole. She gave us stoma bags and glue to stick them on over the stoma, a section of small intestine the doctors had pulled into the outer world and pierced so that stool could exit into the bag. Sutured temporarily to Zhong-hua's side, the stoma bloomed through the incision like a bright red flower bud. He would wear the stoma bag until the next surgery in three months, when the surgeon would remove it and open the man-made rectum for business.

Da Jie spent the last four nights in a rooming house made into an overnight haven for patients and their families. By the time Zhong-hua was discharged, we had been in Boston nineteen days. Da Jie was elated to be going home. She drove all the way across Massachusetts singing Chinese folk songs to cheer up Zhong-hua. The songs sang the praises of a young girl's eyebrows, cheeks, and cherry lips. Zhong-hua's own cracked lips turned up in feeble appreciation. About halfway home Da Jie thought to call her daughter's fiancé, Pete. She had a few numbers programmed into her phone and accidentally called the rooming house. A woman answered and stated that no, she was not Pete. Da Jie tried again, several times. The fourth time, the lady, whose husband had terminal cancer, lost her cool: "I'm not Pete, you stupid bitch!" She slammed the phone down.

Da Jie looked pensive, tilting her head. "Stupid bitch? I is stupid bitch? Good. I like. I think good, but maybe bad. Ellen-ah, what means *bitch*?"

"Well, a bitch is a girl dog, but people also call ladies bitches when they don't like them, especially if they think they are too smart or too strong—you know, like Hillary Clinton."

"Hillary Clinton? OK, good. I am bitch. I like bitch."

We talked for a few dozen miles about her family in China and her bothersome sister-in-law in America, who was in the habit of appearing at her house just before dinnertime with her husband and mother and leaving just before cleanup time. "You know what, Ellen-ah, what is my problem? I too nice. Yes! Too nice! Everybody tell me. Do you ah-gree-ah?"

"No, Da Jie, you are not too nice—you are a bitch."

"Huh?"

"You are a bitch, remember?" Maybe Da Jie did not remember the phone call just minutes ago to Boston or our conversation about Hillary. She was very quiet.

"I'm kidding, Da Jie—*wo zai kai wan xiao*—I'm kidding."

"Oh, yes, yes." Da Jie relaxed and laughed shakily like faint bells. After this there were no more folk songs and no more jokes.

I spoke up when our exit came into sight, but Da Jie said, "No, Ellen-ah. Listen to me. I know. You don't know. I know a lot. Just go straight is good way. I know. Listen to me." I figured eventually she would realize her mistake. She sped on toward New York City and away from home. When we had been driving a full hour longer than the trip should have required, she said, "Oh, home very far this time."

"Da Jie, I think you are going the wrong way. You are now going south to New York City."

"Really? I don't think so." We whizzed past two more exits. "Okaaaay. Maybe you right." She laughed her irresistible silvery laugh. "You know, my brother not lucky. Some people get body like Cadillac, but he get body like old Chevy. Cannot help. But brother this time OK. He not have cancer, not die. This is happy thing. We don't worry about my small mistake. Buy more gas; lose a lot of money, but brother's body OK! Get one good thing, always need lose something, too. This Chinese rule. Lose something, this means luck change."

"Yes, Da Jie, let's change our luck! I think we should take all the quarters we have left and throw them out the window."

"Yes, yes, all throw away!" We both laughed and laughed.

Zhong-hua could not laugh because his Golden Stove was stuffed with gauze and he was cold and in pain. Da Jie took the next exit, paid the toll, and we got back on the highway going north. We left Da Jie off at her house in Albany, and I drove the last leg of the journey.

We arrived home, my husband, me, and our new charge, the hole in his belly. The bag stuck to his side was not as easy to consider an intimate member of the family. We checked dutifully to see if it needed anything done for it, but otherwise, it clung to my husband as a barely tolerated guest. In the morning I looked out upon the cucumber trellises laden with brown vines and obscenely overgrown fruit, bloated and rotten. All the work of hoeing, planting, tying, and watering had come to this putrid display. Nightfall brought consolation with a particularly good view of the rising moon over the pond now that the trees had been razed.

Socrates was dead. My friend had not wanted to tell me over the phone that he had died in his sleep the night after we left for Boston. She had come to feed him and noticed he was listing to the left as he walked. She put him in her car and took him to her house a few miles away. Socrates was sixteen years old and not used to being away from home. My friend said he had barked at the moon for an hour, consecrated the strange surroundings by peeing on the cornerstone, turned a few wobbly circles on the doormat, and settled down with his front paws crossed under his chin. My neighbor Dave drove his truck to fetch him and buried him near the apple tree at the edge of our wilderness.

Twice a day I pulled the gauze from the big hole. What had gone in sterile and white slithered out on the end of my tweezers coated with green slime. I filled the big hole with saline solution, and it became a red-rimmed salt lake the bottom of which was somewhere in the middle of my husband's Sanctuary of Spirits. Dry gauze lowered in on tweezers drank the salt lake dry, and I repacked the chasm with saline gauze and taped over the wound. Every few days we had to peel off the plastic bag from Zhong-hua's side and glue a new one on over the flower-bud anus in his side. His scrotum was cold and hard like dried figs. His penis was black and blue. The slightest touch of my fingertips burned.

Zhong-hua shuffled back and forth between the bedroom and the kitchen. He had lost thirty pounds while in the hospital and had constant cravings. He said he needed to eat the "big-head fish." The fat red dictionary was not helping us determine the English name of this fish. I hazarded a guess: "Catfish?"

"Not. Chinese people know. You must quickly go to Dong Shi, ask for big-head fish. Quickly go, quickly return." I drove the forty minutes to Albany to the Chinese market. The guy who stood behind the counter with his sleeves rolled up gripping meat cleavers looked back at me uninterestedly, shaking his head. He was not Chinese. He was Colombian. I approached the cashier, who definitely was Chinese, and asked her in Mandarin, "*Ni you mei you da tou yu?*" She stared at me, then called her husband over. I repeated the question. He called his cousin over, and they all stared blankly, shaking their heads. I told them it was for Lu Zhong-hua, didn't they know him? My sister-in-law was one of their best customers. "What name? What name? *Ting bu dong ni de yisi.* Not understand your means, OK? Sorry!"

I checked back with the Colombian fellow. "How about catfish?" I persisted. "Don't they have big heads?"

The guy shrugged and made eye contact with his comrade filling the cooler with chicken feet. He answered in the shrug language. The first guy said, "Head not so big. Catfish we get Tuesday and Thursday. No catfish today." I returned on Tuesday, but the catfish were all sold, and only a few small, sad catfish were still swimming in the tank on Thursday. Zhong-hua had specifically instructed me to get a big catfish. I didn't want to greet his gaunt, unsmiling face without a big catfish. I went to Two Brothers Fish Store, Hannaford, Shop 'n Save, and Price Chopper. Price Chopper had a thin white slab of catfish filet on ice. I brought that light offering home. Zhong-hua stared at it.

"What's wrong? This is big-head fish."

"Yes." Zhong-hua could not hide his disgust. His black eyes became shining slits of lightning.

"What's the problem?"

"Where is head?"

"Well it had a head. It's somewhere."

"This big-head fish not have head. Not have skin. Skin very important, very good for healthy. Head very special."

"Zhong-hua, look, just eat this. Tuesday, I will be the first one to Dong Shi and get the biggest catfish for you." That Tuesday the Colombian fellow grabbed a big stud catfish from the tank and swiftly clobbered it on the head with the cleaver. I brought it home, and Zhong-hua boiled it with scallions, ginger, and pepper.

Snake meat would be best, Zhong-hua said thoughtfully. Since the snake lives underground and eats many strange creatures such as stinging insects and frogs with poisonous glands, snake meat provides antidotes to harmful substances and helps bring up the hemoglobin in the blood. Chinese doctors consider snake a "hot" food because it induces a sweating cure. Too much snake causes nosebleeds. I said I couldn't buy any, and Zhong-hua said he was too weak to go snake hunting. Next he went on a peach binge for a week, not long in comparison to the legendary immortals in ancient China, who subsisted for several decades on peaches alone. Even ordinary mortal beings have reportedly attained immortality through regularly eating peach resin.

By this time, anything he ate soon appeared in slightly altered form in the ostomy bag. After the ordeal in the hospital, the sight of yellowish brown sludge oozing into the bag gave us a lot of satisfaction. The doctors had recommended bland foods to prevent another obstruction, things like yogurt, Jell-O, and tapioca pudding. Zhong-hua did not consider these things food and was not about to start eating them. Instead, he ate pickled bamboo shoots and big-head fish. I told him I thought it was a bad idea to eat wood, but he said, "Wood no problem."

The next morning I was awakened by my husband's groans. His

face was beaded with sweat. The bamboo shoots had evidently piled up in his small intestine because there were no shredded bamboo shoots in the bag. I drove him to the emergency room. In agony with an intestinal blockage, my husband lay on a stretcher covered with a thin hospital blanket, shivering. I was in my T-shirt, freezing cold as well. I commented conversationally that microbes didn't grow as rapidly in cold climates, and maybe that's why they kept it cold in the curtained cubicle. My husband moaned. The aide wheeled him away for tests and back again.

For a long time I sat in the semidarkness. At one point I yawned, and I felt my jaw joint pop. My mouth was stuck open. Wide open. I told my husband, "Uh, uh, uh, uh," and walked to the nurses' station, trying to remain dignified and unobtrusive. I told the nurse, "Uh, uh, uh, uh." She looked at me. "Did you break your jaw?" I shook my head and went back to Zhong-hua's room.

The doctor was in there. "Uh, uh, uh, uh," I said. He stared at me. "OK, I don't have much experience with this, but let me try something." He put on latex gloves and stuck his big hands in my mouth, pushing down hard on my lower jaw. My knees bent, but my mouth was still stuck open. "Well, we may have to operate. Better get an X-ray. When it rains it pours, eh?"

Zhong-hua's moans were the sort that called for the universe to witness, not the sort for soliciting sympathy from other people. My ridiculous predicament couldn't even provide comic relief because Zhong-hua was in too much pain. "Are you OK?" he said. "Uh, uh," I said. Tears started down my cheeks. Every time the nurse or technician came in, there I was standing in the middle of the room with my mouth wide open. I sat down and started to massage my jaw with my fingertips. Just as the doctor returned and told me he'd ordered an X-ray of my jaw and would have to start a chart for me, I heard a pop and my mouth closed on its own.

Grateful that my own sideshow was over, I turned my attentions back to my husband. "Please, doctor, he needs some medication for pain." Zhong-hua spent one night in the emergency room and left with admonitions not to eat pickled bamboo ever again.

Zhong-hua's reconnective surgery was only a few weeks away. Da Jie said she was too busy to come this time. My husband was unhappy. He said, "You know, if I go to surgery in China, whole family go to hospital." I could just see the poor nurses trying to monitor the smuggled influx of Chinese cuisine and remove Zhong-hua's father, stepmother, three sisters and their husbands, six uncles, and five aunts from the hospital room every night.

The big hole abruptly sealed itself shut four days before surgery. The doctors had to poke the piece of small intestine resembling a rosebud back into his body and sew up the hole it had been poking through. They had to open up the folded lower end of the small intestine so it could take over the function of the missing rectum. This was a wonderful thing because it meant Zhong-hua could say good-bye to the ostomy bag.

Zhong-hua became paranoid again as soon as we arrived at the hospital. He feared to have me leave the room and the light bothered him, so I resigned myself to staying there. The orange vinyl chairs on that ward were not at all suitable for pushing together for a bed. As I sat there, a childhood memory animated the dim room: One Christmas when I was a little girl of seven, my big sisters blindfolded me and carried me downstairs. They set me down and put a key in my hands. Off came the blindfold, and there was a plywood chest with a hinged lid and a silver padlock. The tag on it said, "Make-It Box— Love, Dad." Inside were paper, metal foil, oil pastels, and charcoal. I felt that I had to make something perfect with these beautiful art supplies, and because of that I preferred trudging up the muddy creek bed behind the house collecting junk: frying pans, plastic doll heads, sardine cans, and rubber wagon wheels. I brought the day's harvest home and made "sculpture" out of it.

As I settled for the duration in the slippery chair and Zhong-hua slept, the memories of my creek art brought back to mind Chinese tales about the Creator's first attempts to make people: these first beings walked around with noses where their toes should be, ears all over their heads like shells, or one leg shorter than the other. Things could go very wrong before they went right. North American trickster tales drifted into my mind, where they combined and recombined like cloud formations: The fog bank moved, and four shreds of mist stretched downward like legs and became Silver Fox running. A dark cloud quickened and rolled over and over to become Raven flying. Raven stuck his beak into his belly button and pulled out dirt. Fox spit on the dirt and rolled it with his paw. Raven poked a hole in the ball, and they both crawled in. After a while Raven complained, "I am tired of smelling your tail." Fox said, "And I am tired of your stick legs scratching me." Fox stretched and Raven flapped his wings until the dirt ball crumbled and they stood on the mound of earth.

"Hey, where are we?" Raven asked.

"I don't know," Fox replied, "but since we are here now, let's make something."

"Let's sleep first."

They slept a few days, and in his dream the lice in his fur taught Fox the words to a song and Fox taught Raven. The song was like a crank in the buckets of their brains stirring up good ideas. A creator had only to sink into sleep or depression, burp, sneeze, scratch off flakes of dead skin, fart, or feel diffuse longing for unheard-of things to come into being. These tales, even in the hacksawed form in which my mind had stored them, gave me the comfort and chiding I needed. I had kept the key to the make-it box in a baking powder tin. Sitting in the pit of Zhong-hua's beleaguering silence, my stomach growled.

The Peaches of Immortality

IT BECAME APPARENT THAT ZHONG-HUA wasn't thinking about anything but food and what it could do for him. When we got home from the surgery that reconnected his small intestine to his handcrafted rectum, the quest for big-head fish was abandoned for pig and chicken feet. Both had a gelatinous, strengthening toe protein—or so Zhong-hua claimed. As fast as the men at the Chinese grocery could stack the packages of feet in the cooler, I snatched them out. I could never sufficiently scrape the thick, fatty pigskin to remove all the elegant golden hairs. Zhong-hua nudged me aside with his diminished mass and leaned against the kitchen sink to scrape the hairs himself. The chicken feet also had all but invisible hairs that had to be properly pinched out. Next the kettle full of claws and toenails must be brought to a boil and the gray scum lifted off the bubbling surface with a sieved spoon. The first water was thrown away and the process repeated. I could not eat pig feet or chicken feet, nor do I remember what I did eat during that time.

At Christmas, Paroda, who had started college, brought over a ham she had won at the restaurant where she worked. All the kids were home for Christmas Eve: Eula, Mavis, Athan, Paroda, and Sweet Sweet. Zhong-hua made multiple Chinese dishes for the holiday dinner, all traditional except for the smoked ham: smoked ham with caramelized onions, smoked ham with ginger and peppers, smoked ham with celery, and smoked ham with tree ears. I cannot recommend any Chinese dish made with ham.

Thinking about the make-it box, my father's gift, finally gave me an idea. It wasn't the brilliant entrepreneurial inspiration I was waiting for, but it was something. I bought some rolls of rice paper and bottles of black and red calligraphy ink and a box of Chinese watercolors. I knew Zhong-hua had carried a collection of his father's brushes with him from China. Soon Zhong-hua had set up a table in the basement studio, where he sat for hours painting. Each roll of paper was sixty feet. By March he had filled six rolls with flowers, mountains, birds, and fish. I bought boxes of ceramic tiles wholesale, and he painted those with glaze, to be fired with the teapots. I watched him and then tried my hand. He had much more control than I did, but my birds were livelier, as I pointed out. I asked him, "How can you paint all these flowers and birds and never look at the real ones?"

"Chinese way and American way different. Chinese artist hold painting inside heart. Just need take out. American artist need same time look at tree, same time paint tree. Try to find tree, how to feel."

"Well, I think some Chinese painters never go outside."

"Hmm, maybe you right. Chinese painter should be sometime go out look."

Before the snow melted that spring, Zhong-hua was outside in his faded pajama pants and black jacket sitting on the upside-down milk crate at the edge of the pond. To his amazement, a school of three-inch goldfish appeared, survivors of the big freeze. He had brought them home from Pet World before the first surgery in August. He sat there smoking Old Golds and saw the kingfisher ride down a swift angle from a high branch, hit the water, and fly up with a wriggling goldfish. He saw the blue heron stand patiently in the mud on one leg, then stretch its long neck to nab a bullhead from the shallows. He saw the twelve-foot blacksnake wrapping itself around the branches of a fallen birch tree that had crashed into the water. Zhong-hua called to me to come see when the female snake, two feet shorter and slightly more slender, joined the male for a horizontal mating dance among the white branches stretched over the water.

At dinner Zhong-hua imitated this handsome snake's technique for baiting the bullfrogs by poking just his head up into sight and wagging it back and forth, back and forth, for as long as it took for one to take the bait and leap into its fanged maw. This choreographed cleverness elicited my husband's esteem. Zhong-hua marveled at the spectacle of the huge frog waving good-bye from the snake's unhinged jaws, his hind legs already swallowed and his oversized head gazing up—clouds traveling unconcerned across the blue sky in each eye. Four hours later, the fingers disappeared at last, and Zhong-hua stood up and stretched in the red afternoon light.

"You watch," Zhong-hua called early the next morning, sitting on his crate. I had draped a rug over the porch railing and was finding satisfaction in the disgusting amount of dirt that fell out as I beat it with a stick. He always used *watch*, *look*, and *see* interchangeably despite my unsuccessful attempts to explain the differences in duration and intent. In Chinese one word covers the bases. I looked. He gestured toward the small, grassy island in the middle of the pond. A small, furry animal was nibbling grass held in its paws. The air was laden with mist, and I couldn't clearly make out—did it have a tail? What was that thing on its face?

"Have flat tail, have beak" declared Zhong-hua.

"A beak?"

"Yes, have," he said.

I peered into the mist again. "A platypus? I don't think platypuses live in North America, do they?" This was amazing. We had the only platypus in North America. Maybe it had escaped from a zoo or arrived as a stowaway in Nova Scotia and swum up the St. Lawrence Seaway. Over the next few days, we tried to get a better look, but the platypus kept turning its back for private nibbling or plopping into the water beak first.

Tarin, a friend from Vermont, stayed overnight during this platypus period. She and I stood on the porch the next morning in sweaters and mittens. A west wind pushed the steam rising off the pond until it merged with the peachy sunlight seeping up between the eastern trees. We gazed into the sparkling meld of fire and water. "We have a platypus in there," I told Tarin. Being a wise woman, she didn't answer right away.

"It has a flat, broad tail and a beak," I continued. "Zhong-hua said he's sure he saw it. I think I saw it. I definitely saw the tail."

"That's certainly unusual. I wonder how it got here."

"Me, too!" My overtired mind welcomed this inexplicable visitation from Australia. My critical faculties were completely out of order, and our pond provided a mystical oasis where marvelous things could happen. Tarin was not inclined to compel reason.

Later that day I saw the platypus on the grassy island he had made his own. I moved slowly toward him, like a walking bush, until I stood with my toes sinking into the soggy mud at the edge of the water. I saw the broad tail. I saw the brown, quivering haunches. I saw the little paw hands. I saw a face that tapered like a mouse's, a rodent face, a beaver face; our platypus had shape-shifted into a teenage beaver. I didn't think there would be enough for him to eat around our pond, especially since Zhong-hua's chainsaw massacre.

In a few weeks, the beaver had gone on his way. By late spring the water level had dropped to only a foot or so, and the bullheads died for lack of oxygen. By early summer the island was surrounded by greenish mud—the pond bed had become a smelly bog.

"We could rent an excavator, you know, one of those big machines that does this." I clawed at the air with my hand.

"No need. We can ourselves do. Just slowly, slowly."

"Ourselves?"

"Yes, no problem. Can. In my young times, when I was village schoolteacher, I did this work."

"You dug out ponds by hand?"

"Yes. Wintertime. In the morning we four o'clock got up. We take off shoes and walk into cold water—one and one and one, like chain. Deep man fill bucket and pass to not-so-deep man. Not-so-deep man pass again—pass, pass, pass—then stand-in-mud man give stand-on-ground man take bucket. Stand-on-ground man give carry-to-field man take. Pond-bottom stuff very good for grow things. Four hours we stand in ice water, then stop. Eat some pounded corn cake and then go back work. We all switch. Stand-on-ground people stand in water. My legs very hurt. Blood pipes all broken. After that I never wear short pants again because legs very ugly blue. I not want another person watch my legs."

My gaze rested on my husband's bare misshapen feet. The bones seemed to have taken an unnatural direction, as if to avoid an obstacle. My husband explained that deformed feet were common among his generation. Their families were so poor that the kids had to accept whatever shoes could be found or traded and wear them for three or four years or until the leather disintegrated. By then the toes had been rerouted. Zhong-hua had the unfortunate position of last in a series of five children—and the only boy. His mother bought or made the eldest daughter new clothes. The second, third, and fourth daughters and then Zhong-hua, in succession, inherited the hand-me-downs. He complained, not about the patched oversized clothes themselves but about the flower-patterned cloth. His mother was sometimes sympathetic enough to refashion the hand-me-downs so that the flowers were on the inside. The other boys could spot the flowers when he turned a somersault or climbed a tree and never missed the opportunity to taunt him.

We accumulated a lot of clothes from garage sales and the Salvation Army. I couldn't suppress a compulsion to corral what we didn't need into bags and donate them back. "Why do this?" Zhong-hua objected. "Just put somewhere—maybe sometime very useful." The edge on his voice signified that this was more than a suggestion. He thought I was insane. Zhong-hua's mother had never thrown away anything. She repaired holes in the blankets with the worn cotton of old dresses and made trousers for her only boy out of the sleeves of worn-out shirts. As he grew, she attached extensions, sometimes in a different color or with the brawl-instigating flowers. Chairman Mao died and the family's poverty gradually abated, but she would not be parted from the scraps of wool and cotton bulging out of the bags under the bed. I tried to regard the alarming plethora of shoes and continual influx from the garment industry from my husband's point of view, as abundance and insurance, not clutter.

Zhong-hua continued his watch at the edge of the big mud pie. There were still painted turtles as big as a man's hand and frogs with gold-rimmed eyes. There were Baltimore orioles, goldfinches, dragonflies, and praying mantises. Day after day, Zhong-hua shuffled in pajamas and slippers between the milk crate and the dank basement studio, where he filled rolls of rice paper with brush paintings. My favorite was of a row of craggy tree trunks blooming red against a snow-covered mountain ridge. High up and shrouded in mist was a tiny hut. I wanted to climb up there with a sleeping bag, and maybe some bacon and a coffeepot.

His favorites were of flowers. He was never satisfied and kept on painting roses and giant peonies over and over. He attacked the problem of the red flowers like a scientist faced with a quantum-layered mystery. Arranging the petals around the intense yellow center, he examined careless strokes and redoubled his efforts in the next flower. Sometimes the blossom was OK but the leaves "not natural," or the butterfly was perfect above a "not pretty" branch. It seemed he had a contract with these flowers he meant to fulfill.

We unrolled the rice paper on the floor, starting in the kitchen and running through the middle of the house to the bedroom. Which flower was good? He wanted to know. I didn't tell him that while he was still in China, I had dug up all the peonies in front of the house and given them to my friend because I hated peonies. They had neglected to take one sickly bush next to the barn door, where Zhong-hua discovered it and promptly transplanted it to the front of the house. We stared into the center of these flowers and peered between the petals. We examined the leaves and the veins in the leaves. Zhong-hua shook his head in disgust: "No good. Not natural. Terrible!" He had a few mountain landscapes, a few birds, some koi fish, roses, and three hundred feet of variations on the peony.

One morning while Zhong-hua slept, I gathered the rice paper rolls under my arm and grabbed my camera. I marched out beyond the garden to the open field. New grass was just pushing up from last year's thatch. I unrolled the fragile paper. It made a lively road that undulated over the contours of the land, a flowery Chinese highway narrowing into the distance. I snapped a roll of pictures. The same day I wrote a proposal to the art center asking for a grant for Zhong-hua to paint Chinese brush paintings of Grafton, New York. When everything was ready, I showed Zhong-hua. He tempered his single nod of agreement with the lament: "I make red flower not natural."

Since the surgeries, I had taken a job as a mental health worker for a supported housing agency and was also still working as a mask maker. When Zhong-hua's vigor did not return, I pondered our situation and decided that my pact with life now required that more education be added to raw willingness to sustain our threesome. I took out a loan and enrolled in a master's degree program at Bennington College in Vermont, reading and writing in the dark hours of morning before leaving the house for work. Zhong-hua dreamed one night that a geyser of hot mineral water had founted from our mud-pie pond bed. In the dream he built a bathhouse around the fountain, and droves of people came to soak their aching bones. He mused, "If this happens, I just need to know how to build this bathhouse. Cement maybe good." If only the pond would fill up again, maybe our luck would improve.

I was not certain that I would be a competent mental health case manager. As it turned out, I did understand the anxiety, depression, and paranoia of my clients from my own experience. It's not easy to feel at home in the world. I wanted to be useful to them, even if only to unveil the mysteries of unclogging a Hoover vacuum cleaner. I met my first client, Arthur, in my office, and he immediately began pacing the floor insisting that someone had been stealing his mail again.

"People tell me it's all in my head. Like they think I'm making it up. How does that help me?"

"Have you considered moving?"

"Jeez, why would I move if it's all in my head?"

"It's in your head, and it's not in your head," I offered.

"Yeah, I know. Thank you! Why can't people understand that?"

We talked for a while more, and I discovered that Arthur loved art. He said he wanted to learn to draw people so that he could paint Saint Francis. I suggested taking a class, but he said no, he would get too confused. When I asked him to tell me the most important thing I could do for him as his case manager, he said, "Slow down. Everybody talks so fast they may as well be speaking Chinese. Jeez. I'd probably sit there for ten weeks and still not be able to paint Saint Francis."

Window-shopping for paint was as close as we got to Saint Francis that day. Driving home, we looked down the long hill that slopes toward the river; the valley below opened up into a panorama of weeping willows, church steeples, and chimney pots under moody tailed clouds tinged purple, pink, and scarlet. Arthur said suddenly, "Look at those clouds! Look at all the colors in there! Look at that gray! Oh, man, isn't that something? We have so much to be grateful for on this planet! So much I can't believe it. Jeez." I learned from Arthur how to ride on clouds. Spending my days with him and other people of high quality was my good fortune.

I had never worked in an office before. Zhong-hua sent me off with bags of long Chinese cucumbers to distribute among the other people there. This cucumber diplomacy was quite effective. People walked up and down the halls happily chomping on foot-long cucumbers throughout August. Everyone raved about them. People whose grinning faces I did not recognize would stop me and say, "So, what other vegetables do you have?"

We had to attend weekly floor meetings that managers declared a "safe space" for expressing any concerns we had. Every week a few people timidly inquired when we might be getting an increase in mileage reimbursement since ours was ten cents below the federal standard and we case managers had to drive up to two hundred miles per week while fronting gas money until our next paycheck. I pointed out that if the cost of gas was eating into an already small paycheck in such a way that an employee could not meet the cost of living each month, then that employee would be forced to look elsewhere. My boss, young enough to be my daughter, later stormed into my office with eyes flashing. She said I had disrespected the administration by giving them an ultimatum. I thought I had only clearly articulated an equation everyone had been openly complaining about.

I went home and hid in the bed, utterly confused. Zhong-hua found me and began vigorously slapping my body up and down with the cupped Qigong hand. "Nothing! Nothing! This just life. Boss always this way. Eat! Eat! You don't worry. Tomorrow tell your boss you is wrong and you is very sorry and you never will do again. Bring her some fresh cucumbers. You know, Ellen, Chairman Mao one time say Zhou Enlai no good. He say, Zhou maybe people's enemy because he have his own idea. Zhou Enlai go down on his knees and beg Chairman Mao to kill him right away: 'You is right; I is wrong. Cut off my head.' Chairman Mao very surprised and laughing. He say, 'No, no, no. Get up, Zhou! Of course I will not cut off your head. You can stay here and help me.' Nobody write down this kind of China history. This just somebody talking. Real

China history nobody know because all people standing next to Mao never can talk, not even after Mao dead. This is government rule. One thing you need to know: you is employee; boss is boss."

I couldn't bring myself to tell my boss that I was wrong. I thought we could both be somehow wrong and somehow right. I left the cucumbers on her desk. Our mileage allotment was soon increased by eight cents a mile, but after that I never opened my mouth at meetings again. My husband needed health insurance.

Zhong-hua maintained his appetite for feet. He put on pounds and walked farther and farther from the house. He even started going to the convenience store or stopping here and there at a garage sale, still wearing slippers and pajama bottoms. Uncut, his hair grew long according to the bizarre currents of multiple cowlicks. The hair next to his ears grew forward horizontally. A shock of hair slanted skyward from his forehead, and another escaped at a stiff angle off the swirl at the back of his head. I offered to trim his hair, but he said, "No need." He seemed oblivious to his appearance. Then a letter arrived from the art center, congratulating Zhong-hua on the award of a painting grant. When it was Zhong-hua's turn to give an acceptance speech, he said simply, "Everyone knows that in my home, Grafton, live many beautiful animals, fly many beautiful birds, grow many beautiful trees and flowers. Thank you!" During the wine and cheese reception after the awards ceremony, a smartly dressed woman approached Zhong-hua and thrust out her business card. "I write a newspaper column," she said. "You really must call me when the show goes up. I can't wait to write a review." The art critic's phone number disappeared somewhere between Troy and home.

My husband navigated a dreamy convalescent plateau of enervation. He was living underground like the blacksnake tunneling beneath the rocky banks manufacturing antidotes to poisonous toads and venomous insects. He disappeared into the moist and populous summer nights, where the throng of tree frogs and the Milky Way enveloped him. At midnight, when I couldn't find him at the basement table or in the bathroom, I pressed my face to the sliding glass door in the kitchen and made out his moonlit form squatting down with a trowel, digging out dandelions. Our lawn lumped and tumbled to a wilderness of field and woods and consisted of mostly dandelions anyway. I let him be.

Another night, missing Zhong-hua at 3:00 AM, I found the door open and heard the relaxed, measured treading of deer over the packed-dirt driveway as they headed for the pond to drink. I glimpsed the pale possum sauntering along the uneven contour of the crumbling stone wall. Nothing minded Zhong-hua standing there, his body rising and sinking on his breath, his fingers tracing trails through the night air. Inhaling, he raised his arms; exhaling, he stroked the air downward. One story claims that a Taoist priest of the thirteenth-century Yuan dynasty learned this circular art in a dream, a practice described as "taking water to the mountain peaks and fire to the bottom of the ocean," causing that which is below to rise and that which is high to descend in a constant flow of yin and yang essences. Feminine essence is *yin* and male essence *yang*. My husband had lately been distressed that the first surgery had irreversibly damaged the nerve that releases the sperm. The thwarted sperm was forced backward into the bladder. Zhong-hua was very sad. The Taoists called the sperm "excellent water" or the "yin of the yin." Some qi masters knew how to change this special fluid to breath and move it up to replenish the brain, thus "taking water to the mountain peaks." Zhong-hua was afraid that with backward sperm, health would elude him. The doctors in Boston said nothing could be done.

The juicy grasses reared upward, evidence of the distance between midnight and noon. The last of the three push mowers found by the curb had failed. For one whole summer, it had roared its way over woodchuck holes and chomped through sumac and burdock stumps as thick as my arm, but lately we had to start it manually by jiggling some wires around. The riding mower Zhong-hua had purchased at a garage sale for $100 no longer worked. Zhong-hua bargained skillfully with the UPS man for another used riding mower, agreeing to pay $250. This was $50 less than the asking price, and then Zhong-hua pointed out that since we had no truck, the price would have to include delivery. The deal was not falling out as the seller had planned. He delivered the mower with a buddy, and they both sat down with Zhong-hua for a men's tea party, Chinese-style.

I gathered that this was my husband's way of making good relations should anything go wrong with the mower. It did. After one half of the lawn was shorn, the mower stopped. Zhong-hua said he would try to fix it first and, if he could not, would tell the UPS man that he had sold a lawn mower that was no good and must return the money. He said in China this was the way things were done. When he finally caught up with the UPS man, the man said no, it had been more than thirty days and he could not refund this money. Zhong-hua just shook his head. He could not understand this terrible American way of doing business.

The creases and whorls of Zhong-hua's fingers blackened with grease, and an array of parts lined up on newspapers spread over the kitchen table. It no longer seemed to be about repairing any particular lawn mower, nor about cropping the grass to match the neighbor's neatly mowed expanse; Zhong-hua seemed to have a commitment to the hidden workings, the blind power in the engine bowels, bound and blocked by some undiscovered malfunction. Time stretched out to accommodate these ritual repairs, which could theoretically ignite the world anew via spark plugs and gasoline. I'm not sure exactly when the grasses bent over from their own weight and Zhong-hua covered the mowers up with black plastic, saying he would fix them in the spring, stating "This not urgent things."

While the lawn mowers waited for resurrection, Zhong-hua turned his attention to the brush paintings he was supposed to be completing to fulfill his commitment to the art center. The show was scheduled for late September; it was midsummer, and he still had to figure out how to mount the fragile rice-paper paintings. Tradition called for several layers laminated with homemade wheat paste and borders of silk. We had spent all the grant money on picture frames, so we made a trip to the Salvation Army and bought a garish cartload of silk shirts. Zhong-hua took these shirts apart stitch by stitch, pressed them, and cut them into three-inch borders. Shirts that were not pure silk bubbled and wrinkled as they dried. Those had to be cut off the painting and the whole process started over. We jointly agreed, "Not perfect is OK. Perfect is not natural."

"You do know that you are supposed to be painting scenes of Grafton, New York, right? I mean, the grant is a *community* grant. When I wrote the proposal, I said you would paint the nature of Grafton."

"Maybe need go out one time look at Grafton Lake."

By now there were a few hundred paintings. Besides the red flower campaign, there were ripe persimmons, ruby-crowned Mongolian cranes, crickets, crabs, shrimp, and numerous small birds, not many of them to be found in *The Peterson Field Guide to Birds of North America* and every one clutching the jointed limbs of bamboo. After several excursions down the road to Grafton Lake, a few attempted lake scenes appeared on the wall. The water was all faded blue, and the pine trees seemed to have been stuck into the shoreline from above, one by one. He kept at it. The hills around the lake steepened into "dragon's tooth" cliffs, and bamboo trees sprouted up between the pines. Chinese fishing boats appeared on the lake, and then the lake narrowed into a river in order to fit in between the dragon's teeth. There was one sprig of pond grass native to our own pond featured in one of the paintings. The stem arched gracefully and exploded into stars. Streamers of petioles trailed downward from the shooting stars. This grass specimen alone represented nature in upstate New York. A yellow bird, visiting from China, swayed on the curve below the starburst.

The painting project had absorbed most of my husband's sleepless nights and afternoons from February to September. We packed twenty of the best ones in cardboard and put them in the car the night before the art show. Zhong-hua wrinkled his brow and touched his chin. "I just think about: if all my paintings nobody buy—this maybe very funny." We looked at each other and burst out laughing at this thoroughly unfunny thought.

I gave Zhong-hua our last fifty dollars to buy moon cakes, sweet Chinese pastries filled with either red bean or lotus root paste, for the opening in downtown Troy. The art center's main gallery was featuring bumper art. There were all-terrain vehicles and motorcycles embellished with roses and skulls and crossbones parked in the atrium. An entire wall displayed artistically lacquered car bumpers. The gravelly voices of motorcycle bums played over loudspeakers, interspersed with engine revving. In a small side gallery hung Zhong-hua's red flowers and scenes of the four seasons. We smiled and stood by the paintings.

Paroda came with two friends from work, and Sweet Sweet brought a camera. Two of my clients arrived in their Sunday best and toured the show as if they were at a White House reception. One murmured over and over, "I love art. I love art," and the other, "Oh, wow! Oh, wow!" An enormous man I'd often seen wandering the streets appeared and washed down a dozen moon cakes with jasmine tea. Then he sat in a chair, pulled out a sketch pad as if he were visiting his aunt Betty, and commenced sketching the face of my client who sat opposite him. She seemed to have forgotten for the moment that she had an anxiety disorder and that relaxing was not in her repertoire. My husband had the effect of causing certain people who came in contact with him to forget who they had been before they met him. He discomfited others into clinging tenaciously to their identity, but no one in this crowd. My in-laws Da Ge and Da Jie burst in and commenced to systematically critique each painting as a judicial duo, moving clockwise: "This one no good. Oh, good, good. This one not too bad. No good. No good. No good. Too expensive; cannot sell like this. Need cheaply sell."

We were packing up the leftover moon cakes when a bearded young man with a video camera arrived out of nowhere and thrust a microphone in front of my husband. "Sir, would you mind telling me, what is art?"

Zhong-hua did not hesitate. He centered his weight and puffed out his chest, hands behind his back, speaking loudly and distinctly. "Art is something the artist do to help you know how is possible to feel or to think—how is possible to be." Everyone in the room turned toward him and froze. "Art need to have this thing that let you feel *how* another thing feel and *how* another thing think. Yeah. Art let you know—this energy is from *world*. Art need let people feel energy of the artist go through these world things. If cannot feel, this not art. If art not do this, then not art: this painting, this poem, just paper, like junk—not art."

Nobody bought a painting, and after the show it started to rain.

Cultural Navigation

THE GROUND FROZE, and the rains looked for pathways in, filling the cellar like a cistern. The foundation
became a mossy indoor waterfall that did not submit to a
"concrete solution." The walls of the house started squeaking,
an unmistakable chorus of creature babies, but we didn't know
what kind. At night the sound of chewing kept us awake, and in
the morning there were rat-sized holes in the Sheetrock ceiling of
the bedroom and living room. I plugged the holes with Brillo pads,
reasoning that rats would not enjoy chewing steel wool.

Zhong-hua sat in the basement painting red flowers while con-
ducting a study of rat behavior. We had two species, roof rats and
Norway rats. They were so dainty-footed that they entered the
Havahart trap, helped themselves to dog food nuggets, and exited
without tripping the door. Zhong-hua resolved to shoot them
with an air gun, but he said that they stared fearlessly down the
barrel of the gun, tilting their heads first one way then the other,
and he couldn't take aim. He identified individual rats as exceptionally smart. We resorted to rat poison.

Rats had never dropped through holes in the ceiling when Socrates was alive. Deer now nosed for apples in the moonlight on
top of his grave. Only a few feet away, Zhong-hua and a bobcat
surprised each other inside the garden fence. The bobcat lunged,

butting its head against the wire fence again and again, until, by chance, it found an opening and bolted.

Without Socrates, Loki, our other dog, spent more and more time under the honeysuckle bush. There was a cool depression under there, made by Socrates turning around and around and landing heavily on his side. Loki was so good-natured that even though he sorely missed Socrates, he wagged his tail and looked hopeful.

In the old days, when I gave the slightest indication that I would be taking a walk, Loki would launch himself off the porch and remain airborne for at least ten feet. Now he didn't even stand up. The vet prescribed some pills and said the dog should bounce back soon—but he didn't. His beautiful head was as sleek and perfect as a harbor seal's, except for the long, troublesome ears, which had always been prone to fungal infection. He no longer barked at deer or chased the cat. Zhong-hua helped me bathe him and carry him inside, where the flies could not bother him.

One day when I came home from work, Loki was thrashing back and forth in delirium. I opened the door, and he staggered out across the grass to the apple tree, where he tried to burrow his head into the ground. I raced to my neighbor's back door and begged him to shoot my dog. Dave was a huge man who intimidated even local toughs on motorbikes. His aim was swift and precise. When I lifted Loki, he was very light and soft, like a stuffed animal, even though he had been fifty pounds a minute before.

The dogs were dead, and the wilderness was closing in. The toaster toasted only one side of the bread. The ignition key would turn but could not start the car's engine. I had an accelerated vision of the reclamation of the house by wind and rain until only a few half-buried stones in a depression in the earth marked our having lived at all.

I wished we could go somewhere slightly removed, a one-dimensional waiting room between the processional order and connecting wires of daily life and a disassembled realm where schedules and toasters have no use. I smiled to think of us wandering stress-free there with our life folded up in our pockets, paper milk crates and a paper pond, like the immortal Chang Kuo-lao, who kept a paper mule in his breast pocket. When he wished to ride, he sprinkled the paper with purifying water to make it flesh again. He always rode backward, facing the mule's tail. If we were immortals, we could disappear for a while, return when we felt up to it, and never add to our suffering by taking ourselves too seriously.

Zhong-hua stacked up the framed paintings between sheaves of Chinese newspapers and turned his attention back to how things work. Our two vehicles had a combined mileage of 360,000. We had already paid a few hundred dollars to Chuck, the auto repairman, to fix the ignition problem in my car. Zhong-hua explained to him that it was a simple situation of two metal pieces missing each other in the blindness of the inner chamber. Chuck said no, it was definitely the starter switch. He replaced the switch; still nothing. Then he ordered a whole new lockset, but that didn't cure it. Finally, Zhong-hua took it all apart himself, stared at the parts on the kitchen table, realigned the two points of metal that needed to touch when the key was turned, and reassembled everything. It worked.

Then Chuck fixed the head gasket, but when he finished, something was still not right. Chuck said he had fixed it perfectly and nothing was wrong. Zhong-hua sat thinking on it for a few weeks and figured out the problem. He told Chuck, "Coolant not going through. Engine very hot."

Chuck shook his head and shot me a look that said, "Get your deranged Chinese husband off my back and give me my money." The malfunctioning part was a twelve-dollar internal thermostat that Chuck had not checked before replacing the seven hundred—dollar head gasket.

After that Zhong-hua ordered needed car parts himself directly from the dealer: "I want to order an elevator for my car. Yes, elevator. One elevator."

"Al-ter-na-tor!" I shouted from upstairs.

"Oh, sorry, sorry! I want one alternator."

My husband's outward focus did not extend beyond the minutiae of metallic mysteries, but at least this concentration was saving us money.

I was trying to help my husband do something I did not know how to do myself—find the right niche, enough space to unfold the paper donkey that could run with the burden of his life as if it were a wren on its rump. Around that time, Zhong-hua discovered that expression "I have no idea" and used it liberally—to my annoyance—as if having no idea were a legitimate excuse for inaction. Perhaps it was the best excuse. I went to my job, and every night when I came home, he was watching Muhammad Ali on the Boxing Channel. If I had been the one lounging at home all day, I would feel guilty, and if questioned on my day's activities, I would say I had dusted, cleaned the bathroom, carried in wood, and, "Oh, lots of stuff." Even though I could see that Zhong-hua had done some chores, when I asked what he had done all day, he said with gusto, "Nothing!"

I kept on prodding: "You have to make connections. The art center sponsored you to teach that free class, and people loved it. Maybe they would pay you to teach again. You should talk to the ladies. Cultivate good relations. My God, I can't do everything."

"What you mean cultivate?"

"Cultivate, like taking care of the garden, turning over the dirt and pulling the weeds so seedlings can grow."

"Yeah, how to do this? In China, maybe smoking together, drinking three bottles, and eat very special food. In China, maybe give expensive gift or money."

"No, that's bribery. You can't do that here."

"Chinese people make things happen this way for a thousand years—make good things happen, make bad things happen, too. Make anything happen. Not do, maybe very bad for you, bad for your family. Not do, maybe lose a lot of business, lose job. Do, maybe you go to jail, nobody see you again, because lately Chinese government make these things illegal. Who they want to catch, they can catch, because they know everybody have to give gift."

Zhong-hua said that a Chinese business spent sixty out of every hundred yuan it earned on gifts to the key players of other companies every year. Individual employees must give gifts to their superiors, their colleagues, and their business contacts at every major holiday. As an employee of the steel company, Zhong-hua never had to worry about apartment rent and always had food and a pocketful of bills, but never knew whether he would be going home at night or going to jail. I asked Zhong-hua if he missed the partial security of cash flow. He said, "You don't understand the mind of Chinese person. The tiger never eats behind. Tiger only eats the food at face's front."

It had been treacherous to navigate the politics of China, and we were having trouble navigating here. The summer camp where Zhong-hua had taught Tai Chi before his surgery didn't call to invite him to teach again. There had been a misunderstanding. A girl had fallen on her hip, and Zhong-hua had rushed over. He was skilled in healing arts such as herbal medicines and massage. He had said, "Do you want me to give you a massage?" She said, "Oh, that's OK," meaning no thanks. The girl told the director later that Mr. Lu had touched her body. She said she didn't mind because she knew he was trying to help her, but her mother had told her to always tell if someone touched her for any reason. The director called me for a meeting and asked me to tell my husband never to touch any student, not even on the shoulder, not anywhere.

Chinese people are reluctant to touch in any casual manner, yet they will readily administer acupressure or massage to a stranger in need. Another cultural fine point requires one to say no when offered anything by another person. The other person is only polite to persist with their offer. "No" usually means "no" to an American but has a different meaning to a Chinese person. My heart sank as the director sternly asserted that she had to protect her institution. I felt confused and defensive, even though I knew this woman was only trying to do her job.

My boss surprised me by suggesting that my husband teach brush painting to my clients. There were fewer land mines for Zhong-hua as teacher in this gentler environment. Zhong-hua started the class by writing a poem in calligraphy on the blackboard. He translated: "Not at home, I think of home and am happy." A few of the clients showed a natural talent for brush painting. Others excelled only at rocks or only at mist. One put the brush down and folded her arms in defeat, while another wrapped up supplies for practicing at home. Arthur made only geometric lines because curved lines upset him. His bamboo forest looked like a bar graph and the sparrows like jet bombers. Despite this, he seemed to identify with the dilemma of a fellow nervous outsider and opened his gracious, magnanimous heart. "I'm no good at this kind of painting, but it's cool. Thanks for coming in and teaching us about this and about China and everything. I really appreciate it." After everyone left, Arthur, who hated messes, chatted with Zhong-hua while helping him clean up the ink spills.

I thought we had come a long way from the time when Zhong-hua wanted to set up a table at the mall to sell his friend's meat grinders—that is, until he announced his desire to make Chinese dumplings and sell them on the sidewalk in front of the state capitol. I assured him that he needed a permit for this, a permit both very difficult and very expensive to procure. "I don't think need" was his answer. A little research proved me right about food vending but also revealed a series of court struggles between Mayor Giuliani and some street artists. Giuliani had appealed all the way to the Supreme Court and lost the appeal. Art is protected under the First Amendment and can be created, displayed, and sold in public places without a license. (Previously, the police could confiscate the art and throw the artist in jail.) And so off we went to New York City to sell our teapots and scarves in front of the Metropolitan Museum of Art.

We stayed overnight at our friend Michael's apartment nearby. Michael helped my husband set up a display that somehow made use of an ironing board and folding chairs and then stood by my husband hour after hour in the cold, kindly urging him to attempt some sort of sales pitch. Zhong-hua slumped down in the folding chair so that his jacket rode up like a turtle shell to shield him from the wind. He stared straight ahead and moved as little as possible. Michael shot me perplexed looks of concern but stood by in faithful silence, a large, bald angel. We didn't end up in jail, but a policeman chased us away the second day because functional art was not allowed. If the item was useful in any way, it was not art. If it had a use but could also be hung on a wall, it could be considered art while hanging there.

We retreated to Michael's for supper, and I remember the impressed look on his face when my husband ate the entire loaf of French bread. Michael hurried down to the street and bought another, which my husband also ate. After that Zhong-hua considered Michael his best friend. He said friends are brothers. You can ask them for anything at any time. You can go to their house anytime and borrow their stuff anytime. Friends will do anything for you, and you have to be prepared to do the same for them.

My husband's early enthusiasm for owning a gas station—convenience store plagued me, because business was the one area in which I had no interest or good sense. He had too many expectations for me as his left hand. I was supposed to be able to translate everything from documents on the sealed vault of a head gasket cylinder to printouts of the vendor rules for the International Gift Fair at the Javits Center in New York City. My mind became very clumsy when fumbling with engine parts or business matters, so I offered a halfhearted hand when he said fiercely, "I *really, really* want to do business!" Boxes bulging with black, red, and white Tai Chi shoes, silk scarves, and tunics occluded the path through the upstairs hallway, and teapots crowded every shelf and cupboard.

Zhong-hua made up his mind to go to the Javits Center International Gift Fair, this time just to look. I found out that only legitimate retail business owners who carried credentials and paid in advance could enter the trade show. "Zhong-hua, you will drive all that way to somewhere you've never been, probably get lost; then, if you find it, you'll get a parking ticket and the door will be shut in your face anyway. And you have no place to stay."

Zhong-hua listened patiently to these reasons not to go, then nodded succinctly. "Yes, you are right." He packed a lunch, filled a thermos with green tea, and waved his hand over his head on the way to the car. "This kind of thing very easy for me. I can go, no problem."

Four hours later he was calling me on his sister's cell phone from inside the Javits Center. I think he said something about the back door. After a few hours of alternating between exploring and enthroning himself in the men's restroom, Zhong-hua left the Javits Center. He soon needed a bathroom again. Since his surgery, this was usually the case. He drove to Michael's apartment in Manhattan. Michael had already told Zhong-hua he would not be home until the next day, but my husband had this exasperating proclivity for stubbornly refusing to accept the most irrefutable facts. "Just try," he said to himself.

"Yes, Michael is at home," the doorman told him. Zhong-hua rode up to the fifth floor but couldn't remember the apartment number, so he called Michael on the cell phone and walked the halls until he heard a phone ringing. Michael had a lady friend in crisis staying with him for the weekend. I don't know who was more mortified—Michael, because he had lied to Zhong-hua about not being home, or Zhong-hua, because he had somehow known all along that Michael was home and had caused him to lose face by showing up. Zhong-hua slept on the couch, and Michael went out to eat with the lady. A few weeks later, the painful awareness that friendship had different parameters in America prompted Zhong-hua to call Michael to apologize.

Zhong-hua went back to keeping late-night company with the Champ, and I desperately hoped my husband understood something I didn't about the ancient Taoist secret of "accomplishment by not-doing." To think that we were sinking, even privately, was an assault on our well-being because I knew from experience that my husband could hear my thoughts, or so it seemed. If I thought I was old and ugly, he became attentive by night. If I thought his hair was looking wild and crazed, he let it become more so. I wanted to convey confidence in my husband's ability to work if that's what he wanted. On the other hand, maybe he needed the pressure off. I wasn't sure which message to send.

Zhong-hua said I thought too much. I recalled that when we worked as gardeners, he had hoped to cure me of this bad habit. A person preserving energy for survival does not have the luxury of entertaining thoughts about terrible things. Terrible things included anything doubtful, impatient, fearful, pitiful, mournful, or sentimental. Thoughts of this nature must be banished. Zhong-hua didn't like me to retell any current news story or gossip about other people's misfortunes. The negative and positive forces in the universe were held in delicate balance and could be tipped the wrong way by one careless thought. Even the playful question "Do you love me?" elicited from my husband a look of startled horror; I had let slip yet another terrible doubt.

Zhong-hua called me a combination of my Chinese name, Ai-lin, and my birth name, Ellen. He said, "Eh-lin." Ai-lin fit me a little too perfectly. It meant "forest mugwort." True, if I were a flower, I would have a woody stem, furry leaves, and a bitter taste. I wouldn't show up at funerals, and my odor repelled mosquitoes. It was hard to tell if a person attracted a name or the name caught the person in its snare. Zhong-hua's name meant "Middle Kingdom," and indeed, he was completely ruled by his stomach. I had an auntie named Sweetie. She was so nice that she let the preacher's widow move in with her and boss her around until she had to die of cancer to escape. Then there was Sweet Sweet, "double sweet." Ugh. "Sweet and Sour" would be more fair.

Zhong-hua had pickled the penis of the first deer he found at the side of the road in a bottle of Chinese wine. My work with schizophrenic and bipolar individuals who lived alone was to help them reduce the terrors of life to true proportions. They did a heroic job, but the true proportions sometimes got the better of me. On the serpentine road home, I tended to look forward to the power of the deer-penis wine to float sad things. The taste was so vile that I only took one swallow, let out a yelp, and continued on my way past the shoe shrine and the peppery pots bubbling on the stove. An hour or so later, I would notice that I could not feel my lips.

Around this time my husband made some mildly critical comment such as "You is not good English teacher because you always want yourself to learn something—forget about student." At hearing this, the deer-penis wine inside me responded with long, damning tirades that reached as far into the past as possible: "Well you are a bad teacher, too. You are the worst Chinese teacher I have ever come across, and I'll tell you why...." During the pause I would try to think of why. Then: "It's because you don't care. Yes, that's true! You don't care! You send me to the Dong Shi to get cow stomach and sheep's lung, and you don't even care that the people don't know what the hell I'm talking about. Why? Because you just don't care. Well, let me tell you something—I will figure it out. I don't need you to teach me how to say *duck head*. I don't need you to teach me how to say *squid*, and I don't need you to teach me how to say *niu pai*—I mean *steak*, right?" By this time my argument had lost forward momentum and began veering to the left and right, pursuing less highly charged topics like the hair in the bathtub and the lack of consistent dinnertime ritual.

Zhong-hua was leaning back, enjoying himself. He held up his index finger importantly. "Have no dinner, you say why no food? Have dinner, you say why nobody eat with me? Somebody eat with you, you say why nobody talking? Woman is you."

"What are you talking about?"

"What is woman? *You* is woman!"

Months after I had ceased grumbling about not having a wedding ring, Zhong-hua came home with a small white box and presented it to me. It was a ring—a gigantic, gaudy, diamond-studded globe. I didn't know quite how to handle the situation. There was nothing in his face to indicate that he was making a joke, and I certainly didn't want to hurt his feelings. After all, it was sweet of him to remember that I wanted a ring and had been without one since the vacuuming incident.

I decided to pretend to like it and wear it. By the third day, it had lost a few of its diamonds from knocking about on my hammer-holding hand. But there were still about a hundred on there. I thought maybe if he'd gotten it at Wal-Mart, we could go there and return it for a small, inconspicuous one. When I tactfully mentioned this, he said no, he had gotten it at a garage sale. Well! Should I be insulted? Knowing how my husband revered garage sales, I thought not. But the ring was so not me that I opted to display it respectfully on my treasure shelf. This worked well for a while as I was realizing more and more that I didn't care at all for rings.

The diamond golf ball glittered lopsidedly there until the first opportunity I had to use it as a weapon. I had hurt feelings over some stupid thing I have no memory of now, so I took the ring, put it back in the box, and stuffed it into Zhong-hua's sock drawer. I didn't really think about it after that. A few weeks later we were driving somewhere with Zhong-hua at the wheel when I noticed with a start that *he* was wearing the ring. I said nothing. He continued to wear the ring, this huge, cheap, lady's ring. He would probably still be wearing it, except that he left it on the sink one day and I snatched it up and hid it. I've forgotten where.

The Keys to the Kingdom

"GOODER is not a word. We say *better*: good, better, best."

"*Better*? Oh, right. Better. Better. What you mean *best*?"

After four years, this word remained alien to my husband. It bounced right off his brain. Paroda was sitting at the kitchen table with Zhong-hua. She had an expository writing course her senior year of college and was interviewing Zhong-hua about the Cultural Revolution. The project included Zhong-hua's giving an oral presentation to the class. He told her about having to carry Mao's Little Red Book under his arm and memorize it. Throughout grade school and middle school, Zhong-hua and his classmates had no textbooks, just Mao's book. Mao said things like, "Firstly, do not fear hardship, and, secondly, do not fear death," and "To die for the people is weightier than Mount Tai, but to work for the fascists and die for the exploiters and oppressors is lighter than a feather."

Three times a day every Chinese citizen except babies had to read passages from Mao's book. Even feeble, bedridden elders would be propped up and the pages turned for them by others. These memorized sayings could be regurgitated as bus fare, train fare, currency at the melon stand, and protection against spittle in the face, brutal beating, or even death. Zhong-hua held his hands behind his back and stood very straight to demonstrate for Paroda how to address a shopkeeper: "*Chairman Mao says if we have short-comings, we are not afraid to have them pointed out because we serve the people. I want one half jin of peppers.*" He laughed and shook his head, ending with an abrupt one-word punctuation: "Terrible."

Zhong-hua told Paroda about shivering through sleepless nights in the countryside. He and other youths had been sent to labor in an area plagued with earthquakes. At night they had to lie on the ground under stick shelters. Zhong-hua had taught the others how to sew their blanket between layers of plastic bags to lessen the ground chill. It was important to cover your face completely from the icy air, but some boys were claustrophobic and could not sleep. Zhong-hua said he was one of the lucky ones. Other girls and boys from the cities had been sent to distant western provinces to herd sheep on horseback through vast uninhabited territory. The bodies of those who suffered injury or illness were often not found until six months or a year later.

After Mao died, Deng Xiaoping sorted out the legacy of Mao-ist thought into piles of horrible mistakes and useful wisdom, condemning the former and upholding the latter. Juxtaposing these polar opposites as fraternal twins was a profoundly Chinese solution to the problem of evil. Zhong-hua remained in awe of Mao for his accomplishment in having forced a vast feudal nation across a bridge of human sacrifice into the modern industrial age. Mao believed that the old traditions condemned China to impoverishment and exploitation by the Western world. Promising prosperity and power, he broke the chain of four thousand years of tradition and pried open the people's minds with the relentless chant of change. Shins and shoulder blades and heaps of ancient bricks piled up at the center of a whirling storm of progress.

I had just gotten to sleep after staying up too late helping Sweet Sweet write yet another essay on *The Great Gatsby* and the American Dream. Zhong-hua came to bed noisily around 2:00 AM and lay on his back with his eyes wide open. After a few seconds, he elbowed me: "Po-li-ti-cal fash-en. How to say?"

"Dammit, Zhong-hua, do we have to do this now? Political faction. Political faction. Can this wait until tomorrow?"

"This very, very important thing for Paroda." He had me there. He would never for his own sake be inspired to stay up half the night in order to enunciate "terrible things."

"OK. Well, political faction is *zhenzhide*, right? That's political. And *zhendou* is faction, a split-off group."

"Oh, not *zhendou*. This word is *douzhen*. *Douzhen*. This mean like fighting ideas. But what you mean *group*?"

"Zhong-hua! How can you not remember *group* or *better* or *exit*, *pot*, *pan*, *cup*, or the name of any American person other than Michael, but you can say 'The antifreeze is probably leaking from the head gasket'?"

"No idea."

He stayed up until three for a whole week with the dictionary. Paroda had always been Zhong-hua's cultural navigator, and he took every opportunity to repay her with life wisdom. Currently, she had a boyfriend problem. It seemed she wanted to spend more time together than he did. Zhong-hua took a study break to elucidate her love life through the analogy of closing a deal on a used car. The short version and essence of this lengthy monologue was: "You need give the salesman more space, Paroda. Take more time. Tell salesman your point of view, talk. Then you need back up, let him think about. Then, salesman will know, for this person most important thing not buy car. Most important thing is respect this person's own mind. He have separate mind, not your mind. Then he will lower the price. Sooo, you can buy car very cheaper." Paroda groaned and covered her ears with her hands. "Mom, make him stop talking about the used-car salesman. I'm so confused I don't know if I'm the buyer or seller." There was no subject Zhong-hua could not analyze in terms related to either the Tai Chi principles of yin and yang, used cars, or all three at once.

When the day for the class presentation arrived, Zhong-hua put on a suit and picked up Paroda at her apartment. Later Paroda called almost crying. "Mom, they wouldn't let him talk. He had so much to say, and the professor stopped him after eight minutes. It was not fair, Mom. Everybody else got twenty minutes. He has so much to teach, and now he can't."

"Don't worry about it. You prepared a good lesson—you and Zhong-hua. If you have something to offer, sooner or later, the world will come and get you—hey, even if you'd rather not go."

Wise words sometimes spoke themselves—probably because I'd heard them somewhere else—and were untainted by association with my army of "terrible things," which could in no way be compared to the Red Army, starvation, firing squads, or anything overtly threatening. My army specialized in negative thinking, a cadre of old soldiers on donkeys who slogged around conjuring a dim outlook from the details of our life: the teapots on the shelves pointing their snouts in the air; my sculptures standing around in unappreciated nakedness; Zhong-hua's unlucrative classes. He still had a few Tai Chi students: Brian, a drummer for a locally famous rock band, and Lenny, a retired Russian anesthesiologist with serious asthma. Zhong-hua called them both "Blenny." Small John, also known as "Have Stomach John," was an office clerk who always pleaded broke but required one-on-one instruction because he was Tai Chi—challenged. For a while, we had a "Big John," a nurse who ultimately found it more relaxing to ride his Honda motorcycle than to learn Tai Chi. Then Russian Blenny quit.

Zhong-hua had another Tai Chi student thirty miles to the east, a seventy-six-year-old man recovering from cancer. Zhong-hua called him "Over-the-Mountain-Old-Man." After the cost of gas and the fees for renting space for the class, this faithful student and the remaining Blenny cost us money. Zhong-hua said, "Over-the-Mountain-Old-Man seems very lonely," and "Blenny very lovely learn Chen-style Tai Chi."

Zhong-hua did not like my worrying. He said, "Do something, need get paid. Who pay you do this worry job? Nobody pay!"

On the ground floor of my office building was a fancy restaurant not frequented by case managers. The fashionably dressed restaurant clientele smoked on the stone steps with the homeless and disabled people served by our agency and left their wraps on the coat rack at the bottom of the stairs. Some of the street people sported very handsome hats.

There was also an elegant meeting room with a chandelier across from a large office in which a handsome middle-aged man sat at a desk, often eating a fragrant lunch delivered by the waiter. Every few days the man could be seen with a bottle of Windex and a towel polishing the massive conference table, where he met portly men whose dignified dewlaps slid about the mirrored tabletop as they nodded and frowned. In order to exit our agency or the restaurant, one had to pass between the chandeliered room and the office. The man left his door wide open and made friendly small talk to everyone who walked by, no matter how sleek or shabby.

One day as I hurried down the stairs from the fourth floor, I bumped right into the handsome man and blurted out, "Who *are* you?" He told me he was Tom Triscari, professor of business at Rennselaer Polytechnic Institute's Lally School of Management. "Business!" I said, quickly blocking his path. "My husband is a businessman from China." I pulled out one of the business cards a friend had created for us the day before Zhong-hua headed for the Javits Center:

Zhong-hua Lu
CULTURAL NAVIGATION
Chinese Culture and Business Consultant
English / Mandarin

The man beamed. "You just made my day. Can you believe I have been waiting for someone exactly like your husband? I want to design a new course for teaching MBA students about Chinese business culture, and I need an expert's help." I called Zhong-hua and asked him if he could come to Troy. Without asking why, he said, "Yes!" and appeared in less than the twenty-minute drive. Professor Tom talked slowly and precisely to explain what he had in mind. Zhong-hua leaned forward and nodded: "I exactly understand." This meeting seemed destined, even though I had kind of pushed it with the fake, yet potentially real, business cards.

Together they conjured an elaborate ruse designed to teach the students that they didn't comprehend Chinese culture and didn't know the first thing about doing business with the Chinese. Zhong-hua would pose as the CEO of a Chinese meat-grinder company called Changshi—a real meat-grinder factory in Shandong Province owned by Zhong-hua's friend. The student-run company, E-Z Grind, had to negotiate the outsourcing of its innovative nonstick grinder to the Chinese. The professor would recruit some Chinese graduate fellows to pose as Changshi executives. While the men talked inside, the mounted policeman outside leaned down from his draft horse and tucked a ticket under Zhong-hua's windshield wiper. He had parked in the building's loading zone, thinking himself lucky to find such a welcoming space close to the meeting.

The black business shoes waited pertly by our kitchen door, newly shined and ready to attend the meat-grinder meetings. Zhong-hua met with Professor Tom and the Chinese company's team a few times a week to map out the details so that the MBA students would not be tipped off that the situation was simulated. They could view the company and the products on the Changshi Web site but, not being able to read Chinese, didn't discover that Lu Zhong-hua was not employed by this company. The first meeting was scheduled for five, when my workday ended. I left fifteen minutes early and passed the meeting room on my way out of the building. The Chinese team was already sitting at the long table in straight-backed chairs, obviously waiting for Mr. Lu. I drove home and spotted the other car in the car shed. I burst in the kitchen door and there was Zhong-hua eating chicken gizzards with wilted spinach. I cried, "Zhong-hua, aren't you supposed to be at the meeting?"

"What time is it?"

"Five o'clock."

"Oh, I need quickly go!"

A few hours later, I heard the sound of his tires on the gravel and looked out the kitchen window to see my husband sauntering toward the house with a cigarette in his right hand and two dead pigeons dangling upside down in his left.

"Give me boil some water."

"Zhong-hua, what the hell?"

"This meat very delicious. In my childhood times, catch this one make me very happy."

"How did you get those birds?"

"Second Street. Just use hands, twist neck. Very easy."

"OK, but I really don't think you should twist pigeon necks in front of Triscari's office anymore."

Zhong-hua laid the birds on the counter and ran cold water into a pot. With one sharp nod, he agreed heartily. "You right."

Triscari was interested in pushing his students. Some of them had a blasé inability to locate Japan, Korea, Thailand, or Cambodia on a map or to operate out of their comfort zone when it came to interacting with people from other cultures. The class he and Zhong-hua designed forced them to do just this. Triscari's candor and effusiveness were not normal, and I'm pretty sure in China he would be considered of unsound mind for those qualities alone. The other faculty members didn't care for him because he made them seem lazy and uninspired by comparison. Zhong-hua thought he was a global visionary, and I thought he was visionary because he saw in my husband the extraordinariness that he made no special effort to reveal.

I imagined Triscari as some kind of a master pickpocket, a spiffy, modern-day Robin Hood redistributing the wealth of our economically depressed town. In my projection, he knew just how the world worked, and that could rub off on us. Silly for me to be looking for a savior under a chandelier after I spent all day teaching my clients to be their own heroes. But at the very least, the elegant, perfectly ordered office, with its paperweights, custom draperies, leather chairs, and framed romantic landscapes, had an air of purpose, and the polished desk shone as a comforting, if illusory, counterbalance to chaos. It was not illusion when I asked Triscari to take the small son of a destitute mother with cancer to a local ball game, and he said, "Of course I will."

When Professor Tom asked Zhong-hua to evaluate the performance of the E-Z Grind students, Zhong-hua told them they had done a very good job but later admitted to me that they had done a very bad job. They leaned too far forward and pressured the Changshi meat-grinder team too aggressively. They talked too loud and too fast. They didn't listen. They sat directly across from the Changshi team leader, which was taboo. Zhong-hua explained his opinions, and I translated them into a compilation we called "Thoughts on the Art of Negotiation." He said things like: "At some point in every negotiation, you will find things are not as you wish them. You need to take a step back from your own interests. If you take more than your share, then nobody will want to do business with you." He emphasized the need to include "vivid" discussions of how to endure prolonged periods of misfortune and loss.

Both Tom and Zhong-hua played this game with great heart and humanity. Maybe this was the point—that business has to have a human heart. Zhong-hua was worried that Triscari wasn't safe because he wore his heart on his sleeve, and conniving people hurt his feelings. There he sat in the open, like a sitting duck, incandescently sincere and exceptional.

Shortly after Zhong-hua came to America, while reflecting on how to do business here, he had said, "I think maybe I need to get a gun." I told him that was really not necessary, but I understood why he was jumpy: Back in China, companies had what he called "knife men." These were hired thugs who hung around outside the buildings where important negotiations were under way. Their job was to make sure the end result was advantageous to their employer. If not, the knife men prevented the visiting negotiators from leaving. Zhong-hua often had to contact his boss and strongly suggest that he cave in to the demands being made. He said he felt in constant danger.

Professor Triscari had to argue with the university to get a modest onetime consultant's fee for Zhong-hua's collaboration in the meat-grinder enterprise, but that only covered about a week of work that spanned a month. The professor had high hopes that the administration would jump at the opportunity to have more mock negotiation classes once they had a chance to see how exciting and effective this one had been. He said they would have to be blind not to realize what a rare resource my husband could be for the school. To this end, we asked Da Jie to videotape the negotiation class.

She showed up in a sweat suit and, after setting up the camera in one corner, spent the rest of the time in animated zigzagging of the room, as if looking for a hidden panel in the wall. Then she inserted herself into the discussions: "Oh, you talk about China? Ask me, I know. I was Red Guard. This is true—I had red armband." The negotiators of both teams, dressed in formal attire and seated at the long table, looked confused. Who was this shrill person? Zhong-hua, being the younger brother, could only suggest behind his hand that his sister stay in the shadows with the camera, perhaps behind that big plant. She brushed him off. "Really? I don't think need. Other people all talking, why not me talk? I am real Chinese person. They need to ask me!" Later we tried to edit her out of the video, but she was everywhere.

Soon after that, a delegation of nineteen engineers from the Three Gorges Company, the biggest hydroelectric power corporation in China, came to study environmental technology at the university. I remembered, when we were in China, gazing up at the painted line on the sheer cliff high above the Yangtze River. The line marked where the new water level would be once the dam was completed. Many farms, villages, and ancient works of art have since disappeared underwater, and submerged factories, garbage dumps, and mines contributed to the toxic soup behind the dam.

Professor Tom paid Zhong-hua out of his own pocket to prepare landscapes of China and large banners of welcoming calligraphy for the classroom. They met the delegation at the airport in the middle of the night, and Zhong-hua helped serve them catered food from the Chinese restaurant on the corner. They asked if there was any decent Chinese food to be had in America and wondered aloud how Americans could eat the most disgusting and dirty animal—chicken. Zhong-hua said he was glad Professor Tom could not understand Mandarin. Tom gave, as always, his whole heart to teaching these people. My husband was very quiet about the Three Gorges delegation, saying only that these elite, top-level engineers had too much power. "Seems very nice, but not. We are just ordinary, so we don't need to spend time with very special people. For us not useful."

When I next saw Professor Tom, his eyes were puffy and his handsomeness obliterated by the bloated misery of spring allergies. His face looked gray and his head a little bald on top—not like his dashing image in my mind. My savior projection was coming home, and the feeling was not unlike finding something I had been sure someone else had taken—finding it right where I had forgotten it. Now maybe I could be Tom's friend. "Cheer up, things will get better," I offered. He said he'd been meaning to call my husband but was feeling out of sorts due to some nasty political infighting at the university that he wanted nothing to do with.

"Tell your husband I'm thinking about him. I still very much want to work with him, but I can't get the university to support me in these cultural education projects. They just don't get it." He had stood up, and his face was floating disembodied at the top of the starched shirt and tie. "Students can't just sit in a classroom reading a case study and expect that they will know how to do business with the Chinese. They have to live this. They have to live it! That's the only way for them to learn that the Chinese have a different culture and they need to adjust themselves. I still want to work with your husband."

"I'll tell him," I said. Zhong-hua was a worthy match for the professor's passionate and kind intelligence, but Zhong-hua was—by choice or circumstance—unsuited, untitled, and autonomous, with his own unapparent destiny.

In the midst of Zhong-hua's brief career as president of Chang-shi Meat Grinder Company, we had to travel to Boston for a biopsy of his ampulla of Vater. Driving to Boston this time was different. We followed the friendly red taillights of trucks through a snow-flurried fog and listened to Elvis Presley. I looked up at the truck drivers' faces. Some of them grinned to themselves, and others just jowl-jiggled comfortably along. While Elvis sang "I'm all shook up," I wondered aloud why great rock stars die young, and Zhong-hua said because this kind of life is very uneven, very hard, very hot.

Zhong-hua slept in the backseat, and I drove. A north wind blew and buffeted the car at a right angle to our direction. I looked straight ahead and tightened both hands on the steering wheel as we sped into the expanding company of stars. That was one way not to connect everything to everything else, to keep a single thought from exploding into instantaneous connect-the-dot lightning. I wanted to admit I had no idea about anything at all and be done with fixing. I thought of the time at work when I had driven to the art museum with Arthur. He raised the subject of the Catholic Church. "They're always talking about how you have to shine a light in the dark. No, you don't! Why can't they get that? No, you don't. Just leave it alone, and it will work itself out. You don't have to shine a light in dark places, all right? Jeez!" I would try to have Arthur's kind of faith.

Zhong-hua's procedure took most of the day; the doctor said he would call us with the results of the pathology report. We went from the hospital to Chinatown, just as always. Halfway home we switched drivers, and I lay in the backseat under a blanket thinking about Arthur's words and chewing on fried squid and a duck head from a carton. I just couldn't understand how a person could sit back and go with the flow and also wrestle the octopus of everyday business. This question made me feel dim-witted, as if I were prying at a knot I myself had tied but could not untie no matter how long I studied it. There were layers and layers of emotion. The petty ones floated on top, like the dirty spume from boiling pork toes that had best be skimmed off. Those were emotions such as resentment, self-righteousness, and indignation. It's hard when you live with a chronically ill person not to think he or she is faking it sometimes. You want to shout, "Get up! Bustle around importantly like me!" At the deeper layers, gratitude and love lay aching like strained muscle on resolute bone. I knew my husband was not well, might never be well.

Suddenly, he said, "I don't want to think every day 'I is sick, I is sick,' because I know this no good for family. I know I is sick, but I need try to do my best. One person not happy, whole family not happy. My happy is one-third of family happy."

Interstate 90 was a long, humming ribbon, mostly out of range of the Elvis station, where we said things we never said at home. "Zhong-hua," I asked from the backseat, "do you like me?"

"Like! Why you need talk about terrible things?"

"What if you hadn't liked me?"

"I never think about."

"Hey, want me to tell you all about when I was little? Ask me something."

"I never want to ask this kind of stupid question."

"Don't you wish I had great big breasts?"

"Go to Price Chopper get some meat is OK. Put there on chest. When all done use, just eat."

That night in bed Zhong-hua held me in his headlock embrace, wrapping the blanket over our heads as if protecting from fallout. I brought up the big-breast topic again. "What kind of meat?"

"Pork, beef, chicken chest—any kind is OK. Use two balloons is cheap way. When done, just take one nail and pop balloon."

"But you can't eat balloons."

"Yeah. But not too expensive. Can buy a lot."

He kissed me.

The Year of the Dog

I T WAS THE YEAR OF THE DOG. According to the Chinese lunisolar calendar, the Chinese New Year began on January 29 and spring on February 4, making 2006 a double-spring year, to follow the previous and unlucky "blind" year without a spring. Zhong-hua had been born in the Year of the Dog in 1958, and Chinese astrologers cautioned that for "dogs," 2006 could be either an especially dangerous or an especially auspicious year. A good outcome required proceeding with care and caution. They noted that dog people are natural leaders but often make bad decisions. Warnings included watching out for falling debris and natural disasters, especially in areas whose names contained *center* and *middle*. My husband was himself one of these danger zones, bearing a name meaning "Middle Kingdom."

Zhong-hua said this was silly and nobody smart believed in it. But then, after holding his chin and pushing out his lips pressed tightly together, as Da Jie did when considering *haochu* and *huai-chu*—that is, good points and bad points—he said probably it was a smart idea anyway for dog people to wear red underwear for luck and protection. He then told me he had already found one pair in my drawer but was finding them a bit uncomfortable.

The art center education director asked my husband to teach a three-hour workshop in Chinese brush painting. She knew it would be popular, because they had turned many people away from the overfilled class he had taught for free as part of his grant. Now she proposed charging eighty-five dollars per student for the three-hour intensive, signing up twenty students, and paying Zhong-hua twenty dollars an hour. Surely this woman could do math. Reading her e-mail, I began to rant loudly until Zhong-hua came in and laughed at my profanities. I typed what I knew Zhong-hua wanted me to say: "Thank you very much. You are nice person. I know my English is not good. I am sorry about this. I will try my best to teach this class."

There was also a message on the answering machine from the secretary of the church where Zhong-hua taught his Wednesday night class: "Mr. Lu, we just had our board meeting and realized you haven't paid us for two years. Please return the key to the door with your back payment."

I turned to him. "Zhong-hua, you haven't paid them any money?" I felt suddenly nauseated. "When you started the class back up, you never paid the fee?"

"Make ten dollars, spend ten dollars buy gas. No money pay church. I just think, what time I get—that time I pay."

"It doesn't work that way here. You have to pay anyway."

"Yes, I told the church lady I want to pay. She told me go figure out how much. Very difficult figure out, because first few months have no students. So many times I too sick, cannot teach. Also, sometimes I just have one 'Over-the-Mountain-Old-Man,' cannot send him home. Because I remember, in my sick times, he worried. He call my home, say, 'Hello.' I very appreciate. So I just think, let him stay—teach him. Other times just have one fireman. He very excited learn Chen-style Tai Chi. If I send fireman home, feel very sorry because fireman try hard. Church lady not like Chen style. She say, 'God lives in here. This is God's house—you cannot make grunting noises in here.' You know, Chen-style Tai Chi need make this kind of noise; get old qi out of body. I tell her, 'Church just want to help people. I teach Tai Chi, just want help people, too. We is doing same work. When I say this, I make her look not happy."

I had made a big mistake leaving Zhong-hua without my help to communicate and interpret protocol. After his surgery, it turned out he had signed "one piece of paper" months before he was well enough to actually resume teaching class. That was a new contract.

I wrote a letter to the church explaining the situation and asking if we could make monthly payments until the debt was paid. Zhong-hua told me to tell them he would clean the bathrooms and mop the floor. He said anyone in the church could come to class for free. He did not want to close this class. When Wednesday came around, he went to the church as usual. A man intercepted him at the end of the class and demanded the key. He said he represented the board of directors. The man said he did not need any money, just please give back the key. Zhong-hua fumbled for it, but it had migrated through a hole in his pocket into the lining of his jacket. When he came home that night, his glasses were smashed and one eyelid was bleeding. Upset and searching for the light switch in the church corridor, he had bumped into the wall corner. He said, "This maybe mean church people want me go away."

"Zhong-hua, you have to give them the key."

"Yes, this probably true." I wished I could push this white church into a hole and bury it, but Zhong-hua seemed incapable of accepting the finality of a bad situation. His years as chief negotiator at the steel company had made him always ready to roll up his sleeves and work at friendly relations across the table. He seemed as baffled at the church's unwillingness to do this as he had often been by the rigid faces of certain barter-impaired homeowners selling tools from their garages—but much more deeply perturbed. He took a handful of pills containing a Chinese herbal preparation and went to sleep.

Sometimes his skin felt like silk beneath my fingertips. Our bodies fit together like persuadable tools—finger hammer tapping a knobby knee, a curved palm sanding block traveling an already

217

smooth thigh, an adjustable thumb and forefinger wrench around a pulsing wrist—tools with no intent but to try themselves tenderly on surfaces of the other. At other times his skin felt like hot, sticky flypaper. Since his surgery, he frequently had chills and night sweats. All I could do was touch and recoil. My beloved lay like an old stump that snorted and blew wind through its knotholes. I fantasized about giving it a shove right off the bed into a creek. I tried gently shaking him, rolling him side to side like a sea lion, and even holding my hand over his mouth. Nothing worked. His snoring was like the sound of an electric blender full of walnuts; it was the sound of someone eating his own nose from the inside out. I tried massaging his breastbone in small circles, but this delayed the uproar only a few seconds.

Sometimes the exhale was a blessedly soft *puff, puff, puff*. I could float my mind almost restfully on the brief exhales, like sliding weightlessly through powdery snow. But then he would stop breathing altogether. At those moments I leaned over him in alarm, holding my breath, too, then calling sharply "Zhong-hua! Zhong-hua!" He gasped for air without waking. His stomach and small intestine rumbled and gurgled. Gas putted out the handcrafted rectum. Quieter rivulets tinkled through our copper pipes and cast-iron radiators as faintly soothing background noise. I vowed to set up a pup tent in the pasture; I longed for stillness broken only by owls calling and wind in the trees. But the silky-thighed god always returned to me, resurrected out of flypaper nights, breathing softly through his nose and pulling me close.

A friend told us about a spa where they might need a Tai Chi teacher. We checked, and they did. For a reference, the spa's director called the church lady, who told her Zhong-hua hadn't paid his fee for a long time. The church lady didn't mention that he had been ill for a year while she had him on her books or that we had offered to pay for the missed months. The spa lady didn't want to listen to explanations, and why should she? Business was business. But American business wasn't Chinese business. In China it was

OK to say, "I'll pay you when he pays me, after the other guy pays him, which will be when the other guy gets paid." Even I was incredulous that such an honor system actually worked.

In China favors are always repaid, except by the immoral, even if it takes years. This kind of elastic time frame and strategic trust is part of *guanxi*, a complex tradition of building social effectiveness through long-term loyalty and integrity. The concept cannot be translated to one word in English, and it was painful to see that its practice could not be translated to my husband's life in America.

We had created this bad situation ourselves, but I still felt punched in the stomach. It pained me greatly that I had neglected to act as intermediary between the world and my husband, with the result that complete strangers thought badly of him. I knew if I had stayed in charge, this would not have happened, and I knew I couldn't have stayed in charge. Not only did my job take me away from home, but I still hadn't forgotten the time Zhong-hua accused me of wanting "to fix him like a teapot." I had tried to step back, let him handle things himself, not wanting us to become a three-legged act. The spa lady e-mailed: "I am certainly not going to open my doors, give out a key or a code to my building to a complete stranger with a bad reputation. As far as I am concerned, we are *not* doing business, your husband is *not* allowed on or near my property."

I answered politely and felt very sorry. Later, I heard Zhong-hua on the phone telling "over-the-mountain-old-man" apologetically that he needed to take a break for a few weeks and would call him when the class started again. The internal stress of this situation Zhong-hua could not take in stride because he felt he had done wrong.

I felt bad that Zhong-hua spent every day alone on the old farm. I also envied him because home is where I wanted to be. He disappeared into the forest to gather firewood on the garden tractor. He filled in potholes in the driveway with gravel and unclogged the pipe from the spring that fed the pond. He sat on the plastic milk crate. After teaching a one-hour Tai Chi class to Blenny on Saturday, he needed to rest for the remainder of the day and all of Sunday. I didn't understand this. Dr. Mayer had said the surgery would cure him. That was a year and a half ago.

Zhong-hua kept house according to his own rationale. A de-ordering principle flourished in his wake. The result was not chaos but an alternate universe. I peered into closets and cupboards I had once been mistress of and saw that everywhere he had redefined the contents, disturbing the labels in my mind and replacing them with families of things having nothing in common: neatly baled dishrags tied up with string and compacted into the bread box with three flashlights, a set of socket wrenches, and a bag of ginseng root.

The Chinese astrologers proved right about bad decisions and falling debris. Zhong-hua called me at work to tell me that a piece of firewood had fallen from the top of the pile onto his head. He said, "Not too much blood. Maybe OK." I knew that if he had picked up the phone to call me, it was probably not OK. He needed twenty-five stitches. The falling wood was a shock, a chunky clap of thunder to the head. It started to occur to me that my husband was not altogether unlike my father, who had once run over his own foot with the lawn mower, another time cut off the end of his finger with a band saw, and—not once but three times—backed out of the garage without remembering to open the door.

The spa debacle compounded Zhong-hua's mortification about the church and left him withdrawn and quiet. With no way to resolve things, we both suffered internally the heartache of erasure. I sat down in front of the television with him and watched an uneven boxing match. The shorter guy was backed up against the ropes with his hands covering his face. The other guy had no discernible method but was nevertheless pummeling him. Zhong-hua was eating a huge bowl of butter pecan ice cream mixed with chopped tomatoes. He was in the habit of rounding up all the food that was about to "get broken," dumping it together, and eating it up so that nothing went to waste. He often made soup of hot water poured over stale heels of bread or boiled milk over rock-hard bean cakes. They were into the third round, and the pummeler wasn't letting up. The ref stopped the fight.

Zhong-hua said this short guy was like him, "always fail." He said it with a kind of matter-of-fact embarrassment, between spoonfuls of tomato ice cream. I had never heard him use this term before, never heard him utter a single word of defeat. How could the world not want this person? How could he be judged by ordinary standards, a person who, shuffling about in faded pajamas having barely eluded death, dipped a brush made of wolf and wild boar hairs in black ink and, by touching it to rice paper, created mountains shrouded in mist, cascading waterfalls, and a teahouse perched on the cliff above where monks conversed? I found myself leaning close to listen to the whispering of the sages while the rice paper fluttered with birds and blossomed with red and yellow.

When you have no idea what to do, it is best to do nothing with a kind of blank reverence. The trick is to do nothing without becoming edgy. Our dear neighbors, Dave and Flippy, for example, did nothing very well. They watched the leaves grow and listened to tree trunks creak. They fed the chickadees. Every night they built a campfire in their yard and watched that. "There's always something interesting to see," said Dave, "like bear droppings." But they were retired. I did nothing the way a praying mantis does nothing. Mine was feigned reverence with a grasping reflex.

On Friday someone at work gave me a three-month supply of unwanted nicotine patches. I brought them home, thinking I'd give them to a friend. I didn't think to offer them to Zhong-hua since he had once mentioned that in China men who don't smoke are looked upon suspiciously, as if they were not real men. Zhong-hua stayed up half the night reassembling the lawn mower.

Saturday morning, without eating breakfast, Zhong-hua began scraping and painting the house. I looked around inside at the gray pall that had settled over everything during Zhong-hua's illness untouched by the dazzling April sunlight outside. I scrubbed the walls and the ceilings, wiped away spiderwebs from high corners, and vacuumed dead flies from the windowsills. I laid the braided rug my mother had made of old clothes in the bathtub and climbed in to slosh the suds with my bare feet. The foot sloshing unbraided the mother rug, and I hung the woolen remnants on the porch rail. I climbed on the toilet and wiped the ceiling with Clorox. I couldn't stop washing, even after I was exhausted. Darkness steeped in the din of tree frogs. I pulled the stove from the wall and stared down at the mammalian dirt that had birthed a half-dozen ballpoint pens, some hair clips, and a toothbrush. Zhong-hua was outside on the ladder with a bucket of yellow paint, making a graceful comeback against a sapphire sky as owls called and bats veered away from his head. He was wearing a nicotine patch on his arm.

That weekend I went along to help Zhong-hua teach the Chinese brush-painting class at the art center, which had filled up to capacity again. Six months earlier, when he had taught the first class, students had complained that they couldn't understand his English. This time my job was to demystify any statements he made to students and elaborate on the answers he gave to their questions, such as, "Mr. Lu, what exactly are those green circles all over the rocks?"

"Yeah, this is green stuff."

"Mr. Lu, I am having such a hard time. I cannot make a nice-looking tree."

"Yeah, this is because you paint no good. You not understand how to paint tree. Need go home plastic a lot."

"Practice," I corrected.

I soon abandoned all efforts to ameliorate his blunt style. The students' faces registered only momentary blankness; they quickly recovered to carry on zealously with ink and brush, much less inclined to distract themselves with inquiry. The class was a onetime gig, so we continued with the job search. He answered ads for metalworkers, cashiers, janitors, and cooks.

Someone at work heard about an opening for an overnight counselor at the drug rehabilitation residence and said Zhong-hua should try for it. The interviewer asked what he would do if someone was determined at 3:00 AM to go out to buy drugs. Zhong-hua said he would talk to them, "let them do another thing." The word *let* in Chinese is *rang* and is energetically coercive, more like twisting someone's arm behind their back. He thought maybe this was the wrong answer.

For both my husband's and my own sake, I preferred to depend on inner resources rather than social finesse. I believed that if a person gave his or her best thing, then the world would at least let the person subsist, if not flourish. I didn't allow myself to dwell on what would happen if the best thing was also the worst thing. Triscari's office was dark, so I went ahead and cut up the scrolls of brush paintings so that Zhong-hua could sell them at the street festival. This was the best I could do to set him up in international business. He sold one for a reduced price and gave one away.

Still trying to recycle the past and avoid having to rebirth ourselves, I told my husband he could tell me the stories of his schoolteacher days and we could write a book. First he gave the traditional "Good idea!" answer and then shook his head: "No good."

"Why not?"

"In my teenage times, I was very crazy person. Very strong. Very fire. One time I really want to write down book. After Mao dead, village officials tell me, 'You can go home. Schoolteacher job end.' I walk back forty miles to my home city. My neighbor, one old man, talk to me I must be write down the stories of my people, my country, he say, because I have special experience and have tell-story gift that is sometime, somewhere very shining, very bright. I want to! For three years, I never see movie, talk to any girl, go to dancing or to drinking with friends. Three years, I every night hurry home from factory job, write down, write down, write down. Sleep just a little, then go back to factory. As soon as I finish fifty pages, I show my neighbor. He say, 'Good! Keep going!' Three years, I all day think about, all night write down. Then, suddenly, neighbor seems not happy. He say, 'This part you write down too well. This stuff you write down very dangerous for you. You need put in garbage. Yes, this is garbage. One day you will get a lot of trouble. Family get a lot of trouble. You need stop right now.'

"One whole week I think about, then decide. I agree with old man. I throw book in fire and all burn. All garbage. Forget. This work done. Never think about again."

The next day Zhong-hua announced, "I want to write down one book."

"What book?"

"Title of book, *Men Have Men*."

"What does this mean, *Men Have Men*?"

"You cannot understand this. Translation not too easy. Women, you know, have babies. Men cannot have babies. Men have men."

"OK."

"Yeah, just this way."

"All men do this?"

"No. You know, sometimes a very good man, a very nice man, does very terrible things. Because he wants to lift himself up higher, protect himself, or protect his family."

"Then?"

"Make her heart dead."

"Not you."

"No, I am not this kind of person."

"Just some men have men?"

"Yes. This title just talk about for man keep heart whole very hard. Talk about man inside fighting with himself. He decide do something help himself, but help himself will make another person get very, very bad situation. Long, long time, China government make many people do this way. Chairman Mao want everyone fighting with each other, fighting with self. He make political games and tell people they must follow his rules. Then change rules. All throw away. He do this again, again, again, until people's minds change. Not just minds change—people's deep heart change. Then they know, every idea can come apart. Every good thing happening have other side, have someone get hurt. Every bad situation you can make better. Nothing is just one way. Chairman Mao let them know, world change, you need change, too."

"This is your book, *Men Have Men*? You mean it is about how a man can keep his heart whole no matter what happens around him?"

"No, no, no. I just make title for fun. This is joke. Yeah, this is like nothing."

I took a day off, and Zhong-hua and I drove over the mountain to return the church key, since the board of directors did not wish to discuss payment schedules or floor mopping. At the mountain pass, the high point where one half of the world rolls away to Boston and the other cascades toward home, I pulled over so that Zhong-hua could find a privacy bush. He said, "Behind part very pain." I said I would make another doctor appointment for him. We stopped at Bennington College on the way home to pick up another financial-aid form for my next semester. I didn't mention the student loan to my husband because I had no idea how I was going to repay it. Back at home, Zhong-hua asked me where he should plant the red flower tree.

"What red flower tree?"

"In back of car. A tree from your college."

"You bought a tree at the college?" Somehow I knew instantly that was not it. "You dug a tree up at the college, didn't you?"

"No need dig. Just pulla is OK." He was already digging a hole near the shed. "Have small red flowers."

"How do you know that? It's still winter, and this tree looks dead."

"No problem. I know this kind of tree. You need every day water, then this tree will. Get other shovel; this one no good."

"Zhong-hua, in China, do red flowers mean happiness?"

"Not mean. Just red color Chinese people like."

"Does red stand for good luck?"

"No luck."

"Red is . . ."

"Means good! Everything fine!" Zhong-hua tipped his chin as exclamation to each word reverberating from the alert center of his body. He clapped his hands. "That's all!"

Whispering Sages

GRADUALLY, my husband seemed less of an apparition and more of a solid being. Still, we were not sure he was well. We had to wait for the next test and the next. These were forays into his hepatic and pancreatic ducts with tiny instruments, like street cleaners equipped with infinitesimal gutter brushes. Whatever stuck to the bristles went under the microscope. "Mr. Lu, you are fine," they said.

Zhong-hua didn't feel fine. They said he could return to work, but he had no work to return to. They said he should go ahead and do the things he wanted to do, but he didn't want to do, he wanted to sleep. I knew by now that visits to the doctor were likely to be a waste of time. Zhong-hua would refuse pain medications, sleeping pills, antidepressants, blood pressure drugs, stool softeners, stool hardeners, muscle relaxers, and tranquilizers, all of which had been prescribed before.

I could not discern physical from emotional pain, which was something he would never admit to harboring. He let me know that the concept of being depressed was a very foolish one in his opinion. I used to be able to fall asleep imagining that his snores were harmless winds rambling through the pines. Now they sounded more like a flooded river clogged with tree branches. His breath gurgled and eddied, struggling against treacherous currents;

it quickened and stopped, rose to voice, and fell back a swallowed rumble. He lurched back and forth, his weight and density uncompromising. He had only to roll against me to cut off my breath by compression. I took to creeping overtop him on all fours and escaping to the floor pallet in the next room with a blanket and pillow. I could still hear the disturbance through the wall.

All our efforts had not been enough to turn the ebb tide that illness had set in motion. And yet, in my eyes, my husband had struggled valiantly, rising to every challenge with a plodding thoroughness torqued with maniacal intensity. Hadn't he confounded the MBA students at the technical institute's mock negotiations with the meat-grinder company? Hadn't he crammed a hundred new words into his head to deliver a talk to Paroda's class about China?

Each night when I came home, Zhong-hua was usually still waiting for his spoonful of energy to fill up. His sleepless nights were followed by dog days. He said, "Body just want sleep." He reminded me of the ancient monk Chen Tuan, a Tang dynasty Taoist master, famous for his sleeping meditation. Chen Tuan spent most of his 118 years this way, waking only when someone ready to benefit from his teaching approached him. His sleep was not sleep as most people think of it but rather a type of internal energy cultivation, a kind of hibernation useful for avoiding evil influences such as fighting warlords, and maybe depression.

If Zhong-hua felt a burst of zeal, like unexpected change in his pocket, he hardly knew how to spend it. He restacked the woodpile or filled in the potholes in the driveway. Zhong-hua was also in charge of the inside of the house and took sporadic initiative. One night over delicious peppered lamb soup with cilantro, Zhong-hua urged, "After eating, you need go to barn, look at books. You need hurry because barn not have electricity."

"Why do we need electricity?"

"I want you see. Today work all day making bookshelf in barn because house too crowded."

Now that he mentioned it, I had noticed the airiness in the house. Most of my books were gone! I was loath to condemn my husband's industry but was a little chagrined that he saw my books as clutter. I supposed words that make no sense might fairly be categorized that way. Not sure which random books had been exiled, I followed Zhong-hua into the darkening barn, where we clambered over the used-lawn-mower collection, seeing by bars of gloaming light slanting in between the barn slats. I wondered where my favorite book, *The Master of Hestviken* (an epic tetralogy by Sigrid Undset set in medieval Norway), had ended up—out here or in the house. "This time just move not-useful books." Zhong-hua gestured toward the inner wall and lit a cigarette, watching my face. The wall had become a mosaic of many different-sized cubbyholes partitioned with scraps of pine. The cubbies ranged from the size of a shoe box to the size of two boxes of corn flakes placed side by side and were packed full of wildlife encyclopedias, poetry journals, oversize hardbacks, and stout paperbacks, stacked horizontally or vertically, but all with the spines facing in so that the titles could not be read. I paused a long time, not wanting to sound unappreciative. "Um, Zhong-hua, why are the books all facing the wrong way?"

"If need turn, can turn."

The first time I needed a book that I suspected had been filed anonymously in the wilderness library, I was not pleased. It was cold out, and the barn was dim by the time I got off work. Surprisingly, by scanning the irregular shelves by flashlight with the approximate thickness of the book in mind, I reached up and, more often than not, found I had fixed on the title I needed. Sometimes I used the library as a kind of daily divination, just pulling down one of the books at random and letting a sentence tinder my mind.

After the book blitz, Zhong-hua resumed his supine position in front of the huge television that I had purchased out of the *Want Ad Digest* from a crippled Vietnam vet who lived in a trailer rusting in a pine woods like a forgotten lunch box in some weeds halfway to Canada. He had made me coffee on a campfire because he had no stove, and while we drank it, his little collie got tangled up in the garden hose, stepped on the nozzle, and sprayed us in the face. The man had laughed uproariously and sputtered, "Welcome to Paradise!" A dog was good medicine.

Here I was again, thinking up cures for my husband, who was possibly only cultivating energy and not depressed. The compulsion to "fix him like a teapot" returned. I knew he liked the large breeds, particularly huge, black German shepherds. Zhong-hua would make a good trainer, but this kind of dog cost plenty. And then there would be shots, food, and the problem of containment. The more I thought about it, the more it seemed an unaffordable remedy.

The medicine we received was less majestic than the fantasy, but it had fur and four legs. One of my clients called to say her son had a litter of mutts that needed homes quickly. They were half poodle and half Jack Russell terrier. I went with Sweet Sweet to have a look. The last remaining puppy was rat-sized and trembling, his eyes completely hidden behind an untidy mop of black hair. He seemed to gaze expectantly from his perfect nostrils. The hair on top of his head was longer than the rest and stuck straight out like bird feathers. We took him to the vet for flea treatment, all two pounds of him, and the next morning a cluster of evicted fleas congregated on top of his head.

Zhong-hua grunted. "This kind of dog not interesting. I just like big dog. If you like this kind of small dog, you can take care. I don't like." I was struck by the intensity of his rejection. Sweet Sweet played with the puppy for a few minutes and then went to her room and shut the door. A few minutes of nipping and licking sated her desire for a pet. Maybe I would have to find this dog a better home.

"What should we name him?"

"Nothing. 'Small Dog' is OK. No need another name."

Maybe this dog was *my* cure. Anyway, I had to leave the medicine dog with his reluctant caretaker while I went to work. When

I came home, I heard the shower running and could not find Small Dog. Then Zhong-hua stepped out naked, holding a wriggling bundle in a towel. He and Small Dog had just showered.

"This kind of dog very dirty. Need wash every day."

I went upstairs to change my clothes. When I came back, Zhong-hua was blow-drying Small Dog. He then sprawled on the pallet with Small Dog in the crook of his arm and enjoyed an evening of watching Tai Chi videos while brushing the furry feet with an old toothbrush.

One day when the weather was just cold enough to have thinly iced the pond, I came home to find Zhong-hua and Small Dog huddled together in a blanket. Small Dog's nose peered out pathetically.

"Yeah, today Small Dog almost go to dead," Zhong-hua reported. "He on other side of pond walking on ice top. Ice start breaking, and he fall in. He cannot swim and just crying 'ee, ee, ee.' I cannot reach, so I get long pole with roll-around paint-house thing at end. I rolling, rolling, rolling, until I get Small Dog back to pond edge. Small Dog terrible cold and shaking. I need hold two hours, stop this terrible shaking. Now I think he OK."

Paroda adored this dog and started visiting after work just to see him. We all stood around in the kitchen while Paroda coveted the dog, cooing and burying her face in his fluffy fur. "This dog no good," Zhong-hua said. "Anyway, I already had this kind of dog in my child times."

"Really? You had a dog?"

"Yeah. Same kind of dog. Wintertime. Family have no food, no warm clothes. Somebody give me tiny puppy because mother dog have no milk, cannot feed. I hold dog inside my shirt on my stomach, because I not have coat. At night I think best way is take dog in my bed, keep him warmer. This seems good way. But morning I cannot find dog. I stand up, looking around, shaking shirt, pants, blanket. Something fall out on floor, looks like black glove. Then I see black glove have small ears, have nose. This means I all night sleep on top of dog, making him like flat pan bread. After this, my whole life I never want another dog."

Small Dog aggravated me by pooping under the piano bench. Since I was absent all day and Zhong-hua was in charge of the home front, I first picked up the poop and next attacked my husband. "This is ridiculous. Why, with all of nature outside, can you not open the door? Good grief, what is wrong with you?"

My husband stood very still, as if he had just swallowed a horse pill and was waiting for it to hit bottom. He looked directly at me and said, "Did you see if poop have small white worms, not?"

Caught off guard, I began to consider this very pertinent question. "Noooo, I don't believe there were any white worms."

"Good! Good!"

In this skillful manner, my husband redirected my tirades toward constructive matters. He could always slip the trap of blame without flinging retaliatory accusations. He had that sleight of hand that, while no good for gambling wins, could shuffle the cards in a flash so that the most important thing appeared on top.

Our situation seemed to be forming a Gordian knot, a pretzel that had no free end to tug on. Meanwhile, I held a meeting with my clients in the park and asked them what kinds of things might improve the quality of their lives, things that didn't cost a lot. Someone said, "Vegas," and another, "Canada." I shook my head, "Can't do it." They prioritized three wishes: coffee parties with Ring Dings, sitting by the ocean (any natural body of water could substitute), and visiting the Indians on the reservation.

"The government screwed the Indians."

"Yeah, we should stick together with them. I send twenty dollars of my check every month."

"Me, too. For twenty years now."

"I've always wanted to learn from them how to live in harmony with nature."

The ocean was too far away, and I wasn't sure if the Indians would welcome us, but I said I would ask. Arthur said he wanted to see the giant windmill on the top of Jiminy Peak. This was within the can-do range, so off we went. I couldn't find where to park, and Arthur said if it were him, he would have known that first, even before he left the house—he would have asked where the parking lot was and made sure so there would be no confusion. We parked and then couldn't find the ticket booth. Arthur said he knew this would happen—that we wouldn't be able to find the parking lot or the ticket booth. When we found it, it was closed: no windmill tours because a group of important wind researchers was visiting. In the end, we hijacked the convoy of scientists, Zhong-hua—style, and rode up through the clouds with them in the eight-person chairlift. We hiked a muddy trail until the huge *whoosh, whoosh* of the propellers quickened our pulse. Like long, slender seabird wings, they cut the mist, shook the leafy heads of fall trees, and made waves in low grasses. It rained the whole time on the red and gold mountain and on us. Arthur hated confusion, dirt, walking, and being wet and cold—but not that day. He had the time of his life, and so did I.

"The world does a person good sometimes," he said.

"Yes, it does."

My husband was not quite sleeping at night, sometimes not quite breathing until I shook him into a great, surprised inhale. It was as if we were on a bridge that swayed endlessly between two points, in the present tense but without presence. Despite this dubious thought, I made the saving gesture and touched my husband where he lay beside me snoring. He gripped my knee, like a vise. Awake, he was there with me—just the other side of skin—of course he was, and together we made a softness that let me abandon all hexing thoughts.

When not tending to things at home, my husband ventured out as a wandering satellite in service to failing engines. I was working in Troy when he called to say his car battery had died just across the river and he needed a jump. As I came over the bridge, I spotted my husband shoveling snow in front of a house, supervised by a round wooly woman in a babushka. I assumed he was just being chivalrous, but I was wrong. He had knocked on the door and asked to use the phone. First the woman said they had no phone, but when Zhong-hua offered to chip the ice from the steps, she agreed to allow him one call if he would also clear the walkway.

My husband told me the story backward as we drove to buy a new battery. I learned that before making the phone call, he had tried to get the car fixed at the auto repair shop down the street where he had an appointment. But the car kept stalling on the way and he was a half hour late. The owner told him gruffly to come back in four hours.

"Can I please wait here?"

"No, you can't wait here. And move your car."

"I cannot start my car, sir."

"I have a tow truck. It will cost you one hundred dollars—cash."

"No need, sir. I have Triple A."

"We do not deal with Triple A here. You use our truck for one hundred, or I can sell you a battery for one hundred."

"Sir, I don't have one hundred cash. Can you please give me a jump and let me move my car?"

"You move your fuckin' car right now or I'm calling the police." The other workers looked on and said nothing. One young man whom Zhong-hua recognized from our small town looked at his shoes.

Zhong-hua answered very softly, very politely. "Sir, I is your customer. You need very nice to me."

"The hell I do! Get out of here, now." The man shook his fist in Zhong-hua's face.

My husband used an even softer and more polite tone of voice. "If you want to help me, I don't want your help. If you want to give me one hundred dollars, I don't want. Call the police, please, sir." That was when Zhong-hua walked down the street to knock on a stranger's door.

My husband's anger rarely manifested as affect but as a disturbing intensity that looked like a chunk of pyrite feels—condensed.

His skin changed color, as the earth's surface changes when a massive bank of clouds rolls in. This took place behind stoic features and a matter-of-fact tone as he related the story. The more contained his response, the more I felt compelled to emote.

"Zhong-hua, that guy cannot treat you like that. I want to go over there and talk to him tomorrow."

"No. No need. This man you don't need talk to. This kind of person in the world few. That's all."

Zhong-hua retreated to small-engine repair. He had a battalion of chainsaws ready to go, including three he had found on garbage day and the one Earnie the local chainsaw expert had performed last rites on and offered to dispose of for free. Zhong-hua took the engine out of one of the two curbside riding mowers and put it in the UPS guy's mower. All it needed was a tiny metal ring somewhere. He had shopped around unsuccessfully for this metal part. Then I came home from work, and he was washing peppers in a suit and tie. "Did you have a job interview?" I asked.

"No. Need buy lawn mower part."

"You wore your suit to buy a part?"

"Right." He was chopping the peppers, and the knife sounded like rapid fire on the board.

"Why?"

"So nobody will get hurts." Six different parts departments had rebuffed him in his usual blue jeans and Tai Chi sweatshirt. He decided to try changing clothes to see if he could get someone to listen to him long enough to find out what part he needed. The formal attire had the desired effect, but he felt disillusioned. He had thought that in America people were treated equally no matter who they were.

Lying in bed at night, Zhong-hua and I both agreed that we could cheat ourselves of happiness by a failure to be contented. The metal ring incident was the first time my husband had ever hinted that he felt like punching somebody. If Zhong-hua had ever felt bitterness, he had never shown it to me. Lately, I sensed he was choking on it.

Da Jie had grown increasingly distant. She avoided her brother. He had always been in the habit of visiting her on Friday evening. "Eat something," she would say, waving from the couch. "I have to go out. I need to play mah-jongg tonight." She still called if the leaves needed raking, the vacuum cleaner broke, or the garage door opener didn't work. "I need you to quickly come," she said. He went. When Zhong-hua first arrived from China, his sister had been zealous with advice, as family tradition mandated. She was the oldest sibling; he was the youngest. She had loaned him the money to buy his first used car and was chastising when it met its end—that is to say, when it met the end of another car.

That was before my husband got sick, and though she was glad to help for a while, she expected him to quickly recover and get a job. Every time he came to see her, she thought he was looking for a handout. The part of the family still in China depended on her for money whenever illness struck, and she alone supported her weakening father and his second wife. Zhong-hua said it didn't matter what she thought; she was his only relative in America, and he needed to try to have a good relationship. He was always thinking how to reciprocate past favors. Every summer since his surgery, my husband had a bountiful harvest of Chinese cucumbers. His sister loved these crunchy treats, so he bagged up half a bushel and drove over to her house.

This time, when he arrived with the cucumbers, there were cars in the driveway, but no one answered the door. Zhong-hua knocked and knocked and at last sat down on the stoop. After two hours, he heard voices in the house. Again, he knocked and called out, but no one came. Anger welled up in him. This would be unthinkable in China. He was the only brother. The world was truly upside-down if they could disrespect him like this.

At our niece's engagement party, she had trouble unstopping the wine bottle, and bits of cork floated in Zhong-hua's glass. What did this mean? Was he dirt? Was he nobody important? He was her only maternal uncle! My husband had stalwartly endured slights from many a shopkeeper, policeman, bureaucrat, and stranger on the street. He always shrugged it off, saying there were few of this kind of rude people in the world. But this he could not shrug off.

He came home strangely animated, nervous, almost electrified. He poured a glass of Chinese wine, the 125 proof that was generally reserved for holidays and for me on a bad day. It didn't take long before he was very jovial and very bold. He called his sister, and soon I heard a dramatic monologue in Chinese that was to continue on and off for the next eight hours. He role-played in a mocking voice, cussed, and delivered a speech that stung with sarcasm.

If his sister hung up, he called back. When his nerve flagged, he opened another beer, which we had in the house only because Paroda had recently graduated from the university and had a yard party. His melodic voice rose and fell melodramatically. "Oh, so this is how it is, I see! Good! Excellent, Sister, excellent! Your daughter serves her uncle dirty wine. I very much love dirty wine. How did you know? How clever of you! You must tell me where to get some of this special dirty wine! Did you already forget in China I was the top manager and people respected me?"

Finally, I hid the phone, and Zhong-hua's head swayed for a while before falling forward onto the table into a puddle of vomit. I fetched a bowl of soapy water and a cloth, unceremoniously lifted his head with one hand, and swiped the front of his face and the table with the other. I wrapped a blanket around his shoulders and went to bed. We never mentioned that night again. In a few weeks, it was time for Zhong Qiu Jie, "Midautumn Festival," an important Chinese family gathering. We sat at his sister's table and ate hot-pot vegetables and moon cakes with everyone else as if nothing had happened.

Throughout the fall and into winter, Zhong-hua continued to inquire into successive jobs with no callbacks. Anxiety, that monkey on my back, returned. Adding to the atmosphere of unease was the actual atmosphere: the winter that seemed never to come, other than a few wet flurries of snow. It was warm, way too warm for December. The wood in the furnace smoldered. Overhead, the geese flew the wrong way. When my husband reached for me at night, I could only feebly pat his shoulder. In my heart I made mad love, but my body was exhausted and my spirit flagging.

The pep talk I was in the habit of giving my husband—"You don't need to start from zero"—was sounding tinny. The myriad selves we had been were dragging us down, and I considered that maybe it was time to start *cong ling,* "from zero," to let fall the edifice of who we thought we were and what we were supposed to be doing.

The grown-up children came for Christmas to join Zhong-hua, Sweet Sweet, and me. It was a Christmas tailored to our pocketbooks. Eula had assigned each of us one other person to give a gift to. This was a new tradition, and Paroda said it would have worked if she had been in charge. As it was, the task befuddled Eula, and she assigned three people to Zhong-hua and nobody to Paroda, the only one who cared about gifts in the first place.

Zhong-hua's Christmas Eve feast was a four-year-old tradition, which now included mashed potatoes and excluded ham. It centered around the mountain of finely sliced cucumbers garnished with toasted sesame paste, garlic, vinegar, and soy sauce. In addition to the array of Chinese dishes made with tofu, pork, and chicken, I prepared a roast. Mavis wanted to bring back another tradition I had started when the children were very small: the lantern walk. Zhong-hua rounded up the bright red Chinese liquor boxes to make instant lanterns. We punched a pattern of holes with an awl and tied string for handles. Each box had a votive candle inside, sheltered from the wind. Zhong-hua carried the one Chinese translucent paper lantern.

Our lanterns bobbed along in the dark like fallen constellations, while Zhong-hua's cast a golden aura bright enough to light the path. He swung it in big circles over his head as we straggled merrily to the woods. This was our version of what my parents had done with a great band of rowdy friends, who marauded the neighborhood singing Christmas carols and then returned to someone's house to share food. Never having had a great band of friends or close neighbors, I had formed my own troupe, back when the kids would still do whatever I said. None of us could sing, so we traipsed through the back fields clutching milk-carton lanterns while Eula beat a big drum and shouted orders.

We had a fine Christmas together. I was relieved that none of the children asked me to make my famous goulash, the dense mixture of hamburger, elbow noodles, and Velveeta cheese they had grown up on and held dear in their adult memories as a delicacy. They each grew up to improvise their own version of goulash, and it warmed me to think that mediocre magic could be improved by the magician's offspring. Mavis left her candle in the middle of the stream that crossed the path, and we laughed and jostled our way home, pausing once to look back at the wee light in its watery darkness.

After Christmas, Zhong-hua had his long-awaited chance at a real job. It was only for a month, but he could make some money doing something in which he was expert, Tai Chi. The job was for the month of January at Williams College, and he had seventeen students signed up. Zhong-hua wanted to do this job "very perfect." I promised to come in halfway through the course to lead class discussions and read the students' assigned papers. The first day, he went alone, because I had to work. This was a fresh start. If he could teach Chen-style Tai Chi to "Have Stomach John," then surely he could teach bright, athletic college students.

Trouble started with the first homework assignment: memorize the English names of the seventy-four forms of Chen-style Tai Chi. These included Walking Obliquely, Looking for a Needle on the Sea Bottom, Buddha's Warrior Pounds the Mortar, Sparrow Dashes Earth Dragon. No, the students protested, this list was unreasonable, absurd, impossible. "Also," they e-mailed impertinently, "this course is a lot more work than the other Winter Study courses. We have to come to class too many hours and then practice at night, too." One miserable boy wrote: "I regret to inform you that I am forced to drop out of Tai Chi because of the overwhelming extreme difficulty of the material and the terrible frustration and discouraging lack of progress that I feel upon leaving class."

Five students quit. Zhong-hua could not sleep. He felt awful. He was breaking the form down into parts, proceeding bit by bit, and repeating many times. He couldn't go more slowly without coming to a complete standstill. Besides, he didn't think memorizing one list of forms was too hard for these smart students, at least not compared with the task his third sister's daughter in China had undertaken when she memorized the entire *Oxford English Dictionary*, complete with alternate pronunciations and multiple definitions. Zhong-hua was baffled and pained by the students' unexpected resistance to hard work.

"Zhong-hua, you need to tell them that if they try their best and come to every class, they will pass. Maybe you should teach them half of the form. They are Americans." Assurances helped class morale, but then two members of the ski team wanted to miss two days of class for a race and pled for release from the unreasonable demands of Tai Chi class. The dean refused. Zhong-hua agreed to let them miss the two classes, but only if they spent extra time with him after class. They did. Less athletic students grappled with the painful challenge of high kicks and complicated dancelike maneuvers. These students were sweating it out.

Homework reading was the ancient Chinese classic *Yenshi jiaxun* (Family Instructions for the Yen Clan), a sixth-century scholar's admonitions against greed, ambition, gossip, and debauchery, which he took great care to write down for his descendants shortly before he died. The students delighted me by not dismissing the opinions of the Confucian bookworm as irrelevant, though most objected to the chapter that condoned hitting young men with sticks to ensure good character development.

Some of them admitted that although they understood what it meant to be physically fit, they were not absolutely clear on the distinction between internal and external nourishment of life. Yen recommended a balance: "Shan Pao took care of his inner self, but a tiger took his life externally; Chang I took care of himself externally, but disease destroyed him internally." Every last one of the students learned all seventy-four forms of the difficult Chen-style Tai Chi, and on the final day, the twelve of them moved more or less in unison, wearing blue shirts, black pants, and expressions of total concentration.

I myself was feeling vulnerable to destruction, from the inside and the outside. Friday I came home, ate one bite of bread, and announced wearily that I had to go to bed. Zhong-hua bustled around preparing to teach his local Tai Chi class. He had only one student at this time, "Small John." Small John had not improved noticeably and routinely neglected to pay for the class. Zhong-hua remarked, "Small John very interesting; come to class nine months, pay one time twenty dollars. Good!" That was the night Zhong-hua was in a hurry because he had to give Small John a ride to class. I had given up reprimands, such as, "One person is not enough to keep a class going!" or "We cannot do business like this anymore. Small John has to pay!" For one thing, it was up to my husband to decide whether he wanted to keep the class open. For another, I didn't really believe that one person wasn't enough. My growing stinginess made me disgusted with myself, so I headed to bed.

Sweet Sweet was watching SpongeBob SquarePants cartoons. That, too, made me groan. What was I to do with an infantile almost-twenty-year-old? I no longer bothered repressing my bad thoughts, like "Get off your ass and help out around here" or "You really need to grow up." But the harshest thing I ever said out loud was: "Hey, how about cleaning up your hair when it gets all over the sink? I don't want to."

I lay down, and soon silence fell, punctuated by her room door softly clicking shut. Sweet Sweet was exhausted, too. I had forgotten that part—she was working and preparing for the English Regents, a state exam she needed to pass in order to graduate high school. She had done badly last time. I dozed off while vaguely prodding myself: "Do something. You need to do something." In my dreams, I sniffed the air and smelled sweet pine. Nice. I liked that smell.

The next thing I knew, I was flying down the stairs and flinging open the cellar door. To my horror, an ominous bank of smoke rose up the stairwell. I screamed for Sweet Sweet, and when her sleepy face appeared, I shoved her out the door. "Get Dave!" I yelled. "Call the fire department!" She disappeared into the freezing darkness. I called Small Dog, but he didn't come. Smoke was scalding my throat and lungs; there was no going back in. I fled the house in long underwear, bare feet, and no coat.

Twenty minutes later, Sweet Sweet and I were sitting in the warm cab of a volunteer fireman's truck hugging each other while the house burned down. "I just lost everything," she said. "I don't care. I really don't care. We can all work hard." Then she took a small bear that dangled from the rearview mirror and danced it in front of my face, singing, "I am very happy because I am alive!"

"What a sweet, brave girl you are." I held her close.

"No, not really brave. Just not afraid."

Fire trucks from four rural stations spun their red beacons in the dark. Snowflakes glittered in the light, and the long hanging boughs of the Norway spruce whipped around like dancing ladies. The men passed back and forth beneath this footless dancing, bulky and yet weightless, like dream workers. An hour or two later, a fireman knocked on the window holding up a subdued bundle from which Small Dog's quivering nose peered.

Some of the men approached my husband and touched his shoulder. That night he was like any other man whose family was in distress. The true bond among all beings is vulnerability. Later we slept on a broken couch at my friend Kathy's house, my feet at Zhong-hua's head to make room for his big chest. Sweet Sweet slept in a room with skulls and crossbones painted all over the walls, left over from Kathy's son's Goth period.

The next day, neighbors we had never met except to wave at piled out of a pickup and boarded up the gaping windows of our house, stepping over Chinese brush paintings and frozen carrots from the fall harvest, photos of my kids, and pages of my notebooks flung from the house. Two men came up to Zhong-hua and gave him one hundred dollars for food. Another neighbor gave him a Wal-Mart gift card, yet another a warm coat, hat, and gloves. Zhong-hua tried to refuse, but they said, "No, take it. This is what we do here." They left their footprints in the snow.

Where Magicians Live

KATHY TUCKED us into her house, which seemed a kind of Noah's ark frozen in ice a few miles from our burned life. We brought only the bags of clothes given to us by friends and neighbors. Zhong-hua wore women's pink velour sweats under his jeans, and I was uncharacteristically stylish in a black fitted shirt threaded with gold. In my displaced mornings, the light shining through the colored glass bottles on the windowsill cast rainbows on the ceiling and cupboards. There was a peach-colored one with a deer head for a stopper, a green one with a hummingbird stopper, and a cobalt one shaped like a car. I found a rag and polished each one with Windex. Easy moments, like the dog licking Kathy's cat's face, deceived me that we were floating in a new world and would soon see the spot for anchor.

The floating illusion gave way to a down-to-earth, deluxe camping out. Kathy's house was a labyrinth of hallways and small rooms heaped with accumulated junk. Mattresses ejected their cotton stuffing, and stacks of old *National Geographics* loomed four feet high. Whole drawers full of rubber bands resisted opening. Nothing worked. The phone beeped loudly and then died. The toaster never got hot. Only half the TV screen functioned, so that the tops of people's heads and their batting eyelashes had to do double expressive duty. There were pliers and hammers in the kitchen, dumbbell weights in the dining room, and Nabokov in the bathroom. The shower didn't work, and the hot water trickled out of the faucet so slowly that it took half an hour to fill the tub. With no railing, the stairwell appeared as a frightening abyss in the middle of the upstairs hall, but soon we were all mincing nimbly around the edges without an involuntary gasp or a tragic thought.

Small Dog didn't know which cat to chase first and ran about in perpetual ecstasy, only momentarily put off by the hostile hissing. We washed Kathy's dishes, sorted her Tupperware, Lysoled her bathroom floor, and scrubbed her shower stall, which disintegrated under the pressure into pieces that looked like bites of meatloaf. Zhong-hua did great heaps of laundry with fabric softener that he mistook for detergent. Kathy thanked him and told him sweetly please not to bother her bins of dirty laundry. She also requested no MSG in the saltshaker. Kathy had no other rules. Since the insurance company agreed to pay Kathy some modest rent, the arrangement conformed to Zhong-hua's ideal of the most good for the greatest number of people.

I watched Small Dog break down social barriers with the three cats, each twice his size and grumpy. First, he sat politely at the foot of the chair or couch where the cat reclined. Next, he rested a paw on the seat of the chair. The process required careful timing of advances, but in the end he curled up, if not touching, at least close enough for companionship. He won over all three cats and developed an amorous relationship with one of them. Zhong-hua shook his head. "This will not work. The dog's pajamas and the cat's pajamas do not match."

I set up an office in Kathy's closet. There was a stair-climber in there, just like the one we used to have in our kitchen for a coatrack, except this one worked. Kathy kept her scuba diving gear in there, too, and the last fifteen years of *Rolling Stone* magazine. When I couldn't think, I got on the stair-climber and looked up at the shelves where she had her video collection: *Man Bites Dog, City of Angels,*

Digging to China. She had recorded them off the TV, so, when played, some of them ended in the middle, while others began in the middle.

I felt apprehensive that our unsubtle presence would annoy Kathy but then remembered there was almost nothing she wouldn't do for me, though I never meant to take advantage of that fact by moving my family in with her. Almost ten years ago, she brought her daughter to me as an alienated teenager who had waded into drugs, alcohol, and dangerous relationships. She wanted to be an artist. Within two years she had surpassed me as a sculptor, and I told her to find another teacher. Kathy believed I had saved her daughter's life. I knew very well that Sarah had saved herself with a combination of talent and heart, but pointing this out did not change Kathy's loyalty.

With mattresses on the floor and food to eat, we had only to navigate the kitchen without tripping on the mousetraps and avoid falling down the stairwell. We resumed the elemental motions of daily life. Zhong-hua's first priority was a large-capacity rice cooker. Then he bought an expensive wok, which elevated our existence with variations on fish, tofu, and vegetables. The wok was an honored sentient being who had likes and dislikes. It did not like being touched by soapy water, sponges, metal, or anyone other than its master. I did touch it but half expected it to cry out "Master Lu! Master Lu!" Kathy rose early to go to her job as a mail carrier and usually prepared breakfast in her sleep. Three times she accidentally left the heat on high under the wok instead of under her teakettle and left to get dressed. Its Holiness was forever maimed after that and no longer nonstick.

Kathy's eight-year-old nephew Zack came over for a Kung Fu lesson from Zhong-hua on Sunday. Zack looked like a miniature version of my husband, who called him "Exactly," not because he looked just like him but because that was how the name registered in him. After the lesson, the two of them sat down over ribs and eggs with hot pepper. Zack never flinched. I heard Zack say, "In

France if you say excuse me after burping, that means you didn't like the food."

"Right, right," Zhong-hua agreed between mouthfuls.

"I learned that in science class."

"Yes, yes."

The next weekend, Kathy and I took Sweet Sweet and Zack to an Afropop dance party. Too shy to dance, Zack stood frozen in place, a plump stoic amid the euphoric multitude, holding his ground for over an hour. Finally, Sweet Sweet took his hands in her own and began to sway back and forth. He didn't move a muscle, not even to escape the understated invitation. Then, after about twenty minutes of allowing Sweet Sweet to dance his limp hands back and forth, he began to bob his head to the beat. Twenty more minutes and he was mini—shuffle stepping to the right and left. There was perceptible twitching going on in his torso, too. By the end, he was swinging, and we all danced right out the door into the parking lot holding hands and laughing. I felt proud of Sweet Sweet, the wonder worker.

Back at work, I remembered an overdue promise to help my unhandy reclusive client hang the curtains we had shopped for together before the fire. I drove by Sam's house, looked up, and saw the dark brown curtains hanging in place. "Wow, that's a miracle," I said out loud. When I stopped in, he admitted that he had astounded himself, that he never thought he could do it. Knowing how to wield a screwdriver is an empowering thing, as good as mastering a multipurpose word. I noticed that the kitchen window was bare. This was the only one that required curtain hooks, and though I had left a small bag, Sam could not fathom them. He said they looked like a strange lethal alphabet. I ripped the bag open, slid the first one into the cloth pocket of the curtain, and handed the rest to Sam. "Absurdly simple," he noted, slipping the next one into place. Strange alphabets, like new dance moves, do sometimes turn out to be absurdly simple.

After work, I came home to Kathy's to find Sweet Sweet at the computer, looking up where to take hip-hop dance classes. After dinner, Kathy, Sweet Sweet, Small Dog, and I huddled together on Kathy's high platform bed munching crackers and watching one of the vintage movies from the closet while Zhong-hua bent over pencil and paper at the table downstairs sketching a house. "For us, very simple is OK," he said. I suggested it at least have a porch and a window to the west. He said that a cement house would be best. I hoped he meant brick, because I didn't want to live in a fallout shelter. The word *brick* had never lodged in his mind, and the Chinese word for brick refused to stay in mine. "You mean the made-of-clay things about this size?" I asked, using Chinese sentence structure and holding my hands out as measure.

"Yes."

"Good idea."

Zhong-hua's first drawings of our dream house looked like a cube of irreducible space in which only magicians could live. But this was just the small house of his beginning mind. By the end of the Year of the Dog, the house of his mind had grown big.

The Thirteen Followers of Life

"DO YOU HAVE TIME, NOT?" he asked me after I returned from work. We drove over to our casserole of pink insulation, fragments of wallboard, and ice-encrusted silk pantaloons. We wrestled free a few cement blocks from the snow. Then a few more. With carpenter's hammers, we tap-tapped the tenacious mortar from the edges and piled the intact blocks by the shed. "Very useful," Zhong-hua said, and turned to denailing half-burned boards, stamping with his boots to flatten out the crumpled sheet metal roofing, and coiling electrical wire around his forearm. We worked in the dark below the severed power lines.

The red chimney bricks were harder to find, buried under asphalt shingles and crisscrossed layers of rafters, broken honeysuckle branches, and soil mixed with kitchen artifacts that were now more aligned with the realm of wood and metal than the realm of human habit. I did my best and was satisfied that I had rescued the bricks that volunteered themselves, ending with a knee-high stack. The next day when I returned from work, I saw that my husband had tripled my pile with his superior archaeological efforts. It wasn't enough for another sky-high chimney; it was only enough for a dwarf chimney or a flueless fireplace, but the point was, it was enough for something. These were building blocks, and I felt better.

The night before the demolition, we crept up the stairs, which were littered with chunks of ceiling, and removed all the windows by flashlight. These, too, went behind the shed. I pointed out that the seals were broken from the heat and the glass clouded. "Doesn't matter," he said. The Dumpsters carted off on flatbed trucks had not been full. I discovered the missing cargo gargantuan in a corner of the barn: smoky pillows and blue-black futons, a melted toaster oven, four dozen ashy teapots, and even a coffee can of charcoaled amaryllis bulbs. When I sputtered my dismay, Zhong-hua said, "Sometime, some part, maybe useful." Among these darkened everyday things, the troll dolls I had lovingly made lay tumbled together in a box with their hair singed and their boot toes burned.

I did not want to see what seemed like evidence of defeat. Could it not just all disappear and make way for the clean and new? But my husband didn't want these things gone. Dumpsters that swallowed the past and rolled it away with all its useful metal and fiber were as inane to him as they were a sweet relief to me. To him these goods were just slightly bruised but still useful, like shoes off a dead man. Maybe he felt no need to divest himself of failure; maybe he didn't even think of this word at all. Having grown up under Chairman Mao, he did not take loss personally. He had spoken of the time when the party officials came to get the furniture and the wooden door of the house to fuel the village steel-smelting furnaces. Then they demanded everyone's cooking wok and iron pots and melted them. Steel made this way was all unusable. Misfortune was universally experienced, and losses were collective and exponential. People who didn't die scavenged the landscape for insects and leaves and aimed their slingshots at the sky.

The hubris of taking unforeseen tragedy as personal failure did not escape me, and I made a determined effort to adopt my husband's practical stance even as I watched the old unworkable life stack up again in a new grotesque formation beside the six broken lawn mowers, of which my husband also said, "Some part sometime very useful. Not whole thing broken, only some part broken, some way broken. Not cannot fix. Can fix." The acrid smell of ash permeated everything, but my husband waved his hand to indicate, this, too, would pass: "Time." Yes, time, I thought, stepping forward, and then, stepping back, I felt I could not bear the rank oppression of entangling junk.

My husband took great pains to save what I thought was trash and clearly intended to keep it for a long time, as long as it took for things to reveal their usefulness. Marriage had increased my capacity for bafflement. I dwelled in the land of the not understood and the not understanding. This was different, I had learned, from the land of the misunderstood and misunderstanding. I like to think it was a state of suspended illumination, and sometimes only the ability to dwell there with some semblance of grace affirmed our relationship. I fell from grace when I called my husband crazy, secretly to myself, or voiced this sentiment to close friends. But if someone else called him crazy, I took offense on his behalf. Under the pressure of defending my husband's sanity, mostly to myself, I got in the habit of comparing dissimilar circumstances successfully. For example, being an artist, I, too, saved things that could be called junk: old cloth, wire, metal scraps, buttons, shattered windshield glass, frayed rope, reeds, roots, horns, bones, and worn-out boots. The stuff of chaos was the stuff of creation.

Zhong-hua tried to tell the demolition man to "go carefully," so as not to break what was salvageable: the radiators, the water tank, and the old floor beams. According to demolition protocol, this man broke every radiator in two. Zhong-hua pronounced him a terrible worker and a boy. The excavation of the new and bigger cellar hole progressed as a battering of shale, gneiss, and bluestone, locally known as "graywacky." The dozer had been working all day. At six o'clock Zhong-hua shook his head. "No good."

"What?"

"No good. This need change."

"Change? For God's sake, why?"

253

"Can't explain. House not straight not OK. This house need exactly north, exactly south."

"But, Zhong-hua, then we will be looking straight down the county road instead of into the woods."

"Look down road is OK. This house need exactly straight, exactly face north, exactly back to south. Also, house with old shed need exactly parallel. Cannot have space become very narrow at one end, become very wide at other end. End of one building need even with end of other building, not one building start halfway in middle of other building."

"It's OK if the shed is not exactly lined up with the house because we will be taking the shed down, won't we?"

"Not. Anyway, you need understand—just one day not parallel not OK. Just one day with this kind of fighting energy can make whole family's life no good. This generation and next, next, next generation all have trouble. Buddhist temple area never have fighting corners."

I studied the shed adorned with hornets' nests, boarded-up windows, and dangling shingles. "Oh, great, this way we will look out the front door right into the wall of a rotting shed. I'm trying to say it's very ugly and will block the kitchen window."

"Yes. Block window is OK. Look into rotting shed also OK. You cannot imagine how beautiful this shed will be."

He was right about that. I was experiencing a failure of imagination—a woeful failure for an artist. I gave in, confident that there would be abundant opportunity to consider the shed's potential, as it really was situated right outside the front door of the new house.

"OK, well, if you have other things, can you please tell me soon, before the building inspector signs off on the plans?"

Zhong-hua's beloved broken-down cars blocked the path of the big trucks bringing gravel and dirt for the septic field. We spent a few hours coaxing the engines to start and shifting the ones that refused to start into neutral. Zhong-hua insisted that they all would work again someday, even though one had no brakes and a door missing, one no transmission, and the last a seized engine. I said we had to have the junk guy come and get the cars. He said he definitely didn't want that. Then he said, "You know, if east wind not pushing west wind, then west wind will pushing east wind."

"Huh?"

"If I don't tell you what to do, then you will tell me what to do. If you don't tell me, then I will definitely tell you. One house have two bosses no good. Traditional way is man is boss."

"But we are both very bossy, so we are equals."

"Ugh. This maybe work."

He was emphatic about wanting to keep the cars, so I gave him a hand and left the subject alone. Knowing my husband, he would find a way to transfer the good transmission to the car with the good engine, even if it were five years in the future.

We walked around the voracious sharp-toothed rock pit. Fronds of chamomile sprouted in from the hard clay and gravel. I wanted to smooth over our differences in opinion and share some joy in this project. "Look, here is our bedroom in the northwest corner. We will see the sun set."

"No good."

"What?"

"Bedroom need on east side. This is must-be thing."

"Zhong-hua, you sat there and looked at the plans yesterday. You never said anything."

"This is must-be thing for children."

"The children don't live here. They are grown up."

"Even one night sleeping in wrong corner is bad thing. A daughter who sleeps in wrong room of father's house can never do well for whole life. Father sleeping where kitchen should be is terrible. Northeast corner is fire corner—cannot sleeping in fire corner. This kind of breaking thousand-year things can throw away thousand-year good fortune. People say they don't believe this old stuff, and I say, 'You don't believe, but you can watch, see, look: these people cannot do very well.'"

I agreed that we needed to do everything we could to invoke good fortune and health. Our one-story, two-bedroom house would have a kitchen in the northwest, a bedroom in the northeast for children and grandchildren, our bedroom in the southwest, and a huge middle room—perfectly square—according to Zhong-hua's specifications.

In the first days, the construction crew, not comprehending my husband's speech, narrowed their eyes, as if that would widen the portals for the sound waves. In just a few days, their inner ears had reconfigured to let in the odd-shaped English words. After that, everyone did fine, except the plumber, who was nearly deaf and generally unnerved by my husband. Communication was an ordeal for both of them. The plumber leaned forward squinting and nodded unhappily. Zhong-hua ended it with "OK, OK, OK," and they parted ways having no clue what had been agreed to and each having his own definite idea of how the pipes should go in. On the side the plumber told me, "Your husband is a nice guy, but only one of us can be up on the ladder at one time, you know what I mean?"

While the men were framing the house, a construction crew five miles away had just removed the steel façade from the Big Lots storefront. They were getting ready to cart it away on a flatbed trailer when Zhong-hua persuaded them to divert one of the beams into the bushes for a small fee. The beam was twenty-four feet long and weighed four hundred pounds. Our discount beam remained in the bushes for a month, and we visited it from time to time until the carpenter cajoled a friend to fetch the beam and deposit it at our new house. The carpenter was not enthusiastic about Zhong-hua's insistence on incorporating a Big Lots beam into the house design, and his noncommittal nod was the worthy equivalent of Zhong-hua's own phrase: "Let me think about."

Zhong-hua showed up at the construction site every day to help in any way he could and clean up in the evening. He reported back that American workers eat too many doughnuts. One day he prepared northern Chinese dishes for them: hot peppers with tofu, pork with scallions and ginger. They sputtered and coughed and sucked air. The next day the boss bought a ham and cheese sub for Zhong-hua. On the day the floor joists were laid on the sills, the crew leader called me at work to say that Zhong-hua was busy hanging up rice-paper banners painted with large red Chinese characters all along the center beam. "He says the words will protect us. Yep. We've never been protected before. It's kind of nice."

Zhong-hua was everywhere on that construction site. He walked beams, climbed ladders, shoveled gravel, and generated opinions about every detail of the project with the single-mindedness of a freight train. The list of "must-be" things grew, and the men started getting edgy. Progress was slow because Zhong-hua questioned everything they did. Sensing that he was making them "not happy," Zhong-hua started his own huge project thirty feet from the house.

He said it was a retaining wall, but I could not discern what it would retain. He had stretched a simple string from the telephone pole by the road to a stake midfield and placed rocks from the cellar hole along the string. He fixed the broken arm of Kathy's wheelbarrow and borrowed it to mix the mortar. He added more and more rocks to make a straight wall quite unlike the lichen-covered walls undulating like giants' necklaces along the forest floor.

I admired those earlier, much better builders of walls, whose arms hefted and stomach muscles tightened in counterbalance just like ours. Even more I admired the generous patience of the first people to walk this land, who took time to learn the language of the birds and offered human words to fire and earth. They knew how to talk to stones. They lifted them red-hot from the fire, placed them in the center of the sweat lodge, and sprinkled them with water. The stones answered the prayers and accepted the human beings as relatives. I hoped they would accept us. I hoped our neighbor would not hate this wall. Zhong-hua was evidently thinking the same thing.

"Maybe this wall make Dave not happy."

"Maybe."

"I need stop now, you think?"

"Maybe you should stop."

"I think continue bit by bit."

"Yes, bit by bit."

"Not one time all finish."

"No."

By dark he was scraping the metal bottom of the empty barrow with his trowel. Traditional New England walls used no mortar, but this one did. Zhong-hua figured one hundred bags of cement and three hundred bags of sand would do it. Finding the rationale behind someone else's words and deeds is hard. I gave myself more time. Swallows, the expert angels of dusk, feasted on insect throngs. The skies rumbled and spat electricity. I threw down my trowel and ran for cover, but Zhong-hua worked on, heaving boulders on the rain-pelted muscles of his will.

Every evening we added sand, cement, sweat, and hours to the bulldozer's harvest of razor-edged stone until a smooth wall emerged from the mist. Made of blue-gray vertebrae studded with quartz crystals, the wall resembled a dragon's back. The ancients in China believed that the subterranean geomagnetic grids of yang energy could be tapped into for telepathic communication and four-dimensional time travel. They called them "dragon currents." The only thoughts we exchanged telepathically were "There is a good rock for that space," and "Slap a little more mortar on here, comrade."

We pried, cradled, hoisted, rolled, and skidded, committing ourselves to the present dimension between ground and sky. Hours went by backward, stewarded by my husband. Besides the less endearing aptitude my husband and father have in common, having to do with cars run amok, falling debris, and man-made disasters in general, they share this mastery of silence. In their companionship, I have explored a vaster interior and more dazzling exterior because of it.

I remembered how my father spent a half hour here and there with me between the once-a-year camping trips. "How about walking over to the post office?" he'd say. Then off he strode without speaking or looking down while I half ran along behind him. We made similar trips to the hardware store, the Dairy Queen, and the library. Conversation? No. I noticed every grassy upheaval of pavement, every glint of chimney flashing, stout-waisted fire hydrant, tilted Stop sign, and rankly alluring alleyway. The silence invited the world closer. And though I sometimes felt yearning, abandonment, even anger in these silences, that was because my body hadn't learned how to carry them, and then, having learned, often forgot. *Cun,* or "meditate," in Chinese, means "to cause to endure," "to retain." Silence, like the stones, retains fields of feeling.

Our dragon current that doubled as a retaining wall sported an oil-changing pit where the dragon's tail forked. A car could be driven up onto the split tail that the mechanic might wriggle into the crevasse below to examine the underbelly of the vehicle. The wall was not done yet, Zhong-hua said, because one fork of the tail needed to curl outward to enclose a small fishpond. Ours was perhaps the only wall in the great Northeast with a utilitarian tail. It seemed my husband had fashioned a miniature "Great Wall" with chambers for sleeping rodent warriors and snakes. Theirs, too, were the hidden stairways, the lookout towers, and the superhighways to the oil pit.

I drive up to the site, where there is finally a foundation for a house, and find Zhong-hua slapping mortar onto the wall and pressing it firmly into the cracks. It is nearly dark. The crickets trill, and swallows dip and dive. Brown and yellow leaves twirl into the open field. He doesn't look up, though I know he feels my presence. Sounds rise and fall along the wall like water, and I realize that my husband is singing. I recall the day Zhong-hua said that singing was an "in-the-past thing" and how those words had contracted my heart. Now I understand, by antilogic, that time is reversible. He is scraping the wheelbarrow with his trowel and singing—not a full-throated song but something low and melodic, delivered in Chinese with head bent to the stones.

I sit in the dark on the wall. "Am I a problem wife?"

"Not big problem. Just have different culture material. You can change."

"Nice to have that as a possibility, but what if I can't?"

"Is OK."

"And you?"

"Never can change. This is me."

"I sometimes have negative thoughts," I said.

"Go ahead." Zhong-hua folded his arms across his chest.

"Well, sometimes it feels so difficult to trust. When I get mad, I follow this image of myself with backpack disappearing down a dirt road, going, going, gone. But I always come back, and you are always here. We must want to be together."

"Yes."

"Now you talk."

"Why me talk? You say everything perfectly. I just say one thing: make good relationship very hard."

"I want to."

"Too, me."

"No, Zhong-hua, it's *me, too*, not *too, me*."

"Listen to me: Just try. Maybe everything OK."

I often think of the thirteenth horse who won the race. According to Da Jie's theory, the twelve who lost all had a change in luck to look forward to, and the thirteenth, the winner, needed to lose something, a shoe or a tooth or the next race. But winning or losing was perhaps not their concern as they stretched their necks to the wind with hearts on fire, following life.

That summer Kathy took me to a lake forty minutes to the northeast, and we paddled across it in her kayaks. On the far side, we slipped into the reeds and steered the winding waterways to a marsh where branchless pines stood around like a gathering of gray old men with big hair. It was a great blue heron rookery. The hairdos were heron nests made of sticks where overgrown babies crowded one another, gawking over the edges into the world's airways. The mystery of where the heron came from and where he disappeared to was partly solved. He didn't just unzip the sky to appease the longings of imagination. He was his own true story.

Acknowledgments

Gratitude to The Ludwig Vogelstein Foundation for a grant that helped me start this book. Gratitude also to my agent, Gillian MacKenzie; Robin Desser, for generous advice on the rough draft; and Dan Jones at the *New York Times* for running an essay based on the book.

Gratitude to the warm, patient, exacting staff at Shambhala Publications, especially to my editor Eden Steinberg and her assistant editor Chloe Foster.

Thanks to my dear teachers Suzette Graham, Tom Bissell, and George Scialabba.

Special thanks to Dr. Tom Triscari, Dr. Robert Mayer, and Kathy Keyser for being the magnanimous characters they really are.

Gratitude to my parents for their soulful zest, my children Eula, Mavis, Athan, Paroda, and Tian Tian for being their own saviors, and my niece Nadine for her expandable love of family. Special thanks to Paroda Loy, who welcomed Zhong-hua with all her heart.

Credits

"I Never Wanted Fame" by Antonio Machado. Reprinted from *Times Alone: Selected Poems of Antonio Machado*, translated by Robert Bly (Hanover, N.H.: Wesleyan University Press, 1983). © 1983 by Robert Bly. Reprinted with his permission.

"Love Doesn't Ask Why," words and music by Cynthia Weil, Barry Mann, and Phil Galdston © by 1992 Dyad Music Limited (BMI), administered by Wixen Music Publishing, Inc. Copyright © by 1993 Universal Polygram International Publishing, Inc. and Kazzoom Music, Inc. All Rights Reserved. Used by permission.

Excerpt from *Taoteching*, translated by Red Pine. Reprinted from *Lao-tzu's Taoteching: With Selected Commentaries from the Past 2000 Years* (San Francisco: Mercury House, 1996). © 1996 by Red Pine. Used by permission from Red Pine.

About the Author

Ellen Graf, Zhong-hua, and Small Dog continue. Zhong-hua is currently studying to be an emergency medical technician. He offers private intensives in Chinese brush painting and Chen Style Tai Chi and Qigong in his home studio. Ellen is working on a collection of essays about improvisation and survival.